# THIS HERE IS A
# STICK-UP

# THIS HERE'S A STICK-UP

## THE BIG BAD BOOK OF AMERICAN BANK ROBBERY

Duane Swierczynski

ALPHA

A Pearson Education Company

*This book is for Meredith, my Bonnie.*

International Standard Book Number: 0-02-864344-5
Library of Congress Catalog Card Number: 2002103783

04   03   02      8   7   6   5   4   3   2   1

Interpretation of the printing code: The rightmost number of the first series of numbers is the year of the book's printing; the rightmost number of the second series of numbers is the number of the book's printing. For example, a printing code of 02-1 shows that the first printing occurred in 2002.

*Printed in the United States of America*

For marketing and publicity, please call: 317-581-3722
The publisher offers discounts on this book when ordered in quantity for bulk purchases and special sales.
For sales within the United States, please contact: Corporate and Government Sales, 1-800-382-3419 or corpsales@pearsontechgroup.com
Outside the United States, please contact: International Sales, 317-581-3793 or international@ pearsontechgroup.com

"Crime is merely a left-handed form of human endeavor."
—Alonzo D. Emmerich (Louis Calhern) in *The Asphalt Jungle*

# CONTENTS

## Part 1: The Men Behind the Masks

*A tour through 150 years of demand notes, pointed guns, and canvas sacks full of money, as seen through the eyes of legendary American bank robbers.*

## Part 2: A Treasury of Bank Heists

*The techniques, the legends, the sweetest heists, the most embarrassing foul-ups, the books, the festivals—and everything else you've ever wanted to know about the art of redirecting funds from major financial institutions. It's all in this part.*

## Appendixes

# PATRICK "PADDY" MITCHELL, BANK ROBBER

## "YOU'VE ROBBED THEM 500 TIMES IN YOUR MIND."

Whatever you do, don't judge this book by its foreword. *This Here's a Stick-Up* is hard-hitting and expertly written. Whereas my foreword may put you to sleep, the rest of the book will keep you wide-eyed and on the edge of your seat.

The only reason for my involvement with this project is that I'm one of only half a dozen of the bank robbers Duane Swierczynski profiles who are still alive and easy to track down. (You'll get to read my profile later in the book.) I was asked to write this foreword from the comfort of my cell here at the U.S. Penitentiary at Leavenworth. Like George W. Bush could never speak for all past U.S. presidents, I cannot speak for all bank robbers. Although I'm sure we all have some common traits, we also have our differences. For instance, in the eight years I have been incarcerated behind these 40-foot-high, 8-foot-thick hallowed walls, I've had the pleasure of talking to dozens of bank robbers. I have not met one who conducted business in the same manner I did, none that used similar getaway routines, and less than a handful who were getting as much money.

If I do say so myself, bank robbers are a different breed of criminal altogether. We consider ourselves to be the elite of the criminal world. Unfortunately, some of the bank robbers Mr. Swierczynski writes about in this fine book were violent—they are the ones paraded across pages of most books, accompanied by grainy photographs of their bullet-riddled bodies—the shoot-'em-uppers; the Bonnies and Clydes, "Machine Gun" Kellys, John Dillingers, "Baby Face" Nelsons; or the slightly more sophisticated souls such as Larry Phillips or Emil Matasareanu, with their panoply of body armor who also paid the supreme price for winning the distinction of engaging a good portion of the Los Angeles Police Department in the most violent shoot-out in American history.

Believe me folks, most bank robbers (this humble scribbler included) subscribe to the Willie Sutton school of bank robbery and use our firearms simply as props. The worst-case scenario for someone like me isn't leaving the bank without the money, but leaving it with someone hurt.

Mr. Swierczynski's book conveys a feeling of on-the-scene reporting. It is filled with vital statistics and delightful anecdotes. But never having pulled off a bank robbery himself, the author has asked me if I would describe the feelings one derives during the course of casing and robbing a bank. He wants to know if it's scary? Exhilarating? Fulfilling? Yes, it's a little bit of all of those—and more.

He wants to know what was like waking up on the morning of the big heist. Was I able to sleep? Was my stomach tied in knots? Was I able to eat breakfast? To me, the day of a heist was a day just like any other day. Yes, I slept just fine, and there was nothing wrong with my stomach—I'd eat a hearty breakfast. You run on automatic, just anxious to get it done and over with. And you are confident that before this day is over you'll be richer by a couple of $300 thousand—maybe more. You know this because you've done your homework by casing that bank every day (Saturdays, Sundays, and holidays included) for the past six months. You know more about the procedures that take place at that bank than most employees, and you've robbed them 500 times in your mind. You keep telling yourself, "Nothing can go wrong."

When you park the car you've stolen near the bank and take one final reading of the surroundings, looking for anything out of the ordinary, you whisper a prayer that everybody does what they are told, and (especially) that nobody gets hurt.

I always stole the armored truck pick-ups or deliveries. I avoided teller's drawers; that's where they keep the explosive dye-packs, marked money, and tracking devices—I left those for the tyros. I'd have to wait until the guards delivered the money. I knew the day and the approximate time the truck would make its delivery from my months of observation. When the truck arrives with the money, that's when the adrenaline starts flowing, and my heart goes into overdrive, thumping against my sternum at 200 beats per minute, maybe faster. After the guards emerged from the bank and the truck drove off, it was show time. I would slip on my mask, drive to the door of the bank, leave my car running, and enter the building.

"This is a stick-up! No alarms! Anyone touch an alarm I'll kill you!"

I'm roaring, I'm cursing, I'm angry and mean, I'm in charge. I cannot be gentlemanly or pleasant. Nice bank robbers are not taken seriously and embolden would-be heroes; employees won't cooperate. In some newspaper articles, I've been referred to as "the gentleman bandit." That was a total misnomer. I've never been gentlemanly while being a bandit.

"I've just come for the money. If everyone behaves, no one gets hurt."

Most times there are no surprises, like a policeman who just happens to be in the bank cashing his paycheck. Now I can lower my voice a few decibels to put the people at ease. Frightened people will do strange things sometimes; they are relieved to hear that I'm here for the money and, providing everyone behaves, they won't get hurt. I know precisely where the bags of money are. I had watched them being delivered to the same location for months. I get the employees busy, putting the smaller deposit bags into the bigger one I've brought with me. On a good day, I'm in and out in under a minute.

I'm out of there, into my hot car, and headed off in a particular direction. I know there will be people looking out of the bank's window, hoping to capture a description of the car and the direction it's traveling. I want them to see both. I always drive in one direction, then double back. Within a minute, I switch cars. The hot car can't look anything like my personal car. (I always had a preference for four-door Cadillac sedans and stole Fords and Chevrolets, always a different color than my own.) Although I've switched cars, I still have to be off the road within a minute or two. Maybe I'll park in a large shopping plaza, an indoor parking garage, or at an apartment complex. More often than not, I'll hop into the trunk of my car, pull down the lid without locking it, and sit it out from anywhere from 8 to 24 hours. I'll emerge sometime later—when the heat has died down. Then I'll leave everything—the outer clothes I wore during the heist, money, gun, and mask—in the trunk, hail a cab to the airport, and fly out of town. I'll fly back in a few days or a week, retrieve my car, and drive out of town.

Now, what does a shrewd operator like me do with all that money? Do I do a sensible thing like invest it in some blue-chip stock or put some away for a rainy day? Not a chance. I've risked life and limb for that money, and I'm going to spend it just as quick as humanly possible. There's always more where it came from. It's party time, folks! We bank robbers are "alpha males" and have an evolutionary advantage over mere mortals for attracting wild and crazy women. And that's what it's all about: sex, drugs, and partying.

Mr. Swierczynski asked me to describe how I feel after a successful heist, when I'm back at my dwelling, cutting open the bags of money a thousand miles away from the city where the authorities are looking for me, and I'm confident I haven't left any clues for the FBI. That's a difficult question. I searched diligently for the words to describe the feeling.

The best I could come up with is a comparison. Imagine this: You've just caught a 20-foot wave while surfing, you're gliding toward your oceanfront abode in Malibu, the sun is setting, and a scantily clad Britney Spears is waiting for you on shore with a cold bottle of St. Pauli Girl beer and a big fat joint, and she just can't wait to make love to you.

Enjoy the book!

Patrick "Paddy" Mitchell
U.S. Penitentiary at Leavenworth
December 11, 2001

# THIS HERE'S AN INTRODUCTION

"Do people still rob banks?"

That's the question a buddy of mine asked when I told him I was writing a book about bank robbery. When, he argued, was the last time you heard about someone knocking over a savings and loan? Didn't criminals these days use laptops to hack their way into global banks to steal billions? And didn't that whole armed stick-up thing go out of vogue somewhere around *Dog Day Afternoon*?

I politely nodded. "That's an interesting point."

As I write this, the biggest crime story in Philadelphia is about a bank robber who led cops on a wild chase down the busy Schuylkill (a.k.a. "Sure-Kill") Expressway on New Year's Eve. "Somebody needs to tell them they need to stop this chase!" barked the 26-year-old heister to a police dispatcher via cell phone. "All that's going to happen is they're going to get somebody killed. If they keep it up, I'm going to hit a car head-on!" That same day, in Boynton Beach, Florida, a man walked into a Union Bank branch and threatened to detonate the bomb he was wearing unless the tellers gave him money—*right now*. About six hours later, in Hallandale Beach, Florida, a nervous bandit tried to rob two banks with the same sloppy demand note; the first didn't pan out, but the second did. Still that same day—New Year's Eve—the NYPD and FBI swooped down on a 46-year-old bank robber hiding at a homeless shelter in Queens who was thought to have pulled two heists in Brooklyn. The day before, December 30, an armed stick-up artist hit a First National Bank in Detroit at 3:53 in the afternoon and escaped with a thick wad of cash. And days before that, a team of European robbers used ropes to swing into a bank in Milan and stole 1 to 1.5 million euros; it was Italy's sixth euro heist in three months.

*Do people still rob banks?*

Did they ever stop?

Ever since men came up with the idea to store money in buildings, other men have dedicated themselves to the pursuit of removing that money from those buildings—no matter how safely the money is guarded, and no matter how technologically advanced the building is. The book you are holding in your hands is a chronicle of that not-so-noble pursuit. For *This Here's a Stick-Up*, I didn't want to write a typical history of bank robbery; instead, I chose the snapshot approach—quick glimpses of the country's most infamous heisters from the past 200 years, along with everything else the casual reader might want to know about robbing banks. Check fraud and armored car heists may be more lucrative, but they're usually not as fun to read about as a good old-fashioned jug heist.

*This Here's a Stick-Up* is not meant to applaud criminal efforts. Then again, bank robbers have always had a special place in the hearts of the American public. As far as criminals go, murderers aren't exactly likeable. Muggers are plain creepy, and that goes double for drug dealers, rapists, and serial killers. And after September 11, terrorists certainly aren't going to win any popularity contests. But bank robbers ... now that's a criminal you can root for. (I'm not talking about the psycho gangbanging punks who get their jollies by intimidating, hitting, or even shooting innocent people; as far as I'm concerned, they can rot in Hell, Circle 7, Aisle 6, Orchestra Seating, No Smoking, thankyouverymuch.) I'm thinking about the classic gentleman bank robber, the dapper fellow in the snap-brim fedora who doesn't want anyone to get hurt, who only wants his $50s and $100s in nonsequential bills—hold the dye packs—so he can snatch a bit of the American Dream for himself.

It's not hard to fathom the appeal. When kids play cops and robbers, who ever wants to be the cop? Who hasn't fantasized about striking it wildly rich? And when's the last time you shed a tear over a bank taking one on the chin? (Hell, I'm still bitter about being charged $2.50 to withdraw my own money from an ATM.) The only criminals in America who can lay claim to being bona fide folk heroes are bank robbers—heisters like Jesse James, John Dillinger, and Bonnie and Clyde. Maybe that's because anyone who's ever struggled over money would secretly like to *be* a bank robber.

Paddy Mitchell notes in his foreword that the author of this book has never robbed a bank, but that's not entirely correct. In 1980, when

I was in third grade, I masterminded the knockover of a small U.S. Treasury. At least, that's what it said on the side of the tin can bank. Technically, it wasn't robbery, since the money inside—mostly silver and half dollars—belonged to me. My mom (rightly so) thought I should save the money for some noble cause, such as a college education. I wanted to buy magic tricks from a novelty shop around the corner. So I popped the top, helped myself to a handful of chunky coins, and spent them on disappearing ink and rubber severed thumbs. I was quickly ratted out, however, and the heat was intense. Mom was not one for plea bargaining. From then on, I was scared straight; I knew I had neither the brains nor the cajones to ever be a successful bank robber.

Nonetheless, I've been experiencing a weird side-effect from writing this book: I can't help but case joints everywhere I go. My own bank branch in downtown Philadelphia, I notice, lacks bulletproof bandit barriers around the teller areas. There are plenty of windows, which can make a take-over more visible than most robbers would like, but they also make it easy to case the place from the landscaped patio right outside. There are a half-dozen surveillance cameras trained on each and every teller station, but that's nothing a wide-brimmed hat and a paste-on moustache couldn't fix. And once outside, it would be very, very easy to blend into the downtown crowds ....

The mania has followed me everywhere. My wife Meredith and I went for lunch at a small diner in Northeast Philly a few months ago. I noticed that the diner didn't accept any credit cards. *Wow,* I thought to myself. *They must deal in a ton of cash here.*

"What?" asked Meredith, who saw that I seemed deep in thought.

"I wonder if these guys have been robbed a lot."

Meredith looked at me funny. We had our lunch, paid the check, then went on our way.

I left a really big tip.

Philadelphia, Pennsylvania
January 2002

## ACCOMPLICES

*Partners, jugmarkers, hired guns, and other assorted riffraff who made this book possible:*

Had I been able to pull off the heist of a lifetime, I would give each of the following people a cool million each. Unfortunately, they're stuck with these heartfelt words of thanks.

**Gary "the Hat" Goldstein** cased, conceptualized, and bankrolled this caper. Its successes are entirely his; its failures are entirely mine. And sitting in the lobby, keeping an eye out for the coppers, was the ever-tenacious **David "Hale" Smith**. If John Dillinger had guys like these on his side, he wouldn't be … well, dead.

**Jennifer "Machine Gun" Moore** double-checked the heist plan and uncovered its many flaws. **Rich "Dick" Rys** and **April "Mad Dog" White** read this book in its earliest form and offered the kind of frank, honest criticism you only hear from prison buddies. **Patrick "Paddy" Mitchell** (and his trusty field op **Jimmy "the Craftsman" Allen**) offered me insights into a world of banditry that a boy could only dream about. **Loren "Pretty Boy" Feldman** taught me everything I know about journalism, and was gracious enough not to fire me as I labored on this book instead of thinking up funnier "News Quiz" questions. **Ron "Baby Face" Geraci** first turned me on to cool Dillinger stories, and forgives me for forgetting his birthday year after year.

I also owe my clean getaway to a **stellar crew of smooth operators** (in no particular order): James Roach (for the Most Dangerous Game), Albin Dixon (for the detective stories), Courtney Dreslin, Tim Haas, Seth Robertson, Myatt Murphy, Jordan "Norman" Matus, "Kid Valentine" O'Connor, Robert Pollock, Will Carr, Mark Blumenthal, Bill Crider, Etienne Borgers, Luca Conti, Mark Sullivan, William Hagen, Jim Doherty, George P. Pelecanos, Paul Challen, Rick Otten-stein, Welling Savo, Eddie Muller, Bill Helmer, Erma Rabusa, Linda Vizi, Ernie Porter, Ron Avery, Tom McGrath, Vicki Glembocki, Sasha Issenberg, Noel Weyrich, Larrie Platte, Bob "the Actuary" Wilkowski, Greg "Luke" Clark … but most of all Mom, Dad, Gregg, Jamie, Marcy, Linda A. Paul (photographer), Sir, and "Super Lou" Wojciechowski.

# PART 1

## THE MEN BEHIND THE MASKS

# 1 THE CARPENTERS' HALL HEISTERS

**Gang members:** Isaac Davis and Thomas Cunningham

**Number of banks robbed:** One

**Estimated lifetime take:** $162,821

**Claim to fame:** Davis and Cunningham pulled the first major bank heist in America

## "I DON'T THINK THEY ARE AFTER ANY GOOD."

Philadelphia in the summer of 1798 was an ideal time and place for a bank robbery. Yellow Fever was sweeping the city and scaring residents into the countryside—even the U.S. government, based in Philly back then, moved to a nearby village called Germantown to escape the creeping, feverish death that would rage on to claim 1,300 lives. And bank security wasn't exactly state of the art back then. There were no video surveillance cameras, no laser beam tripwires, not even so much as a dye pack or panic button. All that separated bank loot from would-be thieves was a brick wall, doors of forged steel, and carefully constructed locks.

That summer, local blacksmith Patrick Lyon received word that the Bank of Pennsylvania needed him for a job. The bank was moving into temporary digs at Carpenters' Hall—where the First Continental Congress first met more than 20 years before. Lyon was torn; he'd wanted to leave town and sail to Cape Henlopen, Delaware, to escape the Yellow Fever. Lyon's own 19-year-old apprentice was already looking pale and had a bad cough. This was no time to hang around town.

But Lyon took the job anyway and helped the Bank of Pennsylvania with the fittings and locks on their new vault. That is to say, new/old vault: The Bank had decided to keep the Hall's existing vault—a brick addition jutting out of the building—and cover it with their own vault doors. Then Lyon quickly packed his bags and hopped on a small boat sailing down the Delaware River.

Lyon and his apprentice landed at Lewistown, now known as Lewes, Delaware, and tried to relax. But the young man was too far gone with the fever and died two days later. To make matters worse, Lyon started hearing some strange gossip around town. Seems the Bank of Pennsylvania had been robbed the night of Saturday, August 31. The score: $162,821—a staggering sum in post-Revolutionary Philadelphia. The act alone was staggering; it was the first bank robbery in American history, according to writer Ron Avery and historian Carl G. Karsch in their articles on the Carpenters' Hall website (www.ushistory.org/carpentershall).

According to gossip, the heist was an inside job. Gossip also had it that Lyon himself was the number-one suspect.

Of course, Lyon knew *he* didn't do it. He had been too concerned with getting out of Philadelphia before he caught the fever. So who did? The locks he had installed were spring and tumbler locks that were impossible to pick. It had to be an inside job. That's when he remembered Samuel Robinson, a carpenter who oversaw the Bank of Pennsylvania's vault move to Carpenters' Hall. Robinson had brought a man named Isaac Davis to Lyon's blacksmithing shop while he worked on the new vault doors. Davis had paid particularly close attention to the workings of the locks and keyholes. And come to think of it, he'd seen both Robinson and Davis boozing it up together before Lyon had departed for Lewes. According to writer Ron Avery, Lyon had turned to his soon-to-be-dead apprentice and said, "I don't think they are after any good."

Being an upright blacksmith and an honest man, Lyon immediately returned to Philadelphia to clear his name. The city constable didn't believe him and threw him in jail, which was teeming with Yellow

Fever. To the constable and the bank president, it seemed suspicious that Lyon had $1,400 recently deposited in the Bank of North America. There was also the matter of Lyon's oh-so-convenient flight to Delaware. Lyon would later write: "I found I was in the hands of those who are not the most intelligent of mankind."

Of course, Lyon had been right: Isaac Davis was the mastermind behind the heist. He had teamed up with the bank's porter, Thomas Cunningham, who had a copy of the new vault key. Davis was caught when his bank—that would be the Bank of Pennsylvania, which he had robbed—noticed him depositing large amounts of money into his account. The genius was arrested, but never prosecuted because he agreed to return the money. Instead, fate meted out justice: Cunningham fell victim to Yellow Fever just days after the heist, and Davis was removed from the list of official Carpenters' Company members. (Maybe it wasn't exactly justice for Davis. But it probably hurt his feelings for a while.)

And poor Pat Lyon? He later sued the bank for wrongful prosecution, and during his trial he was more than happy to recount the horrors of his three months in prison. Lyon would later pen a book about his ordeal, *Narrative of Patrick Lyon Who Suffered Three Months Severe Imprisonment in Philadelphia Gaol on Merely a Vague Suspicion of Being Concerned in a Robbery of the Bank of Pennsylvania with His Remarks Thereon.* Not the snappiest title in the world, but it was from the heart.

Lyon walked away with $9,000 as a result of the first American bank robbery, inadvertently demonstrating the best way to make a quick buck in the United States: Sue someone.

## Cool Fact from the Vault

Today at Carpenters' Hall, where the Bank of Pennsylvania vault used to stand, sits a different kind of green: a sizeable bush.

## 2  EDWARD SMITH

**Number of banks robbed:** One

**Estimated lifetime take:** $245,000

**Claim to fame:** Smith was the first man to be indicted for bank robbery in the United States

## FROM WALL STREET TO SING SING

On March 19, 1831, Edward Smith stole $245,000 in cash and Spanish doubloons from City Bank on Wall Street. Apparently, the native Englishman used a set of duplicate keys he had obtained to sneak into the vault. He was caught after a suspicious spending spree but sentenced to only five years of hard labor on the rock pile at Sing Sing, thus becoming the first American to be indicted for bank robbery. As news of Smith's bold robbery began to spread across the country, however, banks everywhere started to consider something for the very first time: People might actually try to come up with clever schemes to steal what was locked away inside.

### Cool Fact from the Vault

According to one New Yorker's 1896 memoirs, Smith had a partner named Robert James Murray, whom history has largely forgotten. This entry is no exception.

# 3  EDWARD W. GREEN

**Number of banks robbed:** One

**Estimated lifetime take:** A little more than $5,000

**Claim to fame:** Green was the first man to hold a pistol on a bank employee

## ARMED, ALCOHOLIC, AND DANGEROUS

For a criminal innovator, 30-year-old Edward W. Green was sloppy as hell. Green was the postmaster of Malden, Massachusetts, and he had two problems: alcohol and mammoth debt. Green often used the first problem to forget about the second. On December 15, 1863, while on a particularly wild bender, Green staggered over to the nearby Malden bank and saw young Frank E. Converse, the 17-year-old son of the bank president, minding the shop. A dim gaslight flickered to life somewhere in Green's brain and a plot was hatched, right there in the bank lobby.

It wasn't a terribly elaborate plot. Green simply walked home, dug out his pistol, then returned to the Malden bank and pumped two bullets into Converse's head. Green walked around to the bank's tiny safe, helped himself to more than $5,000, and made his way out of town. Then, the former postmaster made the mistake that would doom scores of armed robbers to follow in his wake: Green started spending the loot like crazy. Police were quick to pick up on this and hauled him in for questioning. Most likely feeling sorry for himself,

Green confessed to the crimes. He was sentenced to death and then executed on February 27, 1866—only two weeks after the James Gang committed their infamous first bank job in Liberty, Missouri (see the next entry). Most people think Frank and Jesse James pulled the first daytime bank heist in U.S. history, but Green had them beat by a little more than two years.

## Cool Fact from the Vault

Apparently, Green was partially crippled from a childhood accident and took pity on himself by spending money and swilling booze. (It wasn't easy being Green.)

# 4  THE JAMES GANG

**Gang members:** Alexander Franklin James, Jesse Woodson James, Ben Cooper, Frank Gregg, Red Monkus, Cole Younger, Bob Younger, Payne Jones, Clell Miller, Bill Chadwell, Charley Pitts, James White, and Bob Ford, among others

**Number of banks robbed:** About 12, along with 7 trains and 5 stagecoaches in 11 states and territories

**Estimated lifetime take:** About half a million dollars

**Claim to fame:** The James Boys applied what they learned in military raids during the Civil War to the art of bank robbery, inspiring generations of future bank robbers

## "I AIN'T GONNA SASS BACK TO NO JESSE JAMES. THE MONEY'S YOURS!"

If nothing else, brothers Frank and Jesse James were full of chutzpah. Once, they knocked over a bank in Corydon, Iowa, while most of the town's residents were at church listening to a speech. After helping themselves to $45,000, the James Brothers—along with their usual partners, the Younger Brothers—rode their horses over to the church to interrupt the proceedings. "We've just been down to the bank and taken every dollar in the till," Jesse proudly announced. Then the James Gang doffed their Stetsons and galloped away.

Oddly enough, Jesse James almost didn't live long enough to become the world's most famous outlaw. During the Civil War, when the boys were barely teens, Frank and Jesse's home state of Missouri was run over by the Union Army, thereby inspiring some Confederate loyalists to become guerrilla soldiers, raiding and robbing any Union target they could find. (Even the Confederate Congress wasn't fully behind the bloody guerrillas, who seemed overly fond of robbing and pillaging for personal gain.) Frank and Jesse—only 20 and 17, respectively—hated anything Yankee and were quick to sign up with the guerrillas. Frank was part of the infamous William Clarke Quantrill raid on Lawrence, Kansas, which killed dozens of men and boys and left the town in flames. Later, Frank and Jesse joined Bloody Bill Anderson's guerrilla crew, which raided the town of Centralia, Missouri, and robbed a passing train, slaughtering 25 Union soldiers who were passengers. Two hundred Union troops charged off against Anderson's two hundred twenty-five guerillas … and the Union boys lost—big time. Jesse himself shot and killed the Union commander.

Ultimately, the victory at Centralia didn't matter: General Lee surrendered at Appomattox, and the James boys were forced to give themselves up. Frank was arrested and paroled, but a surrendering Jesse—carrying a white flag and everything—received a .36 caliber slug in the chest from an overzealous Union soldier near Lexington, Missouri. Jesse, coughing blood and almost too dizzy to remain conscious, managed to crawl away into the woods. He was later recovered by the Union troops, but a Union commander took mercy on him, and he was sent home to his mother in Clay County so he could die in peace.

Jesse, of course, didn't die. His mother, Zerelda "Zee" Samuel (she'd remarried after her first husband died of pneumonia), nursed him back to health, and soon Jesse was looking for a little Union payback. So Jesse and Frank decided to rob some banks, especially ones owned by Union men who moved into their territory and took advantage of hard-working yet war-ravaged residents.

Their first robbery went down on Valentine's Day 1866, in Liberty, Missouri. It was an appropriate place to hit: Liberty was where Jesse was heading when he decided to surrender and received a bullet for his trouble. The James boys were joined by 10 other men—many of them former Quantrill Raiders, including a rough character named Cole Younger—all on horseback, strapped with six-shooters and wearing long soldier's overcoats. It was like old times. Three gang members set up watch throughout the town, while Frank and Cole hopped off their horses and walked into the Clay County Savings Association.

*Don't mess with Jesse: The legendary Jesse James (left) poses with members of his gang, most likely two of the Younger brothers.*

Frank slid a $10 bill across the bank counter. "I'd like a bill changed," he said.

The clerk was William Bird, son of the bank's cashier, Greenup Bird. William reached out for the 10-spot, then looked up to see a .44 pistol in his face.

"Actually, I'd like all the money in the bank," said Frank.

Greenup and William were shocked; daylight bank robberies were practically unheard of in 1866. "Make a move and we'll shoot you down," Frank announced, forcing William toward the bank vault.

Cole asked Greenup where the greenbacks were and then helped himself to a stack of Yankee cash, bank notes, and bonds. Together with gold and silver coins from the vault, James and Cole would walk out of the bank with about $60,000, but not before forcing both the Bird men into the bank vault. "Stay in there," one of the robbers said. "You know all Birds should be caged!"

As the James Gang rode away, an unlucky college student named George Wymore happened to be crossing the street. Seeing the speeding outlaws headed toward him, Wymore jumped for cover. But it was too late; one of the gang members didn't want any witnesses and shot four bullets into Wymore's body, killing him instantly. A posse was dispatched, but the gang had already split up. Besides, no one thought to look one town north: Kearney, the home of Frank and Jesse James.

This first bank job—one of the first few in the country—was the beginning of a 15-year career that would encompass 12 banks, 7 trains, 5 stagecoaches, and take the lives of at least half a dozen men. But it wasn't smooth going at first. On October 30, 1866, the James Gang raided the banking house of Alexander Mitchell & Company in Lexington, Missouri. They used the same MO: One gang member asked for change, this time for a $50. Cashier J.L. Thomas, having read about the Liberty robbery, refused. Two more gang members entered the bank, pistols in hand. "You've got $100,000 in this bank," said one of them. "Unless you turn it over, you'll be killed." Thomas claimed not to have the key, and after a rough search, the robbers realized he was telling the truth. The Gang netted only $2,000 from the cashier drawers.

Their next bank robbery, on March 2, 1867, was even more disappointing. The gang rushed into a Savanna, Missouri, bank, but president Judge John McClain refused to produce the vault keys. One gang member shot him in the chest, but McClain still stubbornly refused. The Gang left empty-handed, and McClain survived his wound.

After these disappointing raids, Frank and Jesse decided to vary their technique. Instead of posting ordinary lookouts who might arouse suspicion, they thought the backup gang members should shoot their pistols in the air and raise a general ruckus, frightening local residents who might want to play hero. Also, they thought the gang members were being too nervous and not receiving the amount of loot they would if they had a little more bravado in them.

So on May 22, 1867, the James Gang rode into Richmond, Missouri, and started whooping and shooting. As a result, the raid on Hughes and Madison Bank went smoothly—no bank president hero this time—but the take was only $4,000. And then the mayor of Richmond led a posse after the James Gang, resulting in the death of the mayor and two other citizens (one of them a 15-year-old boy), and the capture and death of a minor James Gang member, Payne Jones.

On March 20, 1868, a cattle dealer from Louisville entered a bank in Russellville, Kentucky and slid a $100 bill across the counter. Cashier Nimrod Long saw the bill was phony and told the dealer so. "I reckon it is," said the dealer, whose real name was Frank James, "but this isn't." Long looked down at a pistol. "Open the vault," Frank commanded. Long ran for the front door and was nearly scalped by a bullet, but managed to escape into the street, crying for help. The gang stole $14,000 and had to shoot their way out of town.

Frank and Jesse were the heart of the James Gang, but they were often joined by the Younger brothers—Cole, who had served with the Jameses in the Civil War guerrilla raids, and his siblings Bob and Jim. (The Jameses and the Youngers were also distant cousins.) While other members were also ex-guerrillas, some were ordinarily law-abiding farmers who would ride with the Jameses for a single job to earn enough seed money for next year's planting. But in December 1869, Frank and Jesse James decided to work alone and robbed the Daviess County Savings Bank in Gallatin, Missouri. For Jesse, it was personal: He'd heard a rumor that the bank clerk was one John Sheets, the Union commander whose unit had shot Jesse as he attempted to surrender. Jesse walked into the bank and asked for change for $100, all the while reading the name "John Sheets" on the clerk's placard. Sheets, meanwhile, was wise to the bill-change trick and reached into his drawer for his pistol. Jesse saw it and quickly fired two bullets into the former Union man, and then grabbed $700 from an open safe. Frank and Jesse were forced to shoot their way out, and in the confusion, Jesse was dragged 30 feet by his own horse before being rescued by Frank. An angry Gallatin posse attempted to gun them down, and Frank and Jesse barely escaped.

The not-so-smooth getaway in Gallatin unnerved the James boys, who decided to hang back for a few years. They had good reason to be nervous: A week after the Gallatin job, the *Kansas City Times* reported that the James boys had been positively identified—at first— and labeled them as "desperate men, having had much experience in horse and revolver work." The reward on their heads: $3,000. Frank and Jesse, however, were safe in Clay County, Missouri, where Mother Zee and various neighbors were more than happy to help them avoid lawmen. Even some of the Jameses' victims—innocent bystanders in held-up banks—couldn't resist admiring the bold out-laws. Reportedly, Jesse would never leave a bank without a sly nod, hand wave, or hat doff. He also was reported to stuff a wad of stolen money into women's purses now and again. What was not to love?

When the James Gang returned, it was with a new, giddy kind of bravado. Their welcome back job was the $45,000 Corydon, Iowa, heist, which was followed a year later by an April 1872, raid on a bank in Columbia, Kentucky, which earned them only $600. Still, the Gang's reputation began to precede them. In November 1873, the James Gang robbed the heavily guarded St. Genevieve Bank in Miss-ouri, and no one resisted. One clerk meekly asked, "You're Jesse James, aren't ya?"

"Yeah, what of it?" replied Jesse.

"Nuthin' sir," said the clerk. "I ain't gonna sass back to no Jesse James. The money's yours!"

By this time, the James Gang had also earned the attention of the Pinkertons, the nineteenth-century detective agency who acted as an unofficial FBI before the FBI existed. They weren't part of the federal government, but to the James boys, they might as well have been; after all, the Pinkertons had been hired by Yankee money to track and destroy them. In January 1875, Pinkerton men stormed Mother Zee Samuel's farm, lobbing either a flare or grenade into the house. Whatever it was, it exploded, ripping away a big chunk of Mother Zee's arm and killing her eight-year-old son—half-brother to both Frank and Jesse. From that point on, the Jameses wanted nothing more than to exact vengeance on the Yankee detectives. And shortly, after a series of lucrative train robberies—a trick they learned from the notorious Reno Brothers (see the next entry)—they saw their chance in a bank up north in Minnesota.

The First National Bank in Northfield, Minnesota, was attractive for two reasons: (1) At any given moment, there was rumored to be $200,000 in its vaults, and (2) its principal stockholders were Benjamin Butler and W. A. Ames, two men who, in the opinion of the Jameses, had raped the South both militarily and financially. On September 7, 1876, the members of the gang set off for Northfield, planning to hit the First National and another bank, if possible. Flush with train cash, the gang was equipped with new pistols and fresh, expensive horses and was itching to beat the tar out of any Yankee hicks who gave them trouble.

But the James Gang grossly underestimated the town of North-field, which was full of Bible-beaters—with particular emphasis on the beating. Residents couldn't help but notice the duded-up strangers who rode into town—a few of them entering their banks, others staying outside with their horses—and decided to arm themselves for a fight, taking strategic shooting positions up and down the street. The fight began inside the First National, when teller Joseph Heywood refused to open a safe for Jesse James, even after a couple punches to the gut with a pistol poking at his head. (Little did Jesse know that the safe was already open.) That's when voices called out, "We have trouble boiling out here!"

When Jesse came running out of the bank, angry residents started firing bullets from every direction. Jesse felt one rip through his duster, narrowly missing his body. Gang member Clell Miller jumped on his horse, and his face was immediately blown away by buckshot.

Charley Pitts caught a round in the shoulder. Frank James felt a bullet slap into his leg. Bill Chadwell was shot in the heart. Bob Younger was shot in his right hand but kept firing with his left. Somehow, Frank and Jesse James, Bob, Cole, and Jim Younger, along with Pitts, managed to ride through the hellstorm of bullets and regroup a few miles out of town.

After barely escaping bloody Northfield, the Jameses and the Youngers agreed to split up, knowing that a posse would be racing after them to finish the job. Fourteen days later, the Youngers were caught hiding in a Minnesota swamp and arrested; Pitts was found dead next to them. The James boys, meanwhile, took the long way home: through the Dakotas, then Iowa and Wisconsin, then Indiana and Kentucky, finally settling in Tennessee, where they set up shop as humble farmers. And for the next three years, they stayed humble.

After three years of planting seeds and moving manure, though, Frank and Jesse had run through most of their stolen money and got the itch again. They were too young—and poor—to retire. So they recruited a new gang, which included brothers Charlie and Robert Ford, who were also from Missouri and wanted to be the James brothers when they grew up. The new and improved James Gang was a smashing success, robbing a train of $40,000 for starters and following up with other admirable strikes, including their last bank heist at the Sexton Bank in Riverton, Iowa, which netted them $5,000. But the new gang wasn't perfect. There was a flawed member—one Robert Ford, who cut a deal with the governor. Noir songwriter Warren Zevon put it best in his 1976 song "Frank and Jesse James":

> Robert Ford, a gunman, in exchange for his parole
> Took the life of James the outlaw, which he snuck up on and stole.

Bob Ford didn't call Jesse out to a gunfight, or anything honorable like that. Instead, Ford waited until Jesse was unarmed in his own home with his wife and children. Right after breakfast the morning of April 3, 1882, Jesse decided to fix a crooked painting on the wall that read "God Bless This Home." With Jesse's back to him, Ford pulled out his revolver and shot Jesse behind his ear. The outlaw was only 34 years old.

Jesse James—or at least his legend—would go on to capture the imagination of Americans for the next century and beyond, inspiring other notable criminals such as the Dalton Gang and Ma Barker, but also any American who admires Jesse's own particular brand of justice, honor, and vengeance.

Frank James, after being acquitted of all charges against him, would go on to host tourists at his family's farm and encourage people to buy pebbles from his brother's grave. He died at age 72.

## Cool Fact from the Vault

Jesse's nickname was "Dingus." It wasn't anything sexual. Once, while polishing his gun before a raid, Jesse accidentally blasted off the tip of his left middle finger. "If that ain't the dingus-dangest thing!" exclaimed Jesse, prompting howls of laughter from his fellow raiders. The name stuck with him the rest of his dingus-dangest life.

## DIGGING JESSE JAMES

Some researchers claim that James faked his 1882 death and lived to be 104 years old. Proving it means going back to where the bodies are buried.

In 1951, an elderly man named J. Frank Dalton moved to Granbury, Texas, and let it be known that "Dalton" wasn't his real name. He claimed to have been born Jesse Woodson James in 1847. "Jesse" also claimed his murder at the hands of Bob Ford had been an elaborate setup, allowing him to escape manhunters and live to the ripe old age of 104 in peace and obscurity. The gossip spread through Granbury like wildfire. Even the local sheriff, Oran C. Baker, believed Dalton's story. When Dalton died later that same year, Baker says he checked the body and "counted 32 bullet holes from his forehead to his knees," presumably reminders of the James Gang's various misadventures. Dalton's gravestone bore the name *Jessie Woodson James*, along with the words: *Supposedly killed in 1882.*

Twenty years later, Jesse's descendants, in an effort to put the rumors to rest, allowed the outlaw's remains to be exhumed at the family burial site in Kearny, Missouri. According to the family, a positive identification was made: The body was indeed Jesse's. Nearly 25 years later, in 1995, poor Jesse was dug up yet again—there wasn't much left aside from a jawbone and some tufts of hair—this time to be subjected to a DNA mapping test. The result: Scientists said the remains were most likely those of Jesse James. Coffin (and case) closed.

But some refused to let the matter die. An Oklahoman used-car salesman and amateur historian named Bud Hardcastle spent years (and $10,000 of his own money) researching J. Frank Dalton, and came to believe the old man was indeed Jesse James. Hardcastle convinced a judge in local Hood County to allow the exhumation of Dalton, and on May 30, 2000, a backhoe dug into the packed soil above Dalton's grave. "It's important to me because I promised some James family members that I'd get the truth out," said Hardcastle to a reporter. "We want to set history straight. They made a big mistake."

And they were about to make another one. On May 30, thanks to a weird headstone mix-up, the diggers accidentally exhumed the steel coffin of Henry Holland, a one-armed man who died in 1927. (Historians are fairly confident that both Jesse and J. Frank Dalton had two arms each.) "It's back to square one," said Hardcastle after learning the grisly news. "But it is certainly something we started and intend to finish."

Then came another surprise: Beneath Holland's steel coffin was another coffin—this one unmarked and made of wood. Hardcastle believes this one contains Dalton's remains and has filed another request in Hood County Court to exhume that body. "I know what I'm talking about, and I'm not going to quit," he told a reporter from the Associated Press in early 2001. "We want to do the same thing we did before. Of course, we're going to move over one spot. It wasn't our fault the tombstone was put in the wrong place."

As of this writing, Hardcastle was still waiting for permission. For now, the original legend of Jesse James rests in peace.

# 5  THE RENO BROTHERS GANG

**Gang members:** Frank Reno, John Reno, Simon Reno, William Reno; also, assorted horse thieves, safecrackers, and counterfeiters

**Number of banks robbed:** Three

**Estimated lifetime take:** At least $150,000, but much of it was the result of train robberies; their largest bank haul was $22,000

**Claim to fame:** The Renos were brutally efficient, politically protected bank robbers and also the first to rob a train

## "APRIL FOOLS!"

Like the James Brothers, the Reno Brothers got their start in the Civil War. Only they didn't start out learning their tricks *in* an army; they committed their first crimes *scamming* one. Back in the 1860s, the Union Army allowed recruiting officers to pay new soldiers a cash bounty. Men who took the cash, fought for a while, then rejoined for another cash bonus were called "bounty jumpers." Frank, John, Simon, and William Reno—by all accounts, tall, dark, and thuggish-looking men—were notorious for pulling this stunt all over the state of Indiana.

Shortly after the war ended, the Reno boys got the idea to gather up a crew of thieves, thugs, and murderers and rob farmers in their native southern Indiana, eventually branching out into Iowa and Missouri. They decided they needed a hideout and found one in the Rader House, a hotel in downtown Rockford, Indiana, which was situated near a railroad line. Soon crooks, thugs, and gamblers from all over convened at the Rader to join up with the Reno boys. (The Rader House was not only handy for planning robberies but also for mugging the innocent travelers who checked into the House, mistakenly thinking it was on the up-and-up.) The Renos frightened honest residents out of town with a series of fires and lined the pockets of local politicians with enough cash to keep them quiet. When greenbacks wouldn't work, fists and guns did the trick. Rockford was theirs.

But the Renos weren't satisfied with their seemingly law-proof operation. They wanted a bigger score. The rumbling of the trains passing through Seymour, Indiana, gave John Reno, the gang leader, an idea. On October 6, 1866, the Renos entered the history books by being the first men to rob a train. They picked a fast express from the Ohio and Mississippi Railroad and watched it loop around Seymour, Indiana. Somehow, Frank and John Reno got the attention of the engineer and signaled for him to stop; amazingly, he did. (Then again, no one had ever robbed a train before.) That's when the rest of the Reno Gang appeared and helped themselves to $10,000 in gold and cash tucked away in the Adams Express car.

Enter Allan J. Pinkerton. By the time he locked horns with the Renos, Pinkerton had gone from barrel maker to personal guardian of Abraham Lincoln during the Civil War. After the war, Pinkerton—along with the famous detective agency he created—turned his sights to bank and train robbers and was willing to hunt them from Atlantic to Pacific. Banks and railroad lines, especially the Adams Express folks, were eager to hire the relentless Pinkerton men. A few months after the Adams Express job, the Reno Gang celebrated by knocking over a bank in Daviess, Missouri, and taking $22,000. Their attention, however, was still focused on train robberies. They soon became fond of planning train heists in the Seymour train station, in full view of the public. This was something the Pinkerton detectives used against them in late 1867 by surprising the thieves at the station and corralling ringleader John Reno into a departing train, at which point the Pinkerton men waiting on the train slapped the cuffs on him. (They didn't want to tackle the whole gang at once and incite a bloodbath.) Most rational criminals would take the hint and flee as quickly as possible. Not Simon, William, and Frank Reno. No, the swarthy brothers quickly commandeered another train, forcing the engineer to race down the tracks after their brother.

Quick-thinking railroad employees diverted the Reno Brothers' train onto another track, and John was delivered to jail as planned. No pocketed politician could help him then; John was given a sentence of 50 years of hard labor. But the loss of their leader didn't stop Frank (a.k.a. "Trick"), William (a.k.a. "Wilk"), or Simon. They robbed another bank in Magnolia, Iowa, this time netting $14,000 and nearly bankrupting the town in the process. Once again, the Pinkertons swooped down. The detectives managed to surprise the Renos at their Iowa hideout and threw the lot in jail.

But they didn't stay there long. The Renos busted out on April 1, 1868. One of them even wrote "April Fools!" on the side of the jail before hightailing it out of there. Exactly one month and 22 days later, the Reno Gang—which by this point had swelled to 24 men—hit another train, the Jefferson, Missouri and Indianapolis Railroad Flyer, for $96,000 in cash, gold, and government bonds. (Even the Reno boys' jaws dropped when they realized how much loot was on board.) At the time, it was the most lucrative raid in the Old West. Suddenly, the Reno boys made the James boys look like tinhorns.

But this audacious raid had cranked up the heat to a white-hot intensity, and it became clear to Frank that it was time to hide the loot and split up. Frank and robbing partner Charlie Anderson fled for Windsor, Canada, while William and Simon hid in the skid row alleys of Indianapolis. Some of the other Reno Gang members tried to pull jobs without the brothers, but the Pinkertons—and an increasing number of vigilante gangs—made short work of them.

Then in the fall of 1868, bad news came to Frank Reno in Canada: His brothers William and Simon had been nabbed by the Pinkertons and were being kept in a jail in New Albany, Indiana. And the Pinkertons were clamoring for the Canadian authorities to round up Frank and extradite him to the United States. This merely made Frank—the same Frank who hijacked a train in a desperate attempt to save his brother John—very angry. He hired someone to kill Allan Pinkerton, hoping to scare the man's private dicks back into their offices. The attempt failed, and the Canadians were ready to wash their hands of Frank Reno. He was unceremoniously shipped out and dumped into the New Albany jail, along with his brothers. The trial was set for late December 1868.

The Reno boys never made it to the courtroom. Early on the morning of December 12, more than 50 men in hoods stormed the jail, overpowering the sheriff and the guards. One brave guard threatened to shoot anyone who dared come any closer.

"We have five nooses," one of the hooded vigilantes shouted back. "Four for the Reno Gang and one for the jailer who gets in our way."

The guard opened the door.

The angry mob found Frank Reno first. "God have mercy on my soul," he gasped as the rope cut into his neck. Next came Simon, and then William, who told the vigilantes his father would be back to haunt them all. No one paid him any mind and they snapped his neck, too. Finally, the mob set upon a quivering, praying Charlie Anderson. But Anderson's rope miraculously snapped mid-hanging, and the outlaw collapsed to the floor, praying to Jesus to forgive his sins.

"It's too late for prayers, Charlie," said one vigilante, who strung him up again. There was no supernatural intervention this time.

The authorities never discovered the identity of the 50 hooded killers, but it is a safe bet that a few of them had been victims of the Reno Gang. They threatened to come back, too, if any other robbers got similar ideas. "Having first lopped off the branches, and finally uprooted the tree of evil which was in our midst," read a printed proclamation from the self-proclaimed Jackson County Vigilante Committee, "we beg to be allowed to rest here. We are loathe to shed blood again, and will not do so unless compelled in defense of our lives."

## Cool Fact from the Vault

Some believe the $96,000 in gold or cash from the Jefferson, Missouri, and Indianapolis Railroad robbery is still out there, hidden by the Renos somewhere in Jackson County, Indiana.

# 6 GEORGE LEONIDAS LESLIE

**Nicknames:** George Howard and "Western George"

**Gang members:** Jimmy Hope, Jimmy Brady, Bill Kelly, Abe Coakley, Shang Draper, Red Leary, Worcester Sam Perris, "Banjo" Pete Emerson, and Johnny Dobbs, among others

**Number of banks robbed:** Dozens

**Estimated lifetime take:** Between $7 and $12 million

**Claim to fame:** Leslie was famous for casing banks by moving among Manhattan's high-society circles, then falling in with underworld gangsters to pull off the robberies

## KING OF THE BANK ROBBERS

George Leonidas Leslie, the self-styled "King of the Bank Robbers," stole more than 10 times the amount the James Brothers ever did. In *Low Life,* a grisly study of the underbelly of gaslight-era New York City, author Luc Sante writes that a police lieutenant considered Leslie responsible for 80 percent of the bank robberies between the end of the Civil War and 1884. "Such estimates must be viewed with suspicion as sounding entirely too convenient," writes Sante. "One set of devious masterminds, after all, does less damage to police prestige than a whole town full of bank robbers. Nevertheless, there is no denying Leslie's prowess." Sante wasn't kidding. Leslie managed to amass an estimated $7 to $12 million by utilizing carefully detailed plans, friends in Manhattan's upper crust, ... and one thin piece of wire.

George Leslie didn't need to rob banks. The son of a wealthy beer baron family in Toledo, Ohio, Leslie was sent to study architecture at the University of Cincinnati, where he graduated with honors. Shortly after, he moved to New York to make his fortune. "He was a fine-looking man," said one police inspector, "with cultured tastes and refined manners." But instead of looking for a job, Leslie busied himself moving in the circles of Manhattan's social elite during the mid-1860s. It wasn't hard work. The Leslie name was a ticket into private clubs and exclusive parties. Everyone loved Leslie, even though no one seemed to know exactly what he did for a living. The young dandy liked to keep his mind active, that was for sure. He was always asking to see the blueprints and architectural plans of his new friends' buildings. Their banks, especially. Leslie's moneyed friends had no idea that instead of studying floor joists and support beams, the young man was studying the banks' structural weaknesses.

Hobnobbing wasn't the only kind of bank reconnaissance Leslie did. He would also visit banks in person, pretending to be a fat cat who wanted to dump a huge amount of money into their coffers. While he was touring the facilities, Leslie was taking careful mental notes of the bank layout. Later, he would transcribe his memories into detailed plans.

Meanwhile, Leslie had made another new friend in Manhattan: Frederika "Marm" Mandelbaum, the top fence in 1860s New York City. Mandelbaum was also known as "Ma Crime," and she was exactly the kind of contact Leslie needed to find the right men to execute his expertly researched and timed robberies. Once he had the men lined up, Leslie simply asked his upper-crust friends—bank presidents, among them—to help out and give one of his down-on-his-luck "friends" a job as a porter. His inside man in place, Leslie then drilled his hand-picked team until each robber could picture the operation, the layout, and the getaways as if they had already pulled the heist a dozen times.

Aside from the contacts, both high and low, and the bank plans and operation drills, there was one more key to Leslie's success: a thin piece of wire he called "the Little Joker." The method was simple: Simply pop off the dial of the safe, push the Little Joker into the recesses of the tumblers, replace the dial, then leave the bank. The next day, a bank employee was sure to open the safe—and thereby record the tumbler impressions on the Little Joker. It wasn't hard to figure out the correct combination from there. Leslie loved that little piece of wire like a brother. It allowed him to abandon a safe if it didn't have enough money, only to revisit it later, with no one the wiser. And it confounded lawmen for years.

Leslie and his rotating gang of robbers are credited with dozens of robberies in Philadelphia; Baltimore; Waterford, New York; Norristown, Pennsylvania; and of course, New York City. Among the biggest was the knockover of Manhattan's Ocean National Bank on June 27, 1869. The take: $786,879. Leslie's biggest score went down in October 1878, when he and his associates stole an obscene amount—$2,747,000—from the Manhattan Savings Bank at Broadway and Bleecker. This was Leslie's masterpiece. He had spent three years ferreting out the plans, which contained secret locations for various vaults. He also laid out $3,000 of his own money for the tools needed to do the deed. But as Luc Sante points out in *Low Life,* the take amount is deceiving: Most of the haul was in the form of non-negotiable bonds, which were of little value to Leslie. The remainder was $300,000 in negotiable securities, but the bank managed to get $257,000 of it back. Only $11,000 was in cash. To make matters worse, Leslie's gang was positively identified by bank guards. Two of the gang members ended up in jail; Leslie got off for lack of evidence.

After his close call with the law, Leslie settled back to a new career as a bank robbery consultant. He would case a bank to the finest detail, then sell his plans to various gangs for anywhere from $5,000 to $12,000 a pop, no matter the outcome of the robbery. As successful as Leslie was at jumping back and forth between high society and low criminals, it eventually caught up with him. He blew tons of his bank loot on women and parties. Eventually, the suave King of the Bank Robbers chose to steal the wrong girl from the wrong thug (Shang Draper, one of his own thieves), and on June 4, 1884, police found Leslie's body, with a bullet in his head, dumped at the bottom of Tramp's Rock in the Bronx.

### Cool Fact from the Vault

Even though Leslie and his associates racked up $2.7 million from their Manhattan Savings Bank robbery, there was still another $2 million sitting on a vault floor. While it is technically possible that a detail-oriented man like Leslie simply missed the money, it's more likely that he didn't have enough room in his bags for any more.

# 7  JOHNNY DOBBS

**Real name:** Michael Kerrigan

**Number of banks robbed:** Unknown

**Estimated lifetime take:** At least $2 million passed through his hands; as a fence, he probably kept a third of it

**Claim to fame:** Dobbs was one of the New York underworld's top safecrackers and fences—and he opened a bar mere blocks from police headquarters

## "THE NEARER TO CHURCH, THE CLOSER TO GOD."

Michael Kerrigan, or as he was known on the streets of nineteenth-century New York City, "Johnny Dobbs," started out as a pickpocket, graduated to working with a band of river thieves, and eventually became known as a master bank robber and fence of stolen property. "He has been engaged in almost all the important bank robberies that have occurred in this country during the past twenty-five years," wrote New York Police Inspector Thomas Byrnes in his 1886 book, *Rogues' Gallery*. "He is known in almost every large city in America, and is considered a first-class workman." Apparently, Dobbs was a first-class killer, too: During one heist in Maine in the early 1870s, Dobbs and his crew threw an uncooperative cashier into a bank vault and slammed the door shut on him. Police found the dead cashier the next morning.

Dobbs spent most of the 1870s and 1880s working heists, being arrested, busting out of jail, and gathering an impressive array of bank burglary tools. After Dobbs was pinched in Lawrence, Massachusetts, on March 3, 1884, police opened up his tool bags and found (among other objects): waterproof fuses, fur muffs to dampen sound, pocket lanterns, 34 steel wedges, 2 jimmies, a spatula for opening window fastenings, 58 hand drills of varying sizes, a system of bellows and tubes that could be filled with gunpowder to blow safes, a map of New England, and of course, 2 bottles of whiskey. After all, bank burglary is thirsty work.

At his peak, Dobbs had enough money to open a saloon on Mott Street in Manhattan not far from police headquarters. When asked why, Dobbs said, "The nearer to church, the closer to God." (According to Herbert Asbury's classic *The Gangs of New York,* many underworld figures opened dive gin joints in the same area.) Ultimately, though, Dobbs' fondness for the sauce—and expensive mistresses—would be his undoing. In 1895, Dobbs was found unconscious in a gutter and died a broke booze-hound in Bellevue Hospital a few days later.

## Cool Fact from the Vault

According to Jay Robert Nash's *Bloodletters and Badmen,* Kerrigan's funeral was paid for with a broach he had given to one of his mistresses.

# 8  THE DALTON GANG

**Gang members:** Grat Dalton, Bob Dalton, Emmett Dalton; also Bill Powers, Dick Broadwell, and Bill Doolin

**Number of banks robbed:** 0

**Estimated lifetime take:** $0

**Claim to fame:** The Daltons attempted to rob two banks at once—and failed spectacularly

## "DON'T MIND ME, BOY. I'M DONE FOR. DON'T SURRENDER! DIE GAME!"

The running headlines in the Coffeyville, Kansas, newspaper on October 6, 1892, told the Daltons' story in spare, hardboiled poetry: "DALTONS! The Robber Gang Meet Their Waterloo in Coffeyville. LITERALLY WIPED OUT. A Desperate Attempt to Rob Two Banks. FOUR BAD ROBBERS KILLED. The Fifth Wounded and Captured. FOUR GOOD CITIZENS DEAD. Marshal Connelly Shot Down Whilst Doing His Duty. A MOST TERRIFIC BATTLE. The Outlaws Beaten at Their Own Game. A REMARKABLE OCCURRENCE. The Whole County Startled by Wednesday's Fight. MOURNING FOR THE DEAD. Business Houses Closed and the City Draped in Honor of the Gallant Men Who Gave Their Lives in Defense of the Property of Our Citizens."

From the screaming headlines, you might think that the Dalton Gang had been terrorizing scores of Old West banks for years. But this wasn't the case at all; the Coffeyville raid was the gang's first attempted bank shot. According to writer Henry Sinclair Drago in his classic book *Outlaws on Horseback,* the Coffeyville raid "made" the Daltons. "If it had not occurred," writes Drago, "they would have passed into history for what they really were—first-class amateurs, at best."

The Dalton Boys, strangely enough, started out on the opposite side of the law. In 1887, Frank Dalton, a deputy marshal in Fort Smith, Arkansas, was killed by a trio of whiskey runners. His brothers Grat, Bob, and Emmett swore revenge and pinned on law badges to catch Frank's killers. They never quite seemed to get around to doing that. Instead, they quit the force and eventually became mired in criminal activities themselves—rustling cattle, robbing gamblers, stealing horses. Bob was the natural leader of the three brothers, "a wild and reckless man, a stranger to fear who could ride like the wind," writes Drago. Grat was the oldest, and Emmett the handsomest. But there was one thing all three had in a common: a lust for outlaw adventure.

In 1890 Grat, Bob, and Emmett, along with other roughneck bandits, formed a gang and started robbing trains. They had some success, stealing anywhere between $11,000 and $19,000 in a half-dozen robberies over the course of 18 months. But they never quite garnered the same attention as their heroes, the notorious James Gang. The Dalton Boys had grown up hearing they were cousins of the Youngers, the long-time James Gang partners, and yearned to live up to the reputations of their famous relatives.

Tired of missing out on the headlines, Bob Dalton thought up the ultimate bank robbery. He remembered reading, as a boy, about the James Gang's ill-fated Northfield, Minnesota, raid, in which Jesse and Frank James had originally intended to rob two banks at once. What if the Dalton Gang could somehow pull off that trick? Surely such a bold move would cement their reputations forever. Bob even had the perfect spot in mind: the small town of Coffeyville, Kansas, where the Dalton boys grew up. They knew the streets, alleys, and getaway roads cold; they also knew that two banks, the First National Bank and the Condon & Company, were practically right across from each other on Union Street.

On the morning of October 5, 1892, a gang of six—Bob, Grat, and Emmett, along with gang members Bill Doolin, Dick Broadwell, and Bill Powers—rode toward Coffeyville. Each gang member was equipped with Winchester rifles as well as fake beards, so no townspeople would recognize the bandits. But on the way, Bill Doolin's horse went lame, forcing him to go off in search of another one. The five continued on anyway, figuring Doolin would catch up with them. (Some historians claim the "sixth man" was someone other than Doolin; in Dalton lore, "sixth man" theories are about as common as "grassy knoll" theories.)

The gang reached Coffeyville shortly after 9:30 in the morning, and right away things started going wrong. Union Street was being repaired, so the Daltons were forced to park their horses half a block away from the banks. Then, for some reason, the gang didn't think to apply their fake beards until after they had tied up their horses. By then, townspeople had already recognized the bandits. The Daltons! Word spread fast. By the time the five men had split up and walked into the two banks—Bob and Emmett into the First National, Grat and the others into Condon & Company—the hardware store was already handing out rifles to whoever wanted one. Townspeople took up strategic shooting positions up and down Union Street.

Inside the Condon bank, Grat shouted, "Open the safe and be quick about it!"

The teller told Grat he'd be happy to open the vault and give them the $18,000 inside, but it was on a time lock, and not set to open for another three minutes. (Actually, the vault had been open since eight that morning.)

"That's only three minutes," said Grat. "I'll wait."

It was a tragic move. A few minutes later—minutes in which Grat, Powers, and Broadwell could have come and gone—bullets came smashing through the bank's plate glass windows. The outlaws ducked for cover. The town had started fighting back.

Across the street at First National, Bob and Emmett were successfully pulling off their end of the job. At first, the cashier tried to weigh their bag down with coins, but Bob was wise to the trick. "Keep that silver out," he said. "I want what's in the vault! The big stuff!"

The cashier complied and loaded $20,240 in cash into the grain sack. Emmett tied the sack with a tight knot and joined his brother to make their getaway. But once they saw the bullets flying, the two quickly turned around and ran through the bank for the back alley. There, a clerk named Lucius Baldwin was waiting for them, pistol in hand. Bob blew him away without a second thought, and the brothers continued running. Edging down the alley, Bob caught a view of the Condon bank, bullets smacking against its façade and windows from all directions. Grat and his buddies looked like dead meat. Bob and Emmett kept running.

Meanwhile, Grat, Powers, and Broadwell saw the two Daltons making a break for it and decided to do the same. Somehow, they made it out the back entrance, trading gunfire with townspeople all the way. Even more miraculously, they met up with Bob and Emmett in an alley a minute later. Bob and Emmett were fine, but the other three had collected a few bullet wounds along the way. Their getaway horses were only 60 feet away. For a brief moment, the Dalton Gang thought they might get out of this one alive.

Then Bob caught a bullet that sliced right through his bowels. He fired at his attacker, but it was a wild shot that missed. Another bullet punched into his body, and he flipped back against a fence and tumbled to the ground.

The same gunman shot Bill Powers right through the heart and then shot Grat in the throat. Emmett and Broadwell made it to their horses, but as they made their escape attempt, three bullets cut through Broadwell. He slumped forward, and his horse carried him for blocks before he finally fell from the saddle and collapsed into a patch of grass.

Emmett was the last man standing. According to some dime novel accounts, published soon after the bloody Coffeyville debacle, Emmett rode back into the hellstorm to rescue his fallen brothers. But a dying Bob, seeing his brother, shooed him away, saying, "Don't mind me, boy, I'm done for. Don't surrender! Die game!" Supposedly Emmett reached down anyway, and the moment before the brothers' hands touched, more bullets sprayed into both of them, killing Bob and seriously wounding Emmett. Other historians say their last moments together weren't quite so melodramatic and that Emmett was probably shot trying to flee.

Whatever the truth, Emmett did end up full of bullets and close to death on the dusty streets of Coffeyville, but he would survive his wounds (and an impromptu lynching attempt). When the firefight quieted, someone shouted, "They're all down." The result: four dead citizens and four dead outlaws. Townspeople came out of hiding to prop up the dead and bloodied gang members for pictures—copies of which can still be purchased at Coffeyville tourist shops.

The entire battle had taken no more than 15 minutes. By that time, legend has it, sixth gang member Bill Doolin had stolen another horse and had galloped hard into Coffeyville but realized something awful had happened. He pulled back on the reigns and raced like hell out of the area. Doolin would live on to lead his own gang (see the next entry).

Emmett Dalton, then only 21, was convicted of killing two of the Coffeyville residents, even though it was most likely Bob who did the shooting. He spent the next 15 years in jail, winning parole at age 36. Later, Emmett would team up with an aged Frank James to produce a stage production about Wild West outlaws, as well as write a book and give speeches about his criminal past. (Talk about milking your 15 minutes.) He died in July 1937 at the age of 66 in Hollywood, California, as broke as the day he was carried bleeding out of Coffeyville.

## Cool Fact from the Vault

Another Dalton brother, the nonoutlaw Bill, later tried to sue Coffeyville for the $900 he claimed his brother Bob carried on him during the raid. People laughed at Bill Dalton, but according to Drago in *Outlaws on Horseback,* an extra $900 was discovered when the returned bank money was counted.

# 9 THE BILL DOOLIN GANG

**Gang members:** Bill Doolin, George "Bitter Creek" Newcomb, Charlie Pierce, Oliver Yantis, Bill Dalton, Bill "Tulsa Jack" Blake, Charles "Dynamite Dick" Clifton, George "Red Buck" Waightman, Roy Daugherty (a.k.a. "Arkansas Tom Jones"), William F. "Little Bill" Raidler and Richard "Little Dick" West

**Number of banks robbed:** Several dozen

**Estimated lifetime take:** $65,000

**Claim to fame:** Doolin's Gang was second only to the James Gang when it came to successful, well-planned bank robberies

## "DON'T MAKE ME KILL YOU."

Bill Doolin became an outlaw thanks to a keg of beer. Doolin was toiling at the Bar X Bar Ranch with some buddies, who on July 4, 1891, decided to head on over to Coffeyville, Kansas, to throw a celebration kegger. There was one problem: Kansas was a dry state, and soon the law showed up. But instead of showing fake IDs, the Bar X Bar boys drew their pistols, and two lawmen were laid out flat. Bang! Doolin was a fugitive.

Soon enough, Doolin became a regular member of the ill-fated Dalton Gang (see the previous entry) and through sheer luck avoided the massacre at Coffeyville. Afterward, Doolin formed his own super-gang, composed of the remnants of various other criminal gangs that had been disbanded, shot apart or captured. (The Doolin Gang even included Bill Dalton, the previously law-abiding brother of the outlaw Daltons.) Only five weeks after Coffeyville, Doolin and his new team rode into Spearville, Kansas, and cracked a bank there for $18,000, then promptly split up. One gang member, Oliver Yountis, was soon tracked and gunned down by U.S. Marshals, who found $4,500 of the Spearville job money on him.

The following spring, Doolin's men held up a Santa Fe Express train for $13,000—another success, despite Doolin catching a bullet in the foot during the getaway chase. The gang holed up in a cave not far from the town of Ingalls, Oklahoma, and would make small trips into the town for food, drink, and a few hands of poker now and again. Word of the outlaws' whereabouts got back to Marshal Evett Nix, recently appointed by President Grover Cleveland to restore law and order in the wild Oklahoma territory. On September 1, 1893, a posse of U.S. Marshals entered Ingalls, and almost immediately the lead started to fly. Doolin, Bill Dalton, and another gang member were wounded and a fourth was captured; three U.S. Marshals were shot to death. From then on U.S. Marshals wouldn't rest until they had Bill Doolin by the neck.

Doolin and George "Bitter Creek" Newcomb, both suffering from gunshot wounds, traveled to Hot Springs, Arkansas, to heal and waited until the following summer before pulling another bank job. This time, it was the Seaborn Bank in Southwest City, Missouri, which yielded $15,000. (For some reason, the bank president, J. C. Seaborn, made the mistake of running out of the bank along with the robbers and was shot. Important tip to bank presidents: Don't try to chase robbers on foot.) The Doolin Gang hit another bank in Pawnee, Arkansas, for $10,000 and feeling flush, decided to hide out for the winter.

Meanwhile, the U.S. Marshals were still hungry for Bill Doolin. One enterprising Marshal named Bill Tilghman—generally acknowledged as one of Nix's best men—managed to track the hopscotching Doolins to Pawnee County, where he hoped to entice some locals into coughing up some information. On a cold January day, Tilghman approached a ranch owned by a man named Will Dunn, who had been sympathetic to the Doolin Gang. He entered a dark room unarmed, and called out, "Hello?"

There was a fire in the middle of the room, and he stopped to warm his hands. When his eye adjusted to the darkness, Tilghman noticed that the room was full of bunk beds. And out of the edge of every bed, the barrel of a rifle was aimed at him.

Tilghman had accidentally entered the Doolin hideout. Eight men who apparently had no problem with killing a U.S. Marshal all had their weapons trained on him.

"Will," Tilghman asked the ranch owner as calmly as he could, "how does one get out of here?"

"The same damn way he got in," came the reply.

Tilghman turned around and walked out of the hideout, unharmed. Later, it was revealed that the gang had spotted the U.S. Marshal on his way in, but Doolin talked his men out of killing him. "Tilghman's too good a man to be shot in the back," he said.

The Doolin Gang carried out only two more robberies, both train jobs, before disbanding in late 1895. It was meant to be temporary, to give the heat a chance to die down, but it would turn out to be the last time the gang rode together. Tilghman somehow convinced Will Dunn—owner of the Pawnee ranch hideout—to secretly become a Deputy U.S. Marshal and rat on the members of the Doolin Gang. One by one, the gang members were shot and/or captured. Meanwhile, Bill Doolin, hidden away under the alias "William J. Barry" with his wife and infant son at a Kansas farm, read about it in the newspapers.

Despite the success in smashing the gang to pieces, Marshal Tilghman wouldn't consider the Doolin Gang history until he had captured its leader. Detective work led Tilghman to Doolin in a bath-house in Hot Springs in December 1895. "Bill, I'm arresting you," said Tilghman, pointing his revolver at Doolin.

Doolin stood up and reached for his revolver, hanging beneath his coat, but Tilghman's free hand shot out and stopped him. "Don't make me kill you," the lawman said. "I haven't forgotten what you did for me in Will Dunn's dugout."

But Doolin pulled his arm closer toward the gun, straining so hard that stitches began to pop along his sleeve, according to Henry Sinclair Drago in *Outlaws on Horseback*. Tilghman knew he was going to have to put a bullet in Doolin, no matter what the outlaw had done for him in the past. "Good-bye, Bill," he said.

"All right, you win," said Doolin, who stopped struggling.

Doolin was such a celebrity that 5,000 people gathered to watch him being led through Guthrie, Oklahoma. Many of them were women, who were looking for autographs, or perhaps even a date. A young woman shouted at Doolin, "You don't look so terrible, Mr. Doolin. I believe I could have captured you myself."

"I believe you could," said Doolin, with a smirk.

Tilghman led Doolin to his room to gather up his things, and saw a pewter cup with the word "Baby" engraved on it.

Doolin pointed to it. "I wish you'd see that the little fellow gets it."

Tilghman, a man of his word, promised he would deliver it to Doolin's boy.

Not long after landing in prison, Doolin escaped, and 37 other cons followed him out. After a hideout stint in New Mexico, Doolin and his wife relocated in Lawton, Oklahoma, and by all accounts tried to lead a quiet, law-abiding life. But the U.S. Marshals refused to forget about Bill Doolin. In August 1896, Marshal Heck Thomas received information that Doolin was planning to sneak his wife and son out of the country and arrived in Lawton in time to see Doolin packing his wagon.

"Hands up, Doolin!" called Thomas.

It's not clear if Doolin could place the voice, but it didn't matter. Doolin whipped around, rifle in hand, and opened fire.

Thomas shot back, and Doolin was thrown to the ground, his chest riddled with buckshot. He died soon after. Inside the wagon, packed away carefully, lawmen found the tiny pewter cup that Doolin had given to his infant son. It had been delivered by Tilghman, as promised.

### Cool Fact from the Vault

According to legend, Heck Thomas found Bill Doolin already dead of consumption. Knowing there was no reward money for hauling in a dead man without any bullets in him, Thomas pumped a couple of slugs into Doolin's corpse, then brought him in. Then again, another legend has it that Thomas gave the $5,000 reward money to Doolin's widow and boy.

# 10 BUTCH CASSIDY AND THE SUNDANCE KID

**Gang members:** Robert Leroy Parker, Harry Longbaugh, Tom McCarty, Matt Warner, Elza Lay, Harvey Logan, Bill Carver, Joe Walker, Ben Fitzpatrick, and Jack Ketchum, among others

**Number of banks robbed:** At least seven, in addition to numerous lucrative train and payroll robberies

**Estimated lifetime take:** Although Cassidy's Wild Bunch Gang made most of their big money from train robberies, they made at least $75,000 from bank jobs

**Claim to fame:** Did Butch Cassidy die in a Bolivian ambush in 1908, or did he survive—as some maintain—to live to a ripe old age in 1930s Nevada?

## "GENTLEMEN, THROW UP YOUR HANDS. BE QUICK ABOUT IT AND DON'T MAKE ANY NOISE."

When Robert Leroy Parker was a teenager, he made a long trip to buy a new set of clothes, only to find the store shuttered. So Parker broke in, selected the items he wanted, and left a note for the shopkeeper, explaining that he would pay in full upon his return. The law was summoned anyway, and young Parker suffered the humiliation of an arrest before the charges were dropped. Some say this sparked a hatred of authority in the man who would one day become Butch Cassidy.

Whatever the cause, banditry certainly didn't run in the family. Maximillian and Ann Parker were law-abiding Mormons from

Circleville, Utah, and gave birth to Robert on April 13, 1866. When Parker turned 13, he helped support his family by working for a local ranch and later a dairy farm where he met Mike Cassidy, an older rancher with a shady outlaw past. Cassidy became young Parker's mentor, teaching him the pleasures of sharpshooting, playing cards, and rustling cattle. Cassidy invited Parker to join his cattle rustling gang, and the teenaged Parker eventually took over the gang when Cassidy disappeared after gunning down a Wyoming rancher.

In 1887, Parker—now calling himself "Cassidy," after his mentor—met Matt Warner, another Utah Mormon boy, and Tom and Bill McCarty, two budding train robbers. The four young men agreed to rob a train together and chose the Denver and Rio Grande Express on November 3, 1887. They piled stones on the tracks, forcing the train to come screaming to a halt and then boarded the train, making their way to the safe. But the guard claimed not to be able to open it—only stationmasters had the combination, he explained.

"Should we kill him?" asked one of the McCarty brothers.

"Let's vote on it," said Cassidy.

Fortunately for the guard, the vote was 3 to 1 in favor of letting him live. The total take was a meager $140, scooped up from passengers.

On March 30, 1889, Cassidy, Warner, and the McCarty boys decided to take their first bank: the First National Bank of Denver. Tom McCarty walked right up to the bank president and leaned in toward him. "Excuse me sir, but I just overheard a plot to rob this bank."

"Lord!" the president exclaimed, looking nervously around the bank. "How did you learn of this plot?"

"I planned it," McCarty replied, and produced his gun. "Put up your hands."

Within minutes, the gang stole $20,000. Warner used his cut to open a saloon and nailed a $10,000 bank note—the one bill the gang couldn't cash—right on the wall.

The gang hit their next bank on June 24, 1889. The four men spent the day hanging out in saloons in Telluride, and kept an eye on customers coming in and out of the San Miguel Valley bank. When it drew near closing time, one of the gang members entered the bank and told the teller he wanted to cash a check. The teller took the bait, and the next thing he knew his face was smashed against the desk. "Let us take what we want," hissed the outlaw, "or risk instant death." The teller didn't so much as blink, and the gang rode away with $10,500 into the area known as "Robber's Roost," which offered difficult passes and easy lookouts to prevent the law from sneaking up on them.

Posses sprang up in reaction to the robbery, and the gang decided to cool their heels for a while. Cassidy spent the next two years working ranches in Colorado and Utah, even putting in some time as a butcher. That was the odd thing about Butch Cassidy; every so often, he seemed to feel the need to live the straight life. Even his alias hinted at the schism: "Butch" most likely came from his lawful job as a butcher, while "Cassidy," of course, was adopted in honor of his outlaw mentor. He was by all accounts an expert marksmen, but there's no evidence he ever shot anyone.

Soon Cassidy had enough of ranching and butchering, and once again it was time for crime. He teamed up with a cattle rustler named Al Hainer to pull an extortion racket that would eventually become a Mafia favorite: If ranchers paid Cassidy and Hainer protection money, then their cattle would remain safe. If ranchers refused, the cows would suffer the consequences. The scheme worked until 1894, when ranchers got fed up and sicced the local law on Cassidy, who was cornered in his cabin, grazed on the scalp by two bullets, and knocked unconscious. Both Cassidy and Hainer were sentenced to two years at Wyoming State Prison in Laramie City.

Jail was the best thing that could have happened to Cassidy's budding career. While inside, he heard stories about the "Hole-in-the-Wall," an outlaw oasis in Wyoming that was even harder to reach than the Robber's Roost. The place was full of bandits who had eluded the grasp of the law and teamed up to perform heists and raids throughout the Old West. Perhaps this is what inspired Cassidy to apply for early parole. During a hearing with Wyoming governor William Richards, Cassidy pleaded his case.

"My time is three-fourths done," he said. "A few more months won't make much difference. I've got some property in Colorado that needs looking after, and I'd like to get a pardon."

"If it's your intention to go straight after you get out," said Governor Richards, "perhaps it could be arranged. Will you give me your word that you will quit rustling?"

"Can't do that, governor," Cassidy said, cutting right through the cow manure. "If I gave you my word, I'd only have to break it. I'm in too deep now to quit the game. But I'll promise you one thing: Give me a pardon, and I won't commit any more crimes in Wyoming."

Amazingly, it worked. Cassidy was sprung on January 19, 1896, and he promptly made his way to the Hole-in-the-Wall. There Cassidy found an outlaw Who's Who. There was famed bandit "Big Nose" George Curry, and months later arrived his protégé Harvey "Kid Curry" Logan, generally regarded as the cruelest killer in the country. There was also Elza Lay, who would become Cassidy's right-hand man in the capers he planned for the Wild Bunch. (Matt Warner, Cassidy's previous number two, had taken a fall after an ill-fated bank robbery with the McCartys, and after a long prison term would go straight, eventually becoming a lawman himself.) It didn't take long for the charismatic Cassidy to take charge of operations. Under Cassidy, the Wild Bunch became masters of the meticulously planned operation, which included knowing how much money there was to be stolen on a particular day and stashing food, water, and fresh horses along a carefully plotted escape route.

And while Cassidy's Wild Bunch might have knocked over banks, trains and company payrolls without a second thought, the gang wasn't without a code of honor. Once, Cassidy approached a man on a horse who seemed like a lawman, and Cassidy prepared for the worst. But the man turned out to be a priest, and Cassidy was so ashamed, he gave the priest directions to the nearest town and offered a generous parish donation. (The priest politely turned it down.) Another time, a gang member stole a horse from a young boy. Cassidy was so outraged that one of his men would steal from a child, he banished the outlaw from the Hole-in-the-Wall forever.

While these stories might be apocryphal, Cassidy was definitely a man of his word. As promised, Cassidy steered clear of Wyoming. On August 13, 1896, he led two members of the Wild Bunch to the Montpelier Bank in Idaho. One guarded the door, while two others covered their faces from the nose down with bandanas and burst into the bank. An employee claimed not to have any money. A gang member promptly smashed a gun butt into his face and proceeded to bag the loot anyway. The trio netted $7,165 worth of cash, gold, and silver and split before a posse could catch up with them. Not long after, the gang robbed a bank in Belle Fourche, South Dakota, and stole nearly $5,000.

Cassidy, Lay, and the Wild Bunch followed that up with a series of train robberies over the next few years, but a July 11, 1899, train job near Folsom, New Mexico, resulted in the capture of Elza Lay, and once again Cassidy was left without a righthand man.

Enter Harry Longbaugh, a Pennsylvania boy who lammed out when he was 15 to seek adventure in the West and, like his eventual partner, fell into horse thievery. While still in his teens, Longbaugh was caught and sentenced to two years in the Sundance jail, which supplied his nickname. He would go on to rob a train in 1892 with future Wild Bunch members and then a bank in South Dakota on June 27, 1897, but Sundance was captured along with Harvey Logan. Both escaped on Halloween 1897 and made their way toward the Hole-in-the-Wall. Butch and Sundance became fast friends, most likely because they shared the same laid-back view of life. They were careful professionals who always knew when to lay low and didn't let greed or frenzy run them straight into prison. It's not exactly clear if the two spent a lot of time goofing around on bicycles, as in the Paul Newman/Robert Redford movie, *Butch Cassidy and the Sundance Kid,* but their casual manners probably weren't far off the mark.

Even their heists tended to be reasonably friendly encounters. On September 19, 1900, Butch, Sundance, and another gang member rode their way to Winnemucca, Nevada. At noon, employees at the First National Bank were startled to hear a gentle request: "Gentlemen, throw up your hands; be quick about it and don't make any noise."

Two of the bandits covered the employees and customers with revolvers, while a third took two cashiers to the vault with a Winchester rifle leveled at them. One of the cashiers claimed he couldn't open the safe because of a time lock but was suddenly able to work miracles when threatened with a slashed throat. (Okay, maybe Butch and Sundance weren't *that* friendly.) The robbery netted the gang $32,640. This impressive take would be almost doubled the following year when Butch, Sundance, and three others stopped a train near Wagner, Montana, and stole $65,000. This was the famous train robbery scene featured in *Butch Cassidy* in which the gang blew up one of the train cars—and nearly themselves—with one too many sticks of dynamite.

By this time, however, Butch and Sundance had attracted the attentions of Pinkerton detective Joe Lefors, who had been hired by train companies to track and destroy the bandits who had been costing them so much damn money over the years. Butch and Sundance, who had split from the rest of the group to make a clean getaway, were pursued by a posse of a hundred lawmen. They barely made it out of Montana alive. Feeling the heat, Butch and Sundance, along with his new girlfriend, school teacher Etta Place, went on holiday in New York City, then hopped a passenger ship to Buenos Aires in South America. (Incidentally, no one knows Etta's real name; "Place" is Sundance's mother's maiden name, which the two used later while hiding out.) The couple and third wheel Cassidy built a cabin together and then settled down to do some serious farming. Not the usual career path for bandits, but then again, Butch Cassidy always did enjoy a run at the straight life now and again. The era of the Wild Bunch was all but over, but the most interesting part of the Butch and Sundance story was yet to come.

Joe Lefors had lost track of Butch and Sundance after the Wagner train robbery, but in 1905 he started hearing stories about two *gringo* bandits who had knocked over two banks in southern Argentina. Butch and Sundance, either bored with farming or running low on funds, were up to their old tricks again, this time using Etta Place as an advance scout to report back on bank layouts. Two banks were apparently enough for the former school teacher; most historians believe Etta abandoned the pair in 1906. By 1908, there were reports of Butch and Sundance robbing mining payrolls in Bolivia. They robbed either too many payrolls or the wrong payroll, for they were set up for the kill upon their arrival in the town of San Vicente on the night of November 6, 1908.

The room they had been given only had one doorway—the front. As soon as their host, Bonifacio Casaola, showed them their room, another man ran to the nearest Bolivian soldiers and told them the gringo bandits were in town. Butch and Sundance had barely settled themselves in for an evening meal in the room when they heard a voice.

"Surrender, señors!"

Both outlaws spun around to see a Bolivian captain. Cassidy—who prided himself on never having shot anyone—snatched up his revolver and blasted away at the captain, who fell over dead. The two made their way to a window and saw that the place was surrounded by Bolivian cavalrymen, some of whom were rushing toward them. Butch and Sundance started firing. A bloody gunfight ensued, and the end result was two dead gringo bandits. Contrary to the film, Butch and Sundance didn't race out from their hiding place, gun blazing, ready to die in a glorious fusillade of Bolivian bullets. The bodies were found some hours later. Some think Butch plugged a mercy bullet into Sundance, then one into his own brain when he realized there was no way out.

Or did they die at all? Like Jesse James, there have been numerous reports that Butch Cassidy survived the ambush to live to a ripe old age in Nevada. In *Digging Up Butch and Sundance,* an excellent investigation into the Butch Cassidy life-after-death theories, author Anne Meadows examines various Cassidy sightings, even some from Cassidy's own sister, who swore Butch visited her often long after his alleged death. In the 1930s, Butch Cassidy sightings were as popular as Elvis Presley sightings would be in the 1990s.

And Meadows's conclusion? Best evidence—including original accounts from Bolivian newspapers—suggests Butch and Sundance did indeed die in Bolivia. According to Meadows, Butch's sister even "implied to at least two researchers that she was just having fun with her stories."

## Cool Fact from the Vault

Whatever you might believe about Butch Cassidy surviving the Bolivian army's assault, it is true he once witnessed his own funeral. In May 1898, a posse surprised a gang of resting bandits and shot two of them. One was identified as Butch Cassidy. News spread, and the real Butch Cassidy—very much alive—convinced a buddy to sneak him by the mortuary, covered by straw in the back of a wagon, to watch crowds of people line up to the see the corpse of "Butch Cassidy." (Later, the dead guy was positively identified as another, lesser-known outlaw.)

# 11  ADAM WORTH

**Number of banks robbed:** At least three; most likely a dozen

**Estimated lifetime take:** The Pinkertons estimate $2 to $3 million from every kind of theft, including bank robbery

**Claim to fame:** Worth was a cunning, urbane thief who could swindle or rob anything he encountered— including one of the most secure banks in Boston

## "ADAM WORTH WAS THE NAPOLEON OF THE CRIMINAL WORLD. NONE OTHER COULD HOLD A CANDLE TO HIM."

Adam Worth was largely forgotten until writer Ben Macintyre happened across an old police report about Worth written after his death in 1910 and decided to pursue a full-length biography, *The Napoleon of Crime* (1997). Worth ran criminal operations on three different continents, and his greatest heist was the theft of the portrait of the Duchess of Devonshire, one of the most expensive and sought-after paintings in the world.

But before he became an international terror, Worth launched his spectacular criminal career as a bank robber in gaslight-era New York City. Bank robbers back then didn't have the hardscrabble Robin Hood quality of the depression era, nor the violent desperation of modern-day stick-up men. Thanks to supergeniuses like George Leonidas Leslie (see "George Leonidas Leslie"), bank robbers were like rock stars. And like a journeyman guitar player venturing to the big city to make it in a band, Worth left his hometown of Cambridge, Massachusetts, for New York in the mid-1860s, which Macintyre describes as an island brimming with "pickpockets, con men, whores, swindlers, pimps, burglars, bank robbers, beggars, mobsmen and thieves of every description."

Worth started out as an apprentice pickpocket. Desperate for bigger money, he started hanging out at the parties of Marm Mandelbaum, New York City's top fence. But none of the established gangs—including George Leslie's—would give him a shot. "It was hard for a young man to get a foothold with an organized party of bank robbers," wrote Sophie Lyons, a one-time con woman who ended up a gossip columnist. "The more experienced men were reluctant to risk their chances of success by taking on a beginner." Worth was on his own. He recruited his brother John in 1866 to break into the Atlantic Transportation Company on Liberty Street in New York. The two spent all night trying to figure a way to blast open the safe, but nothing worked. Worth left disgusted.

He tried again at an insurance company back home in Cambridge, and this time made off with $20,000 in bonds, which he proudly brought back to Marm Mandelbaum to fence. As per the usual deal with Mandelbaum, Worth only pocketed 10 percent—$2,000. Despite the paltry haul, it established him as a player in the underworld, and Worth soon became "a master hand in the execution of robberies," as one newspaper account put it.

Worth's most notable bank heist took place in 1869 at the Boylston National Bank, easily the biggest in Boston. Along with two accomplices from Mandelbaum's circle, "Piano Charley" Bullard and Ike Marsh, Worth presented himself as William A. Judson, a health tonics dealer, and rented the building next door to the Boylston Bank. His product, "Gray's Oriental Tonic," lined the front windows of the establishment. ("Quite what was in Gray's Oriental Tonic has never been revealed, since not a single bottle was ever sold," writes Macintyre.) The trio quickly figured out where the vault sat against the common wall, then hacked away at the bricks and mortar for a week. Once the steel vault was exposed, Worth used a drill to punch one-inch holes in the vault, forming a circle, which would eventually yield an 18-by-12-inch opening. On Sunday, November 21, Worth wormed into the vault, then started passing the safety deposit boxes back to his partners, who pried them open and took the contents.

The haul, which the Pinkerton Detective Agency estimated at being nearly $1 million in cash and securities, was packed into trunks marked "Gray's Oriental Tonic" and loaded on a train for New York. The next day, Monday, bank managers opened the vault and had the biggest shock of their lives. "Yesterday morning Boston was startled," reported the *Boston Post* on Tuesday. "There is no discount on the word .... The infinite cleverness with which [the burglar's] operations have been conducted from beginning to end indicate him to be a man of no ordinary ability, and it seems very probable that, having so far succeeded in eluding police, he may escape altogether."

Worth did indeed get away, but felt compelled to flee to Europe—New York would be too hot for him, and the frontiers of the Old West seemed too dangerous for a man of his new wealth. The Pinkerton Detective Agency was immediately hired to find the culprits, which began a 30-year cat-and-mouse game between Worth and Pinkerton himself. By the time Worth was arrested in 1899, it would be for more high-profile crimes. Feeling in a retrospective mood, Worth even confessed many of his earlier crimes to Pinkerton, including the Boylston heist, long past the statute of limitations.

"Of course you cannot tell," Worth said to his nemesis. "I wouldn't want to be tried on it, although thirty years have elapsed."

## Cool Fact from the Vault

Worth is generally acknowledged as the real-life model for Sherlock Holmes's criminal nemesis, Professor Moriarty.

# 12  HENRY STARR

**Nickname:** "Bearcat"

**Number of banks robbed:** "I've robbed more banks than any man in America," claimed Starr (about 21)

**Estimated lifetime take:** $60,000

**Claim to fame:** Starr is credited with being the first bank robber to use a getaway car. In Starr's case, it was a stolen Stutz Bearcat sports car—hence the nickname.

## "YOU TOLD ME YOU WERE THROUGH ROBBING BANKS, AND HERE I FIND YOU PULLING A DOUBLE-HEADER."

Henry Starr is the missing link between galloping bank robbers of the Old West and gas pedal–punching robbers of the depression era. Part Cherokee, he was born in Fort Gibson in Indian Territory on December 2, 1873, and grew up hearing he was the cousin of Belle Starr, notorious "Bandit Queen" of the Old West who was a horse and cattle thief, a fence and sometime lover of bank robber Cole Younger. Starr would later dispute this—"I never so much as met the lady"—but he seemed to follow in the Starr tradition. In the 1890s, he formed a band of outlaws and began stealing horses and knocking over stores.

In 1893, Starr shot a U.S. Deputy Marshal named Floyd Wilson, who was about to arrest him. Other Marshals claimed that Starr killed Wilson in cold blood, but Starr told a different version, according to Henry Sinclair Drago in *Outlaws on Horseback*:

> *"Throw away that gun and put up your hands or I'll kill you," said Wilson.*

*"All right," Starr replied. "I'll lower my gun and give you a chance to shoot first, and you'd better make a clean job of it. If I kill you, it will be in self-defense. Shoot!"*

Wilson took his shot, but the bullet whizzed harmlessly past Starr's ear. Starr then put a bullet in Wilson's heart and galloped away.

Now no longer a penny ante horse thief, Starr joined a gang of robbers for a while before forming his own gang. This new team only worked together for one job, and in the words of Starr, it netted them "trifling pay for such a desperate venture." On June 5, 1893, Starr led his men into Bentonville, Arkansas, to raid the People's Bank, but it all went to hell in the first minute when an instant posse appeared with rifles and started shooting at the bandits. A six-person human shield Starr had arranged quickly dissipated, and Starr's men were left to blast their way out. When they finally caught their breath and counted the loot stolen from the counter, it amounted to $11,000. Split seven ways, it was only $1,500 a man.

Demoralized, the gang disbanded, with only one member, Kid Wilson, accompanying Starr to Colorado Springs, Colorado. There, Starr married Mary Jones, and the couple honeymooned at the Spaulding House under the names "Frank and Mary Jackson." That didn't fool a local businessman, who recognized Starr and called the law. Starr was arrested at the hotel, while Kid Wilson was found in a nearby whorehouse. Both were returned to Fort Smith. Starr was tried and sentenced to dangle at the end of a rope for killing Marshal Wilson. But an appeal to the U.S. Supreme Court overturned the case, and Starr was granted a new trial.

The second trial, however, also resulted in a death sentence. Starr's lawyer appealed again and somehow won a *third* trial for his client. This time, Starr escaped the noose and was given 25 years at the Ohio State Penitentiary. While at the Fort Smith prison awaiting trial, Starr had quelled a prison riot when he disarmed riot leader Cherokee Bill, with the understanding that the Fort Smith guards would agree not to kill Bill. In 1905, this display of bravery would earn Starr parole from President Theodore Roosevelt himself. In gratitude, Starr even named his firstborn son Theodore Roosevelt Starr. Starr and his wife Mary set up a real-estate business in Tulsa, and led a quiet, law-abiding life.

This would have been the end of the Henry Starr story if not for one minor historical detail: Oklahoma became a state on November 16, 1907.

What's the big deal about that? The state of Arkansas never forgave Starr for raiding the bank in Bentonville. But as long as he lived in Tulsa, which was in Indian Territory, Starr could not be extradited. Once Oklahoma achieved statehood, Arkansas immediately set in motion plans to nab their man. Starr fled for the hills, quite literally, and hooked up with some outlaws and started hitting the banks again. First was a bank in Tyro, Kansas, which netted him $2,500, followed by a small farmer's bank in Amity, Colorado, which yielded $1,100. At the same time, a bunch of Oklahoma banks were robbed, too, but Starr maintained he had nothing to do with them. "The newspapers printed scare-head stories that I had got off the reservation again," wrote Starr, "with forty kinds of war paint on."

But the Tyro and Amity jobs were enough for a sheriff's posse to capture Starr and his men in Arizona. He was returned to Colorado and sentenced to 25 years in the Cañon City Prison. While in jail, Starr wrote his autobiography, *Thrilling Events: The Life of Henry Starr*. It was a rousing read, but Starr should have held off a couple of years. The most thrilling events were yet to come.

Once again, model prisoner Starr won parole and walked out of Cañon City Prison on September 8, 1914. He stayed a reformed man for 16 days. On September 24, his seventeenth day of freedom, he knocked over the Keystone State Bank, netting $3,000 and kicking off an astounding six-month run of Oklahoma bank robberies. Six days later, it was the Keifer Central Bank ($6,400). Seven days later, the Farmers' National Bank in Tupelo ($800). Eight days later, the Pontotoc Bank ($11,000). Six days later, the Byards State Bank ($700). Starr took off for nearly a month before robbing the Farmers

State Bank in Glencoe ($2,400) on November 13. Seven days later, it was the Citizens State Bank in Wardville ($800). Another month-long rest, then the Prue State Bank ($1,400) on December 16 was robbed. Four days after Christmas, Starr robbed the Carney State Bank ($2,853). The Oklahoma State Bank heist in Preston a few days after the New Year's 1915 was a bit of a washout—there was no money taken. (But Starr's hold-up did cost the bank $1,200 in vault repairs.) To make up for the lack of cash in Preston, he hit the First National Bank in Owasso ($1,500) the very next day; seven days later, the First National Bank in Terlton ($1,800) and the Garber State Bank ($2,500) on the same day. Feeling like he was on a lucky streak, Starr robbed the Vera State Bank ($1,300) the next day.

Starr may not have robbed the most banks in history, but he certainly did his best to squeeze in as many as he could in a five-month period. And while lawmen were combing the Osage Hills looking for him, Starr was safely ensconced in Tulsa, at 1534 East Second Street, just down the street from the county sheriff and four blocks away from the mayor. After all, the closer to church, the nearer to God.

By late March 1915, Starr was feeling so confident, he decided to attempt what the Jameses and Daltons couldn't: rob two banks at one time. "When I came to Stroud to look things over," said Starr, "I saw it was just as easy to rob two banks as one, so I decided to kill two birds with one stone."

The Stroud jobs weren't as easy as Starr thought. Starr and five other men rode into Stroud, tied up their horses, left one man behind, then marched down Main Street. Giving his men a signal, they split up into two groups of three. Starr and two others entered the Stroud State Bank, then whipped out their guns: a short rifle for Starr and six-guns for his companions. The robbers scooped up $1,600 from the drawers, and then moved for the big money.

But when Starr ordered a bank employee to open the safe, he was told he was too late: The time lock had already been set.

Meanwhile, Starr's partners across the street were able to shove $4,215 in cash and silver into their grain sack. Both teams took hostages and emerged from the banks. The group moved up the street, with Starr facing backward to keep the entire town at bay. From here, there are two versions of the story. One has it that the residents of Stroud decided to defend their town à la Coffeyville (see "The Dalton Gang") and started blasting away at Starr's men. (In this version, Starr supposedly used a bank vice president as a human shield and, at one point, told him to "Stand aside and let me get that bastard up there.") According to *Outlaws on Horseback,* the town of Stroud took up strategic shooting positions, but never fired a single bullet at Starr or his men.

What happened next, however, is not in dispute. A 16-year-old boy named Paul Curry, having seen what the six bandits were up to, ran to a nearby butcher shop and took a sawed-off shotgun that was ordinarily used to slay hogs. Curry hid, waited for Starr to pass his line of vision, and then pulled the trigger.

The bullet caught Starr in his left thigh, shattering his leg bone and flinging him to the ground. "I'm done for, boys," he said, realizing he was momentarily paralyzed from the waist down. "Save yourselves."

His gang members fled with the money, and Stroud residents immediately set upon the fallen bandit with a mind to lynch him. Before that could happen, someone called U.S. Marshal Bill Tilghman, who arrived three hours later. Tilghman and Starr had run into each other before. "Henry, I'm becoming convinced that you are going to live and die as a criminal," Tilghman said. "You've broken every promise you ever made me. You told me you were through robbing banks, and here I find you pulling a double-header."

On August 2, Starr pleaded guilty and was sentenced to 25 years in the Oklahoma State Penitentiary but was yet again paroled early. Writer Henry Sinclair Drago points out that while Starr had been collectively sentenced to more than 65 years in jail, he had barely served 15.

*Starr and stripes: A prison snapshot of Henry Starr, the link between bandits of the Old West and modern-day heisters.*

And even those 15 years hadn't properly reformed Henry Starr. On February 18, 1921, a little more than a year after his parole, Starr and two armed men stormed a bank in Harrison, Arkansas, about 100 miles east of Bentonville, the scene of his first bank job. "This is a hold-up," Starr announced, then herded the two bank employees into the vault. Starr planned to take the money, then lock the employees inside to make for a clean getaway.

But one of the employees, William J. Meyers, had an anti-robbery device hidden in a corner of the vault: a double-barrel shotgun. While Starr went for the money, Meyers lifted the gun and shot the outlaw in the back. Starr screamed and fell to the floor of the vault, and his armed companions fled. (Their identities remain unknown.) Starr lived for four more days and bragged to his jail doctors that "I've robbed more banks than any man in America." He died on February 22, 1921.

The Harrison bank job might have been the end of a career, but it was also a symbol of things to come. Starr and his companions had driven to the job in a high-powered touring car, a Stutz Bearcat, which the two survivors had used to flee. The getaway car, pioneered by Henry Starr, was an innovation that bank robbers continue to use to this day.

## Cool Fact from the Vault

Starr is the only bank robber to appear in a movie about his own criminal exploits ... playing himself. After his parole in 1919, Starr's friends convinced him to get into the movie business. He ended up producing and starring in *A Debtor to the Law,* which was about the Stroud double robbery. It was a success, and reportedly Starr earned $15,000—a bigger take than most of his bank heists.

# 13 JOHN ASHLEY AND THE EVERGLADES GANG

**Gang members:** John Ashley and Hanford Mobley, among others

**Number of banks robbed:** 40

**Estimated lifetime take:** $1 million

**Claim to fame:** Ashley had the support of his neighbors—and the perfect hideout

## "BOB, I COULD HAVE KILLED YOU WITH EASE. WHY DON'T YOU STAY OUT OF THESE WOODS?"

Outlaw John Ashley had the perfect hideout: 4,000 square miles of the Florida Everglades. Ashley would pull a bank job in a small Florida town, then run into the Everglades, where he knew every lily pad, waterhole, frond, sinkhole, and bullfrog like the back of his hand.

Ashley learned the area when he was a teenager and earned good money trapping otter and raccoon along Lake Okeechobee. One day in 1911, however, Ashley came across an Indian named DeSoto Tiger who had a canoe packed full of otter hides, ready to be traded for a nice chunk of cash at the markets in Fort Lauderdale. Ashley made a quick decision. He shot Tiger, took the hides, and left Tiger's corpse floating in his own canoe.

A short while later, shopkeepers in Fort Lauderdale were confronted by a group of Indians who'd found Tiger's body ... and no otter hides. That's when the shopkeepers remembered a certain John Ashley bringing in a huge pile of otter hides to sell. Palm Beach County Sheriff George Baker, a colorful lawman who was fond of his beaver Stetson hat, went out with his son Bob and arrested Ashley at his home. Ashley was sentenced to die at the end of a rope, but Baker apparently felt bad for the guy and let him make a run for it before his execution date. Baker would soon come to regret his generosity.

Ashley soon rounded up a gang of thugs and started to rob everything in southeastern Florida that wasn't nailed down. Between 1911 and 1924, Ashley's criminal gang would steal over a million bucks from 40 banks in the Palm Beach area. He was famous for two things: being able to hide in the Everglades at will and never planning ahead. During one heist, Ashley didn't bother to supply a getaway car, figuring a bank employee would have a car and be willing to drive for them. Advance planning? Please. "Advance planning" for John Ashley meant making sure the bank was going to be open the day of the heist.

Nonetheless, the Everglades Gang had Florida banks so terrified that some managers would immediately start packing up large sacks full of cash the moment they saw Ashley and his boys pull up. Ashley would simply walk in, accept the money, doff his hat, and race off to hide in the Everglades, where few law officers would offer pursuit. Banks feared him, but some South Floridians came to see Ashley as a folk hero, a Palm Beach version of Jesse James. Some said that Ashley even resembled James.

Not Sheriff George Baker and his son Bob. The two dedicated themselves to undoing their dire mistake by hunting down Ashley. George died before he got the satisfaction of seeing his greatest mistake back behind bars, but Bob continued the pursuit, organizing bands of deputies to comb the Everglades for signs of the Ashley band. Bob Baker found only one: a handwritten note from John Ashley himself, nailed to a tree. "Bob, you and your posse passed by me about 30 feet away, and I could have killed you with ease," it read. "Why don't you stay out of these woods?"

Ashley loved the Everglades, but also the state of Florida itself. That might be why it upset him so much to see out-of-state bootleggers making inroads into his home turf. This was Prohibition, and Ashley had no problem with local bootleggers trying to make a buck.

But he hated the idea of gangsters from up north muscling in on business. The common trick back then was to establish ships along the U.S. coastline, far enough away to be legally out of the country, but close enough to race boats back to the mainland for transportation to speakeasies.

Somehow, Ashley pinpointed the tiny island of Bimini in the Bahamas as the home base for out-of-town gangster rumrunning, and one day in 1924 he decided to sail over to do some robbing. Ashley and his nephew Hanford Mobley ended up swiping over $65,000 from gangsters, who didn't think they needed guns in their Caribbean hideout. The raid was a smashing success but also an international incident. As L. R. Kirchner points out in his book *Robbing Banks,* this was "the first time in over a century that an American privateer had raided a British Crown colony." The Brits were mad. Northern gangsters were mad. Local law enforcement was mad in public, but secretly pleased that Ashley had single-handedly busted a major rumrunning ring.

Still, the heat was intense, and Ashley decided to stick to stick-ups from that point on. Ashley and three other gang members took off for another state by car but were surprised by a roadblock on a wooden bridge near Sebastian, Florida. Someone had tipped the cops off. The car was stopped; dozens of bullets were fired. The result: four dead Everglades Gang members, including Ashley himself.

Later, a conspiracy theory emerged: Northern gangsters, in retaliation for the Bimini raid, had paid off Florida cops to bump off John Ashley and his men. It was even rumored that the sheriff first tied up Ashley's gang, roped them to the back of their cars, and drove around for a while before pumping bullets into their still-living bodies. To some residents of South Florida, their Jesse James had been murdered.

## Cool Fact from the Vault

While robbing the Stuart Bank in Palm Beach County, one of the Everglades Gang members dressed up as a woman.

# 14 HERMAN "THE BARON" LAMM

**Number of banks robbed:** Dozens

**Estimated lifetime take:** More than $1 million

**Claim to fame:** The Lamm Technique

## THE LINK BETWEEN BUTCH CASSIDY AND JOHN DILLINGER

Modern-day robbers who plan their bank jobs down to the last detail have the Prussian Army to thank. That's where Herman K. Lamm— a.k.a. "the Baron"—learned how to pull the perfect twentieth-century heist. His "Lamm Technique" would practically become a Dale Carnegie success guide for budding bank robbers in the 1930s, and it helped Lamm's gang net more than a million bucks over the course of a decade.

Herman K. Lamm was born in Germany in 1880 and immigrated to the United States right before the turn of the century. One of his first gigs: acting as a relay horse-holder for Butch Cassidy's infamous Wild Bunch—in essence, acting as a getaway driver before the advent of getaway cars. But when Butch and Sundance split for the greener pastures of Bolivia, Lamm and other Wild Bunchers (including William "Wild Bill" Cruzan, William T. Phillips, and Norman E. Weaver) formed their own robbery team, hitting trains in Idaho and Colorado in 1902 and 1903. A year later, Lamm cooked up a new team of bandits that operated in Utah, knocking over stores, trolleys, and private houses. Lamm's bold doings are sketchy after this time; some believe he and a crew of Wild Bunchers followed Butch and Sundance's lead and hightailed it to South America to pull other train and bank heists.

In 1914, Lamm returned to Germany and joined the Prussian army when it looked as if war was ready to break out. But before Baron Lamm—he earned the title in the Prussian army—had a chance to pack a pistol in defense of his homeland, he was caught cheating in a card game and sent packing. In 1916, he returned to Utah in shame and returned to bank robbing with renewed vigor—and skills. Why not, thought Lamm, treat bank heists like military operations?

It was a revolutionary idea, and for a while, it worked: Lamm managed to rob a series of banks. But he was caught in 1917 and sent to a Utah prison.

No matter. Baron Lamm spent his time in jail perfecting his technique. He realized that bank-robbery schemes, like military campaigns, should be flexible enough to respond to unforeseen obstacles. The James Gang had also treated bank robberies like military raids, but not to Lamm's obsessive extent. For Lamm, a perfect heist meant prepping teams on the bank's floor plan, pinpointing safes, assigning each "team" member a specific objective and time frame in which to accomplish it, and mapping a series of retreat plans. The most important rule in what would come to be known as the "Lamm Technique": Leave the scene of crime at the pre-arranged time, no matter how much—or how little—you've collected in your burlap sacks.

To Lamm, the getaway was as important as the heist itself. The car itself had to be plain-looking but souped-up to outrun anything the local police force had to offer. The driver had to have racetrack experience. And the getaway route had to be pasted to the car's dashboard, detailed to speedometer readings for each block and alternate turns to take in case of emergency.

The homework paid off. Once Lamm was sprung from jail, he formed a new bank-robbing gang and drilled them like crazy using a stopwatch. Soon, his supergang started knocking over banks, and the Lamm Technique worked like a charm ... until December 16, 1930, that is.

That's when Lamm's gang knocked over the Citizens' State Bank in Clinton, Indiana. The robbery itself went off without a hitch, with $15,567 packed in sacks and typewriter covers, but the getaway was another story. Driver F. H. Hunter panicked when he saw a vigilante in the street with a shotgun and decided to hell with the plan. Hunter wrestled with the wheel, pulled a mad U-turn, then bumped over a curb and blew out a tire. Lamm and his men jumped into another car, but it had been fitted with a device called a "governor" to prevent it from picking up speed. They abandoned that car for a truck, but it didn't have enough water in the radiator.

Things were getting ridiculous. Lamm and his men tried yet another car, but it only had one gallon of gas in it. As a result, more than 200 Illinois police officers and vigilantes were able to block and surround Lamm's getaway car. Pistols were drawn, bullets started flying, and both Lamm and Hunter were shot to pieces. Another gang member, a 70-something bandit who once allegedly rode with the Dalton Gang, shot himself to avoid capture. The remaining two, James "Oklahoma Jack" Clark and Walter Dietrich, were sentenced to life at Indiana State Prison.

And that's how the Lamm Technique managed to survive the grave. For at Indiana State, Clark and Dietrich met up with a young man named John Herbert Dillinger, who was intensely curious about how The Baron managed to pull so many bank jobs for so many years without getting caught.

## Cool Fact from the Vault

Some historians believe the fugitive expression "on the lam" originated with the Baron. (Either that, or with bank robbers who were overly fond of sheep.)

# 15  THE NEWTON BOYS

**Gang members:** Willis Newton, Joe Newton, Jess Newton, and Dock Newton

**Number of banks robbed:** About 80

**Estimated lifetime take:** "I don't want to say how much money it all added up to," wrote Willis Newton, "but it was more than Jesse James, the Dalton Boys, and Bonnie and Clyde got, all put together"

**Claim to fame:** Careful planners to the end, the four Newtown brothers prided themselves on the multitude of banks they knocked over in the course of five years

## "BETTER 'THERE HE GOES' THAN 'HERE HE LIES.'"

If there are any bank robbers you'd want as family members, it would be the Newton Boys. Unfailingly polite, nonviolent, and professional heisters, the boys had the smarts to pull over 80 bank heists in 10 states and 2 countries without getting caught. They were eventually arrested after a 1924 train robbery went awry, but even that can be blamed on the non-Newton who had been recruited to help. If the Newtons had kept it in the family, they might have been robbing banks along the same dusty Texas roads as Bonnie and Clyde a decade later.

Two of the Newton Boys, Willis and Joe, both lived past 80 and toward the end of their lives dictated their memoirs to writers Claude Stanush and David Middleton. "Lots of things been written about us," Joe Newton told the writers, "but none ever told the real story." While the Newton Boys were famous during the Roaring Twenties, if it weren't for Stanush and Middleton's subsequent documentary and memoir, their lucrative exploits might have been completely forgotten.

The 1998 Richard Linklater film *The Newton Boys*, starring Ethan Hawke, Matthew McConaughey, and Vincent D'Onofrio, would bring the Boys back into the public consciousness. (By the way, the real Newton Boys looked nothing like Ethan Hawke and Matthew McConaughey. Vincent D'Onofrio, maybe.)

Willis and Janetta Pecos Newton of Uvalde, Texas, had 11 children, but only 4 became bandits. Willis Jr. was the natural leader of the gang and was always eager to crack bigger and better banks. Joe, on the other hand, was the baby of the gang and a reluctant robber, never quite comfortable living life as an outlaw. "It was the biggest mistake of my life," he said. Jess was the laziest of the four outlaws, pretty much going along with whatever Willis thought best. Dock was a hellraiser and was the first Newton to run afoul of the law.

In 1910, Dock was arrested for stealing cotton. Willis was thought to be in cahoots with his brother, and both boys were sent to the Texas State Penitentiary for two years. While Dock repeatedly hatched mad escape plans, Willis served his time until his mother petitioned Texas Governor O. B. Colquitt for his release so he could help back on the family farm. But hot days of picking cotton wasn't exactly the life Willis had hoped for, so on New Year's Eve 1914 he and a buddy hopped onto a train 30 miles west of Uvalde and robbed the male passengers of their cash and watches, netting $4,700. It sure beat picking cotton.

After Willis was caught trying to unload a bundle of stolen clothes, he was sent back to prison to serve a fresh two-year sentence. Remembering what had sprung him the last time, Willis cooked up what is perhaps the smartest jailbreak ever: He wrote letters to the sheriff who had caught him and the judge who had sentenced him, asking if they would sign a petition for his parole. As expected, they both told Willis to take a flying leap. But now Willis had their signatures and used them to forge a petition, which was sent to the Governor's office. Amazingly, the phony petition worked. Willis was sprung again.

Some time later, Willis began to get serious about crime. No more petty clothing heists or watch-snatching. It was time to rob banks, which he felt was morally justifiable. "Some of them banks out in West Texas didn't care about hurtin' us poor farmers," recalled Willis in his memoirs. "So why should I care about hurtin' them?"

And as for partners? Willis had heard his share of stories about thugs who would rat you out to the law in exchange for a lighter sentence. So he decided to make it a family act.

Jess and Dock were more than willing to join their brother in his new venture. (By this time, Dock had finally successfully escaped jail and was looking for fundraising opportunities anyway.) Joe was the tricky one. Willis wasn't completely sure he'd be up for bank robbing, so when he wrote him a letter from Tulsa, he simply asked Joe to help him out with a job. Joe, thinking it would be some kind of cattle gig, showed up in Tulsa with his saddle and riding gear. Upon picking him up at the train station, Willis laughed. "I got a job for you," he said, "but it ain't that kind of job."

At first, the Newtons were strictly nighttime robbers, which minimized the risk. If there was even a hint of the law, the Newtons would ditch the plan and go home. "Better to say, 'There he goes' than 'Here he lies,'" quipped Willis. Timing was important, too; the Newton Boys mostly struck rural banks deep in the night in late fall, when piles of cash from selling crops had been deposited and when the chilly weather kept curious bystanders home in bed.

Once inside, the Newtons' success depended on the kind of bank safe inside: They would only crack the ones with square or rectangular doors, since nitroglycerin could be easily poured into the grooves. (Safes with round doors, on the other hand, were virtually nitroproof.) After some experimenting, the Newtons became quite good at guesstimating the amount of nitro—or "grease," as they called it—needed to peel a safe door. It was a delicate, dangerous way to make a living. Pour too little, and the door would merely "hang up," twisting itself at an angle, but still able to prevent hands from grabbing the loot inside. Pour too much, and you could blow your head clean off (or the safe door across the room and out of the front of the bank, like the Newtons did at a bank in San Marcos, Texas—the explosion was so powerful that money fluttered through the air and landed across the street).

By the 1920s, many banks had updated to round-door safes, but a good number of small town banks hadn't. Those became the Newtons' targets. There was the bank in Deer Trail, Colorado ($6,000), and another in Moosomin, Saskatchewan ($8,000). The Newtons were also able to pull off what the Jameses and Daltons dreamed of: two banks in one night—and not once, but twice. First in Hondo, Texas, the Newtons used their grease to peel the safe in one bank, then walked one block down the street to repeat the perform-ance in another. Then in Spencer, Indiana, the Newtons decided to do two banks at once instead of wasting time with consecutive strikes.

The Spencer double-shot had some comical results (as portrayed in the Linklater film). While Dock stood guard, Willis used the grease on one safe, while Joe did another. Then, unexpectedly, an innocent bystander started walking down the street. Dock did his damnedest to shoo him away, but the guy refused to listen. That's when Willis's nitro blast went off. Terrified out of his wits, the bystander hauled ass up the street ... just in time to walk past the second bank as Joe's charge exploded. The man turned on a dime and ran back past the first bank, where there was yet another explosion. Thinking he had stepped into the middle of a war zone, the frenzied bystander screamed and ran off into the night.

Dock couldn't help but laugh through tears as he explained to his brothers what had happened.

Soon, the Newtons and their methods became famous, with accounts of their robberies appearing in newspapers across the coun-try. "Some banks claimed we took $25,000 when maybe we took $15,000," recalled Joe. "We had a suspicion they claimed that to collect more insurance." During the off-season—remember, the Newtons only busted safes in cold weather—the brothers would live like celebrities, eating fine food, wearing the best tailored suits and attending ball games, carnivals, and social events. They were fond of wearing diamond stickpins, both for aesthetic and practical reasons. If a cop were to stop a Newton for questioning, there was nothing better than a glittering diamond to buy a bit of freedom.

By 1922, Willis was craving a challenge, and talked his brothers into doing daylight jobs. Joe was skeptical: "We were getting out of our line." But Willis insisted that such a job would be a quick way to build up funds, and besides, a certain bank in Braunfels, Texas, looked like a "lead pipe cinch."

On the chosen day, at high noon, Willis and Jess marched into the bank with six shooters and barked orders at the employees. "Lay down here!" (Years later, Willis said it was all part of his nonviolent strategy: "If you talk rough to them, then you don't have to hurt nobody.") Everyone obeyed, lining up on the floor. Willis leaped over the wooden rail and helped himself to the vault.

After stuffing a flour sack full of Liberty bonds and cash, the brothers were readying to leave when a bank employee returned from lunch. This particular bank employee happened to be a former Texas Ranger, and he was ready to bolt back outside when Dock, who was standing guard outside, herded him back inside at gunpoint. All three then left the bank and were speeding down their preplanned escape route before any lawmen had a chance to pursue them. The risky daylight job paid off, netting the brothers $104,000.

Despite their new success at daylight jobs, their continuing success at nighttime safe raids, and the occasional bank messenger hold-up, Willis was always looking to expand the family business. In June 1924, he received a hot tip on a mail train out of Chicago that was loaded with cash, bonds, and diamonds. Naturally, Joe had his doubts; it seemed too big a heist, and the bigger the heist, the more likely something could go wrong. But Willis insisted on pulling the job and even recruited an outsider to help. That would be Willis's first miscalculation.

The team split up into two groups: Willis and Jess disguised themselves as rail employees and hopped the train ahead of time; meanwhile, Joe, Dock, and the new gang member drove two Cadillacs to the town of Roundout, which was 30 miles north of Chicago, where they waited by the tracks. Willis and Jess pulled guns on the conductor and told him to stop the train at Roundout, at which point the others would jump on and proceed to take as much cash and diamonds as they could carry.

"Ain't this a helluva way to make a living?" Jess joked to the conductor.

But the conductor was so panicked at the sight of the guns, he forgot to stop at Roundout. And somehow, in the confusion of running for the train, the new gang member accidentally opened fire on Dock. "Every shot hit him," Joe would recall years later. "Two went into one side and one each into his jaw, right hand, and shoulder."

All Dock could do was struggle to collapse on top of a stack of mail, bleeding, while the rest of the gang went about their business of tear gassing 17 armed mail guards and robbing the train. When the gang doubled back and realized what had happened to Dock, they knew their getaway was going to be next to impossible. "As you can guess, we was pretty mad," recalled Joe. "No Newton had ever hurt anybody and no Newton had ever been hurt." Still, the Newtons loaded the loot into the cars, sped away to various stash locations to hide it, then rocketed to Chicago, where they hoped an underworld sawbones might treat their fallen brother.

Even though that decision saved Dock's life, it landed all of the Newtons, except Jess, in the hands of the Chicago cops. Jess had hightailed it to Texas to bury some money. Unfortunately, he got so drunk he forgot where he hid it, and he was later captured, too. (Someday, a lucky kid from San Antonio might be digging in his backyard and find $35,000 from the Roundout robbery.) The only thing that saved the Newtons from a lengthy stay in the Gray Bar Hotel was their willingness to trade the stolen money—some

$3 million worth—for time. Willis and Dock were sentenced to only 12 years in Leavenworth, Joe got 3, and Jess only 1. And none of the Newtons served their full sentence.

Fate, however, had a funny way of making sure the Newtons—Willis and Joe Newton, anyway—paid for their bank-robbing sins. Fifteen years later, both were jailed for a bank robbery they didn't commit. Even local law admitted as much to them: "Maybe you didn't rob this one, Willis, but you robbed others and got away with it."

Jess Newton died of lung cancer in 1960. Dock Newton, despite the violent way his last raid ended, got drunk and tried to rob a bank again in 1968. The 77-year-old shot it out with lawmen who surrounded the bank in Rowena, Texas, and was arrested after one cop smashed Dock over the head with his gun butt. Dock spent eight months in a prison hospital and then entered a nursing home, where he died in 1974.

Both Willis and Joe led law-abiding lives and later became professional beekeepers, making money by selling the honey. When their bees didn't produce as much as expected, the two surviving Newton Boys would make their last raids together: stealing honey from wild hives. "I may be too old to rob banks," recalled Willis, "but I can sure rob beehives."

Willis died in 1979 at the age of 90. Joe died 10 years later, at 88.

## Cool Fact from the Vault

Sterling Hayden's 1955 western, *The Last Command,* features a cameo appearance by Joe Newton. The movie was shot at a mock village near the Newton Boys' hometown of Uvalde, Texas, and Joe would often hire himself out as an extra. In *The Last Command,* Joe had two roles: first, as a Mexican soldier charging the gates of the Alamo, and second, as the Texas defender who shoots that same Mexican soldier. (Talk about killing yourself for a role.)

# 16  HARVEY BAILEY

**Nicknames:** "Old Harve," "King of the Heist Men"

**Known accomplices:** Nick "Chaw Jimmie" Traynor, "Dude" Richardson, Alvin Johnston, Jimmie "Wolf" London, Curly Santle, Frank "Jelly" Nash, Eddie Bentz, Al Spencer, Thomas Holden, Francis Keating, Vern Miller, Freddie Barker, Alvin Karpis, among others (Bailey rarely liked to work with the same crew twice.)

**Number of banks robbed:** 29

**Estimated lifetime take:** More than $1 million during the 1920s alone

**Claim to fame:** From 1928 to 1933, Bailey was the elder statesman of bank robberies. When he finally got nailed, it was for a crime he didn't commit.

## "THEY'VE ACCUSED ME OF THE DENVER MINT JOB, THE LINCOLN HEIST, AND EVERYTHING ELSE THAT'S HAPPENED IN THE LAST TEN YEARS."

Like George Leonidas Leslie and "the Baron" Lamm before him, Harve Bailey was the consummate, careful pro. "Where the bank robber was considered the top man of crime," writes Jay Robert Nash in *Bloodletters and Badmen,* "Bailey was considered the only bank robber in the nation without peers." It's unlikely that Bailey sat down and studied the Lamm Technique (see "John Ashley and the Everglades Gang")—after all, it was locked away in the brains of two ex-Lamm gang members who were up in the big sneezer in Indiana. But independently, Bailey came up with his own version, which included a getaway method called "running the cat roads."

Author L. L. Edge described the method in his 1981 book, titled (appropriately enough) *Run the Cat Roads*: "[Bailey] would spend days driving on farm-to-market roads surrounding an area where he was planning a robbery. He referred to these roads as cat roads because cats were about the only ones who could use them after dark. Using a foot-pedal odometer, he measured distance between points and recorded them." Only amateurs and pikers would rush into a bank knockover without a carefully detailed getaway; the best heist men—the Harvey Baileys—would have every inch of their escape recorded in logs and memorized.

Bailey started his criminal career in Iowa running not cat roads, but illegal hooch, back at the dawn of Prohibition in 1920. Bailey was famous for his huge black Buick that could not only outrun the local law but also held an absurd amount of booze in the trunk. (Countless frat boys would later duplicate this technique.) The car was so popular that some criminal buddies asked if they could borrow it to burgle a clothing shop in Maryville, Missouri. But the suit-nappers were nabbed, and Bailey's ownership of the car was uncovered. It would be his first—and for over a decade, last—arrest.

Bailey jumped bail and decided it was time for a change of pace. Safecracking seemed more profitable than rumrunning, so he teamed up with other criminals to pull a series of nighttime bank burglaries in Iowa and North Dakota. Soon, Bailey graduated to daylight jobs, and on September 28, 1922, Bailey pulled his first big score: Hamilton County Bank of Ohio, for $265,000 in cash, securities, and bonds.

That haul, however, would be eclipsed less than two months later. On December 18, 65-year-old Federal Reserve guard Charles T. Linton was closing up his truck in front of the Denver Mint when a black Buick came speeding up. Two guys with sawed-off shotguns popped out and started blasting away. Other Federal Reserve guards returned fire. Ninety seconds later, the Great Denver Mint Robbery was over, leaving Linton dead, two of the robbers wounded, and $200,000 in fresh, unmarked $5 bills missing.

While the crime has never been officially solved, most historians credit Bailey with the hold-up. A month after the robbery, police found the getaway car, rotting away in a garage. And inside was the rotting body of Nick "Chaw Jimmie" Traynor, a known Bailey associate. (Other Bailey men were also implicated.) Bailey, however, insisted he had nothing to do with it—shooting and killing wasn't his style. Plus, it wasn't smart to go after government money. "They'll spend a million to recover a penny," Bailey said. If Bailey was telling the truth about the Denver job—that he'd been hitched to a crime he didn't commit—it wouldn't be the last time.

A few years later, Bailey did something un–bandit-like: He teamed up with a partner and opened a pair of gas stations. It was an attempt at the straight life for the sake of his wife and two boys. Of course, the gas station business didn't stop Bailey and associates from taking a LaPorte, Indiana, bank for $140,000; a Rochester, Minnesota, bank for $30,000; a Vinton, Iowa, bank for $70,000; a Washington Court House, Ohio, bank for $225,000; an Atlantic, Iowa, bank for $55,000; a Sturgis, Minnesota, bank for $80,000; and a Clinton, Indiana, bank for $52,000 within a two-year period. After all, a man needed to have his fun, keep his mind alive.

But his legitimate gas stations did so well that Bailey and his partner were able to sell them to invest in real estate, buying two farms in Wisconsin. By 1929, Bailey was making so much money that he started to think about laying off bank robbing for a while. After all, he only stole when he needed to replenish his reserve funds, lying low between jobs to avoid capture. Maybe it was time for the King of the Heist Men to go straight.

Then the stock market crashed in October 1929, and most of Bailey's money, which was socked away in banks and other investments, was wiped out. It was a cruel finger-in-the-eye from the fates. Bailey, pushing 40, was forced to start over and run the cat roads once again. Along with old friend Tommy Holden, "Jew Sammy" Stein, and some new guy named George Kelly, Bailey stormed the bank of Willmar, Minnesota, on July 15, 1930, and stole $70,000. It was a rough comeback; shots erupted, and Stein ended up catching a bullet in the head. (It would also be the first bank heist for George "Machine Gun" Kelly; for more on him, see "'Machine Gun' Kelly.")

Bailey's next gig, the knockover of a savings bank in Ottumwa, Iowa, went much smoother and netted his gang of five more than $40,000.

Eight days later, there was a bank robbery so huge—$2,678,700 from the Lincoln National Bank in Nebraska—that the law assumed only Harvey Bailey could be behind it. But Bailey claimed he was cooling his heels in Minneapolis on the date of the robbery. (And it is thought that master planner Eddie Bentz, #23 on this list, cooked up this caper.) As with the Denver Mint Robbery, known Bailey associates were also linked to the Lincoln National job. Involved or not, Bailey did profit from the heist in at least one way: He helped unload the hot securities.

One of the keys to Bailey's success was his insistence on not working with the same crew twice. He reasoned that rotating men kept the law from branding a certain group "the Bailey Gang" and decreased everyone's chances of getting caught. Bailey also had a rule about not involving wives or girlfriends in official business—a rule that would infuriate Kathryn Kelly, the woman who practically invented the killer rep of her husband, "Machine Gun."

In 1932, in search of a fresh set of faces, Bailey traveled to Kansas City to meet up with Freddie Barker and Alvin Karpis, who had a job lined up in Fort Scott, Kansas. That robbery, which took place on June 17, 1932, rapidly devolved into chaos when a teller tripped an alarm. Some historians say that Freddie Barker went psycho, threatening to kill people left and right, forcing the calm, collected Bailey to hold things together. Karpis's own account is a bit different. "There were a lot of crises we didn't count on," he writes, saying nothing about Barker flipping out. (Then again, Karpis and Freddie Barker were best friends; for more, see "The Barker-Karpis Gang.") Two female hostages were taken, bullets were exchanged, and the team barely escaped with their $47,000. Bailey left the job with only $4,000, vowing never to work with Barker or Karpis again. Looking to blow off some steam three weeks later, he went golfing.

Golfing was big with some of the 1920s heist men. Bailey was fond of the sport, as were Tommy Holden, Frank Keating, and Frank "Jelly" Nash, all old-time pros who worked with Bailey now and again. After Fort Scott, the four met up for a couple of holes at the Old Mission Golf Course, a public course in Kansas City. Little did Bailey know that the FBI were wise to their nine-iron addiction and had been snooping around public courses for months.

Bailey, Holden, and Keating had just finished putting out when they heard a voice behind them.

"Hold it, boys."

An FBI agent popped out of the trees along with six other cops. Bailey, Holden, and Keating were arrested without resistance. After all, it's hard to conceal a pistol in your finest golf duds.

At first Bailey insisted he was a guy named John Brown, but cops found one of the Liberty Bonds from the Fort Scott job in his pants pocket—just that morning, Bailey had absent-mindedly put it in his pocket, intending to unload it later. Bailey's apartment in Kansas City was searched, and weapons used in the Fort Scott job were found.

After a decade of eluding capture, the King of the Heist Men was sentenced to 10 to 50 years—a comparatively light sentence, since Bailey was a "first-time offender." Bailey hated that a lame heist such as Fort Scott had gotten him into this mess. Mostly, he regretted working with the Barker-Karpis guys. "Their kind of heat burned everybody," he would say years later.

Little did he know that his golf course take-down was the beginning of a long string of rotten luck.

Bailey entered the Kansas State Penitentiary in August 1932. At the age of 45, it was his first taste of life behind the walls. The following spring, Bailey was approached by a spastic, mean-looking con named Wilbur Underhill, who wanted the King of the Heist Men's help in busting out. Reluctantly, Bailey agreed, but he was wary of Underhill's blood lust. (For more on Underhill, see the next entry.) "Let's get one thing straight right now," Bailey told him. "There'll be no gun play at all or else we're dead men."

Underhill said nothing. Bailey took that as agreement.

On Memorial Day 1933, Bailey, Underhill, and eight other convicts broke out of Kansas State, taking the prison's warden and two guards hostage. Underhill badly wanted to blow the warden's brains out—seems he had an old grudge to settle. But Bailey, who had been shot in the kneecap during the escape, refused to let him. "No sir, there ain't no killin' gonna come off here," said Bailey, according to *Run the Cat Roads*. "You make one move and I'll christen you."

"All right," Underhill said. "If that's the way you want it." The warden and the two guards were allowed to leave unharmed.

Within the month Bailey's knee healed, and in mid-June he picked up a copy of the *Daily Oklahoman* and saw that he was, yet again, the number-one suspect in a grisly crime. This time, it was the infamous Kansas City Massacre, where five lawmen and one criminal—notorious thug Frank "Jelly" Nash—were blown away when two unidentified gunmen tried to rescue Nash. (Some claim the gunmen were there to kill Nash, and things got out of hand.) "They've accused me of the Denver Mint job, the Lincoln heist, and everything else that's happened in the last 10 years," Bailey complained.

By July, Bailey's knee was back to normal, and he decided it was time to get back to work. Thus began the unlikeliest crime team in U.S. history: the Bailey-Underhill Gang. This bank-robbing odd couple, along with other Kansas State escapees, knocked over two banks before splitting up. Bailey couldn't stand Underhill for much longer than that. First was the First National Bank in Clinton, Oklahoma. One gang member stayed with the getaway car, one manned the door, while three others herded the bank employees into a back room. The gang made off with $11,000 cash. Then on August 9, the gang took the People's National Bank of Kingfisher, Oklahoma, for $6,024.

All the while, Underhill remained the violent, angry *yang* to Bailey's cool, calm *yin*. "He always wanted to kill someone," Bailey later said. "We'd drive through some town, and every time he saw a cop, he wanted to kill him."

It was bad luck to hook up with a violent psycho for a partner. But the worst luck of all was just around the bend.

For the Kingfisher job, Bailey had cashed in an old favor with "Machine Gun" Kelly and borrowed one of his trademark tommy guns. After the heist, he traveled back to Kelly's hideout in Paradise, Texas, to return it. Unwittingly, Bailey had walked into Machine Gun's life at the worst possible moment: Kelly and his wife Kathryn had just kidnapped an Oklahoma oilman named Charles Urschel, and the big heat was on.

In fact, the Kellys weren't even around; Kathryn's stepfather Robert G. "Boss" Shannon greeted Bailey when he showed up at the Paradise ranch. Bailey called Machine Gun and Kathryn, who were in Oklahoma City, and the two urged Bailey to split. "Things are pretty hot now," explained Machine Gun.

But Bailey had traveled a long distance, and his knee was acting up again. "I'll catch a little shut-eye and keep moving," he told him.

The next morning, Bailey woke up with the barrel of a shotgun tickling his nose. FBI agents had the ranch surrounded.

"All right, Harvey," one of them said. "It's all up."

"By God, a man's gotta sleep sometime, hasn't he?" Bailey quipped, still rubbing the sleep from his eyes.

When Bailey went to trial, he was found guilty of taking part in the Urschel kidnapping, even though he'd never so much as laid eyes on the oil baron. The damning evidence: $1,000 in cash found on Bailey, which was a loan repayment from Machine Gun Kelly. (Moral of the story: Never lend friends money.) Bailey was huge news in August 1933; his capture was the first big feather in the fledgling FBI's cap. He was even bigger news when he managed to crash out of a supposedly escape-proof prison in Dallas, Texas.

But the run was Bailey's last. Within hours, more than 100 cops had him surrounded in Ardmore, Oklahoma, and returned him to Texas in chains. Bailey, who had long been accused of big, violent crimes he swore he didn't commit, was sentenced to life in prison for the Urschel kidnapping, a crime he definitely didn't commit.

Upon his parole in 1965, Bailey said, "I may starve, but I'll never steal again." As far as anyone knows, he was telling the truth. He became a cabinet maker in Joplin, Missouri, married the widow of an outlaw named Herb Farmer, and even hired a ghost writer to pen his autobiography, *Robbing Banks Was My Business*. Old Harve ran that great big cat road in the sky on March 1, 1979, at the age of 91.

(Bettmann/CORBIS)

*Bail(ey) is denied: Harvey Bailey, back in the hands of the law after his final prison break in Oklahoma City.*

## Cool Fact from the Vault

Bailey and his gas station–owning partner are credited with inventing the first conveyor system for scrubbing and polishing automobiles. That's right: The King of the Heist Men was also the King of the Car Wash. (Insert your own "clean getaway" joke here.)

# 17 WILBUR UNDERHILL

**Nicknames:** "The Tri-State Terror," "The Southwest Executioner"

**Number of banks robbed:** 9

**Estimated lifetime take:** $29,750

**Claim to fame:** Underhill was a violent, slightly insane bank robber who officially kicked off "Bloody 1934"

## "TELL THE BOYS I'M COMING HOME."

The Underhills were a divided family: All of the women in the family were kindly, decent, and law-abiding citizens, the three youngest daughters going on to marry into good families. But the men—father Wilber and sons Earl, George, Ernest, and Wilber Jr.—all had rap sheets and spent many years at the unofficial family resort: the Missouri State Penitentiary. By the time Wilber Jr. (he later changed it to "Wilbur" because he thought it sounded more manly) was arrested for burglary and sent to prison in 1919, brothers Earl and George were already there for similar crimes, and brother Ernest was in for murder.

Young Wilbur, however, was by far the most vicious of the lot. He turned so mean after a childhood injury that even his mother had to admit: "I don't think [the accident] left him quite right." After winning release from prison, Underhill became known as the "Lover's Lane Bandit," robbing amorous couples who'd made the mistake of parking on his stalking grounds near Joplin, Missouri. He was captured in a sting and sent back to his brothers but won release in 1926. Underhill promptly recruited a partner and tried to knock over a drug store in Okmulgee, Oklahoma, on Christmas Day 1926, minutes before midnight. But the owner's wife carefully hid the sack of money between her legs, and said the only cash in the store was in the register.

Underhill started pawing through the till, which contained about $25, when the door opened, and three customers entered. The bandits lifted their guns and ordered the men to raise their hands. One of them, George Fee, saw the guns and chuckled. "Is this a joke?"

Underhill shot Fee in the chest, and the 19-year-old dropped to the floor like a sack of brass doorknobs.

Both men escaped without taking any money and were caught two weeks later in Tulsa. Underhill was awaiting trial when he used smuggled hacksaw blades to escape and went on another robbery spree, this time killing his 16-year-old street robbery victim and an older eyewitness. Once again, he fled to Tulsa. Once again, he was caught and returned to prison—this time, sentenced to life behind bars.

For four years, Underhill focused on nothing but crazy, rabid escape plans, causing his fellow inmates to give him wide berth. He spent weeks upon end in solitary confinement, which made him even meaner. Finally, on July 14, 1931, Underhill saw his chance for his second jailbreak. While working on a road gang, he hid under a bush, then eluded the posse that had been sent to recover him, diving into a river through a hail of bullets. In the following month, the escaped lunatic would be dubbed the Tri-State Terror, a bloodthirsty robber who loved to knock over gas stations, grocery stores, and even movie theaters in Oklahoma, Arkansas, and Kansas. When cornered by a cop named Merle Colver, Underhill didn't hesitate in blowing him away. By September 4, 1931, Underhill was back in jail for the murder.

It was here in the Kansas State Penitentiary that Underhill met Harvey Bailey, with whom he hatched a successful escape plan (for more on Bailey, see the previous entry). After two bank heists together, Bailey split and Underhill was left to rob banks on his own. First was the People's National Bank in Stuttgart, Arkansas ($1,000), followed by a measly $550 robbery at the Farmers' and Merchants' Bank in Tryon, Oklahoma, a few weeks later. But later in the same day, Underhill made up for it by stealing $2,000 from the American National Bank in Baxter Springs, Kansas. Two days later, on October 11, Underhill and four accomplices hit the International State Bank in Haskell, Oklahoma, for a pitiful $400.

Underhill finally saw a five-figure payday when he led his armed gang into the Citizens' National Bank of Okmulgee, Oklahoma, on November 2. Shortly after noon, Underhill approached the bank's vice president, J. H. McElroy, and calmly told him: "A robbery is taking place." As customers entered and employees returned from lunch, Underhill and his men lined them up along one wall of the bank, loaded $13,776 into a sack, then fled with McElroy and a cashier standing on the running boards of the getaway car. Both were allowed to step off three blocks from the bank.

The fat take—fat for Underhill, anyway—might have persuaded him to take it easy for a while. Underhill promised his childhood sweetheart Beatrice Hudson that he'd get hitched and try to live the straight life. He marched into a courthouse in Coalgate, Oklahoma, on November 18, 1933, and applied for a marriage license under his birth name: Henry W. Underhill. The Tri-State Terror even gave the clergyman the address of his new in-laws in Oklahoma City and told him to send the marriage license there. When law officers learned about this, they staked out the home. Sure enough, Underhill and his bride showed up, but they were gone by the time the FBI agent returned to the scene after calling for backup. And despite Underhill's promise to his bride, he robbed the First National Bank of $3,000 less than a month after getting married; perhaps it was Underhill's wedding gift to himself.

The day before New Year's Eve 1933, Underhill got up early in the chilly morning to dress. He and Beatrice, along with partner Raymond Roe and his girlfriend, had rented a cottage in Shawnee,

Oklahoma, for the holidays, and Underhill had a New Year's Day appointment in Oklahoma City to cash $5,300 in stolen bonds. But before Underhill could even put his pants on, he heard a voice say: "Stick 'em up, Wilbur. We're the law."

Underhill spun, grabbed a Luger pistol from a dresser, but by then it was too late. More than 24 agents had his honeymoon cottage surrounded and started blasting away. Walls, window, and curtains were sliced to shreds. Underhill reached out his pistol and squeezed off a few shots blind. Roe and his girlfriend scurried into a closet, but a bullet cut through the wood and landed in the woman's stomach.

Finally, Underhill raced out into the cold air wearing nothing but longjohns. The surrounding agents trained their fire on their moving, barely clothed target. A bullet smacked into Underhill's right shoulder and sent him spinning to the ground. Somehow, Underhill rolled with the blow and got back up on his feet. Another bullet hit him in the left shoulder, followed by two more bullets. But Underhill kept running, bleeding and barefoot, through the icy snow. He had his eyes on a cornfield. If only he could get to the stalks, maybe he could zigzag his way out of this.

As he reached the field, a bullet struck him in the head.

But that didn't stop Underhill, because the bullet failed to penetrate the man's skull. There was a lot of blood, sure, but no brain damage. He kept running. He ran so fast that he managed to put serious distance between himself and the pursuing agents. Through bloodied eyes, Underhill saw a furniture shop in downtown Shawnee. Just a little farther. Just a little farther.

A short while later, a call came into the Shawnee police station. "Someone wearing nothing but his underwear is trying to break into the Owens Furniture Store!"

The FBI found Underhill inside, shot all to hell, but somehow still alive. In fact, Underhill survived a two-hour operation, and even joked about the shoot-out with reporters two days later. "Actually, I only got hit five times, but them shots made eleven holes in me," laughed Underhill. "I counted each one as they hit me. When I set sail, they sure poured it to me." He also survived a 70-mile ambulance trip to the Oklahoma State Penitentiary at McAlester on January 6, 1934. "Tell the boys I'm coming home," Underhill told a prison guard during the journey. The Tri-State Terror may have been referring to buddies in the slammer, but he might as well have been talking about the devils in hell. Underhill died 12 hours later.

It was one of the strangest, most prolonged deaths in outlaw history, but it was only the beginning. The year 1934 was going to be a bloody one.

## Cool Fact from the Vault

One prison warden was so frightened of the psychotic Underhill that he had a special gas bomb installed above his office door, just in case the Tri-State Terror decided to pay him a surprise visit.

# 18  BONNIE AND CLYDE

**Full names:** Bonnie Parker and Clyde Champion Barrow

**Number of banks robbed:** 5

**Estimated lifetime take:** Not much more than $5,000

**Claim to fame:** The most famous criminal couple in history, Bonnie and Clyde raced, robbed, and killed their way through depression-era America—with emphasis on the killing

## "THIS HERE'S A STICK-UP!"

Back in the 1930s, nobody much liked Bonnie Parker and Clyde Barrow—especially their bank-robbing colleagues. "They're just a couple of cheap filling station and car thieves," said "Machine Gun" Kelly. "Pretty Boy" Floyd hated how they treated innocent civilians. John Dillinger once referred to Bonnie and Clyde as "a couple of punks. They give bank robbing a bad name!"

Yet, the outlaw lovers are probably the most famous bank robbers in history. "Sixty-six years after they went down in a hail of bullets in Gibsland, Louisiana," proclaimed *Texas Monthly* in a February 2001 cover story, "Texas' bank-robbing lovers are hot again." Every year, Bonnie and Clyde fanatics gather in Gibsland, Louisiana, to discuss such arcane tidbits as Bonnie's shoe size and the color of the 1934 Ford V8 in which Bonnie and Clyde were cut apart by Texas Ranger bullets. (Three and Cordova gray, for the record.) Much of their present-day fame is probably thanks to the 1967 Arthur Penn movie *Bonnie and Clyde,* which presents the bandits as highly likeable and attractive counterculture heroes.

No matter what you think of Bonnie and Clyde—a couple of fun-loving kids or "a couple of rats," especially that "dirty, diseased woman," as J. Edgar Hoover called her—the fact remains they were lousy bank robbers. The biggest haul of their five recorded bank jobs was only $2,500. When Clyde first met 19-year-old Bonnie at a mutual friend's house in January 1930, he was already a wanted man, but only for small-town grocery and filling station stick-ups throughout Texas. The petite, blonde-haired Bonnie promptly brought her jug-eared man home to meet her mother. That's where cops found Clyde, sleeping on Emma Parker's sofa. (Not exactly the best first impression a young suitor can make.)

Clyde, then 21, was shipped off to prison in Waco, Texas, and his new girlfriend promptly shoved a .32 revolver between her small breasts and smuggled it in to him. Clyde escaped, but was caught a week later and sent to Eastham Prison Farm, where he served two years and became desperate enough to chop off two of his own toes to escape work detail. Bonnie stayed faithful, writing him long mash notes. Clyde was paroled on February 2, 1932, and limped home to the joyous arms of his Bonnie. "The instant she looked up and saw Clyde," recalled Bonnie's mother Emma, "it was like he had never been away at all." The two promptly joined Ralph Fults, a prison buddy of Clyde's, in a hardware store heist that went wrong in every possible way. Night watchmen surprised them, their getaway car got stuck in the mud (as did Bonnie's shoes), and a pair of hijacked getaway mules refused to budge.

Clyde managed to get away, but Bonnie was horrified to find herself captured and thrown in jail. While her boyfriend continued perfecting his criminal techniques, Bonnie retreated into poetry, writing "The Story of Suicide Sal." It was no doubt based on her foiled robbery attempt with Clyde, but it was also high fantasy:

> I got on the "F.B.A." payroll
> To get the "inside lay" of the "job";
> The bank was "turning big money"!
> It looked like a "cinch for the mob."

*Eighty grand without even a "rumble"—*
*Jack was last with the "loot" in the door.*
*When the "teller" dead-aimed a revolver*
*From where they forced him to lie on the floor.*
*I knew I had only a moment—*
*He would surely get Jack as he ran;*
*So I "staged" a "big fade out" beside him*
*And knocked the forty-five out of his hand.*

The narrator, "Suicide Sal," goes on to take the fall for her man, just like Bonnie did. But at that point, even Clyde had never attempted a bank robbery, much less even laid eyes on "eighty grand." Still, one could see that Bonnie's heart belonged to Clyde, even if he'd abandoned her to the law. After her release from prison in the summer of 1932, Bonnie was sitting at home with her grandmother when news reached them: Clyde and a prison buddy named Raymond Hamilton had gunned down two cops outside a dance in Stringtown, Oklahoma. When Clyde showed up hours later and asked Bonnie to join him, she did not hesitate. Right then, Bonnie and Clyde began a robbing and killing run that would not end until their deaths nearly two years later.

Heading north, Clyde got up the nerve to try his first bank robbery on November 9. Along with Bonnie and two others, Clyde hit one in Orango, Missouri. "This here's a stick-up!" he announced, but only got $115 for his trouble. Disgusted, Clyde carefully cased out his next bank, situated in another small Missouri town. He planned to burst in, gun in hand, while Bonnie manned their getaway car. But when Clyde did burst in, he found a sad old man sitting in the corner of an empty lobby. The bank had closed four days ago.

In fact, Bonnie and Clyde, along with their new 16-year-old outlaw partner W. D. Jones, were far more successful at killing people than robbing banks, a point that the 1967 Arthur Penn movie tactfully skips. Throughout their run, 12 people—lawmen and innocent civilians—would fall victim to Clyde's beloved collection of firearms, most of them stolen from National Guard armories. Clyde also loved fast cars. He even wrote a fan letter to Henry Ford at the Ford Motor Company in Detroit, Michigan:

> While I still have got breath in my lungs I will tell you what a dandy car you make. I have drove Ford exclusivly [sic] when I could get away with one. For sustained speed and freedom from trouble the Ford has got every other car skinned and even if my business hasen't [sic] been strictly legal it don't hurt anything to tell you what a fine car you got in the V8.

> Yours truly, Clyde Champion Barrow.

It was a Ford, in fact, that first sicced the FBI on Bonnie and Clyde. At the time, bank robbery wasn't a federal crime, but transporting a stolen car across state lines was. According to declassified FBI files, an abandoned Ford in Jackson, Michigan, was traced to Pawhuska, Oklahoma, where they found another abandoned Ford, which had been stolen in Illinois. Inside the car, they found a prescription medicine bottle, originally filled by the aunt of one Clyde Barrow. Further digging led the FBI to discover that Bonnie Parker had been along for the ride. On May 20, 1933, a federal warrant for Bonnie and Clyde's arrest was issued in Dallas, Texas. At the same time, the couple was starting to receive national attention. Even *The New York Times* started covering their outlaw doings.

By the summer of 1933, Clyde was happy to welcome his brother Ivan (a.k.a. "Buck") into the fold. The two began their criminal careers together, but Buck had spent the past couple of years in jail while his faithful wife Blanche had waited for him. Now the Barrow Boys were together again, along with their respective paramours and fifth wheel W. D. Jones, which gave Clyde the guts to try another bank job. On May 8, 1933, the gang hit the Lucerne State Bank in Indiana for $300, which was merely a warm-up for their most lucrative heist on May 16 in Okabena, Missouri.

*Happy together: Bonnie Parker gets the drop on Clyde in this playful photo from 1932.*

The robbery went smoothly enough at the outset, but the bank happened to be the most prominent building in town, according to author John Treherne in his book *The Strange History of Bonnie and Clyde.* "Everyone in town seemed to know about the hold-up before we did," complained Clyde. "There was a regular reception committee waiting for us when we came out, everybody shooting right and left."

One old man valiantly tried to push a log in front of the getaway car. Clyde told Bonnie to blow the man's head off, but Bonnie demurred. "Why honey," she said, "I wasn't going to kill that nice old man. He was white-headed."

Still, the Barrow Gang escaped, and the take was $2,500—the largest amount Clyde would ever see in his career. On June 22, the gang robbed a bank in Alma, Texas, for a small amount of money, then robbed a Piggly Wiggly store in Arkansas.

These were the relative glory days of the Barrow Gang. But as the summer of 1933 dragged on, everything started to rocket downhill. Police cornered the gang at their hideout apartment in Joplin, Missouri, resulting in a blistering shootout that left Clyde winged and W. D.'s head "spouting blood," according to Bonnie. A few weeks later, Clyde crashed their stolen Ford into a ditch, which caught fire and severely burned Bonnie before Clyde was able to wrench her from the wreckage. (The pain was so bad, Bonnie begged Clyde to shoot her; another gory detail left out of the 1967 movie.) This was followed by another shoot-out at a tourist camp in Platte City, Missouri, which left Buck with a gushing head wound and his wife Blanche blinded by sharp glass. The gang made it out of the area but were pinned down the next day in a field in Iowa. A dying Buck and feverish Blanche were nabbed—"Daddy, don't die!" she pleaded—while Bonnie, Clyde, and W. D. ducked bullets and somehow escaped.

Life for Bonnie and Clyde became a brutal routine of avoiding police traps and recruiting new accomplices to steal enough money to scrape by. In January 1934, Clyde led his most successful operation: busting his old friend Ray Hamilton and other inmates out of the Eastham Prison Farm. Together, they mounted what would be Clyde's last bank robbery in late February in Lancaster, Texas. Clyde held a shotgun on the teller and two customers, while Hamilton scooped the cash into a sack. It is not clear how much was stolen that day—accounts range from $2,400 to $6,700—but it is known that Clyde and Hamilton argued over the split and how to run the gang. The two parted company on bitter terms. (According to the *Texas Monthly* article, the slurs "small-time twerp" and "yellow punk" were thrown around.)

Meanwhile, officials in Texas were tired of the bloodshed—and the image of Bonnie and Clyde as a wild fun-loving couple, thanks to

Bonnie's poems and dozens of photos discovered by police in abandoned Barrow hideouts. These are the same images that are reprinted to this day: Bonnie chomping on a cigar, even though she abhorred the things in real life; Bonnie pretending to "get the drop" on Clyde, leveling a rifle to his belly. If not for the piles of bodies the two left in their wake, including two Texas highway patrolmen gunned down on Easter Sunday 1934, Bonnie and Clyde seemed like such nice, fun-loving people.

The public ate the photos up; the lawmakers hated them, and decided enough was enough. Lee Simmons, head of the state prison system, lured former Texas Ranger Captain Frank Hamer out of retirement and gave him the job of bringing Bonnie and Clyde in, dead or alive. "I'd be foolish to tell you how to do your job," said Simmons, "but the way I look at it, the best thing you can do is put them on the spot, know you are right, and shoot everybody in sight."

That is exactly what Captain Hamer did 102 days later. On May 21, Hamer gathered up five local cops and set up an ambush south of Gibsland, Louisiana, the family home of Henry Methvin, an accomplice of Bonnie and Clyde. "We had been tipped off that Clyde was planning to rob a bank at Arcadia," explained deputy sheriff Bob Alcorn to the *Dallas Morning News,* "[We] had information that led [us] to believe the pair would come this way. So we laid down and waited." For two days, the six-man posse waited, lined up behind bushes, armed with automatic rifles, shotguns, and pistols. They almost gave up the morning of May 23 when someone heard a Ford approaching. It was Bonnie and Clyde, returning from breakfast.

Clyde slowed when he saw what looked like Henry's dad standing next to his truck, stalled on the side of the road. It was. When the old man moved out of the way, the first shots exploded. The back of Clyde's head was blown away. His foot slipped off the clutch, and the car rolled forward. Bonnie screamed, and felt dozens of bullets drill through her body, ripping away at her scalp, her jaw, and fingers on her right hand. At least 25 more rifle slugs cut into Clyde's body.

The fusillade was so intense, the car rocked back and forth on its suspension as it moved, until it finally came to a dead stop on an embankment.

"Be careful," someone shouted. "They may not be dead."

But they were dead, and then some. Souvenir seekers swarmed the scene, knowing that someday Clyde's shattered sunglasses or the true detective magazine Bonnie had been reading would be worth a lot of money. Schoolchildren marveled as the dead outlaws were dragged— still in their shot-up Ford V8—through town.

Bonnie, in her final moments alive, may have thought about the last poem she'd written: "The Story of Bonnie and Clyde." It was as if she'd predicted their grisly end:

> *Some day, they'll go down together*
> *And they'll bury them side by side*
> *To a few, it'll be grief—*
> *To the law, a relief—*
> *But it's death for Bonnie and Clyde.*

Bonnie, 24, and Clyde, 25, were buried in separate graveyards, which was Bonnie's mother's idea. "He had her for two years," she explained. "Look what it got her."

## Cool Fact from the Vault

If one posse member hadn't stopped him, a ghoul at the death scene would have hacked off Clyde's trigger finger and kept it as a trophy. Another man offered the Barrow family $50,000 for Clyde's body; he wanted to mummify it and take it on a road tour.

## WHERE *BONNIE AND CLYDE* WENT WRONG

The classic 1967 Arthur Penn flick was a lot of fun, but it played fast and loose when it came to historical fact.

**The movie:** Bonnie (Faye Dunaway) meets Clyde (Warren Beatty) when he tries to boost her mother's car.

**The reality:** Bonnie met Clyde at the house of a mutual friend.

**The movie:** Bonnie wears short skirts.

**The reality:** The real Bonnie Parker always wore ankle-length skirts. Short skirts were fashionable in the 1920s, but by the Great Depression, style had turned in a more somber direction.

**The movie:** Buck Barrow (Gene Hackman) does an amazing series of leaps over a 12-foot bank tellers' cage to help himself to cash.

**The reality:** John Dillinger pioneered that move.

**The movie:** Clyde asks a poor farmer if the cash on the bank counter is his; the farmer says yes, and Clyde tells the farmer to keep it.

**The reality:** Dillinger did that, too.

**The movie:** Blanche Barrow (Estelle Parsons) is a hysterical woman prone to crying jags who can't believe she's married to a gangster.

**The reality:** Blanche Barrow was a willing and helpful member of the Barrow Gang.

**The movie:** Bonnie and Clyde are sold out by the father of their partner, C. W. Moss (Michael J. Pollard).

**The reality:** "C. W. Moss" was a composite of W. D. Jones and Henry Methvin. Furthermore, even though popular legend has it that Henry's father, Irvin, sold out Bonnie and Clyde, the best evidence is that Frank Hamer's men forced him into it, even at one point shackling him to a tree.

**The movie:** Bonnie eats half an apple before being shot to death.

**The reality:** Bonnie ate half a sandwich before being shot to death.

**The movie:** Bonnie and Clyde are happy-go-lucky bandits who were kind to innocent civilians.

**The reality:** Bonnie and Clyde killed one heck of a lot of people, including innocent civilians.

## PAYING FOR THEIR CRIMES

The most money Clyde Barrow ever stole at one time was $2,500, which wouldn't be enough for Clyde to buy his own hat today. Here's a Bonnie-and-Clyde memorabilia pricing guide, according to the most recent auction data:

◆ Clyde's death hat: $12,650

◆ Clyde's blood-soaked death shirt: $85,000

◆ Bonnie's sequin death hat: $4,600

◆ Rifle ammo clip taken from the death car: $6,900

◆ Manuscript of a Bonnie Parker poem: $63,250

◆ Letter from Clyde to his mother, November 12, 1931: $7,475

◆ The sign-in book from Bonnie and Clyde's funeral: $2,000 to $3,000

◆ Buck Barrow's Elgin pocket watch: $1,610

# 19  JOHN DILLINGER

**Gang members:** Harry Pierpont, Charles Makley, John "Red" Hamilton, Russell Clark, Harry Copeland, Ed Shouse; Hamilton, "Baby Face" Nelson, Homer Van Meter, Tommy Carroll, Eddie Green

**Number of banks robbed:** 11

**Estimated lifetime take:** $310,000

**Claim to fame:** "Dillinger" is the first name that comes to mind when someone says "bank robbery"

## "WELL, HONEY, THIS IS A HOLD-UP."

John Dillinger spent most of his adult life behind bars, and he didn't commit a crime worth noting until a year before he was gunned down. In fact, if a meteor had dropped out of the skies in May 1933 and pounded 29-year-old John Dillinger, he would have been remembered only as an Indianapolis kid who once mugged an elderly grocer and received a long stretch in jail for it. But less than a year later, "Dillinger" would be a household word, a master bank robber who would cause entire states to panic and call out the National Guard.

Dillinger was born in the Oak Hill section of Indianapolis to a middle-class family and soon became a perpetual headache to his hard-working grocer father and stepmother. Along with a gang of neighborhood boys who called themselves "the Dirty Dozen," the young Dillinger heisted candy, then loads of coal, and finally whiskey. As a teenager, Dillinger quit school to work in a machine shop, then used his pay to stay out all night carousing in the city. Thinking the city was going to ruin his son, the elder Dillinger moved his family to a farm near Mooresville, Indiana. Rural life didn't cure Dillinger of his wild streak—nor did a hitch in the Navy, for that matter—but while living in Mooresville, Dillinger met Beryl Hovius, a 16-year-old girl who would become his wife. In 1924, the newlywed couple moved to Indianapolis, and soon Dillinger was looking for quick cash to make life in his favorite city more enjoyable.

Dillinger found it in a Mooresville grocer named B. F. Morgan, a kindly old man who once caught a teenaged Dillinger stealing pennies but let him go with a friendly warning. Dillinger knew that Morgan always gathered his cash up Saturday nights before heading uptown for a haircut. On Saturday September 6, 1924, Dillinger and a drunkard pool shark named Ed Singleton decided to rob Morgan. Dillinger repeatedly clocked the old man over the head with a huge bolt wrapped in a handkerchief and demanded the money. Morgan screamed and tried to grab a .32 revolver from Dillinger, which accidentally went off. Dillinger fled, thinking that he'd shot his victim. When he reached the corner where Singleton was supposed to be waiting with a getaway car, Dillinger saw he was alone.

Both Dillinger and Singleton were quickly rounded up and set to face Judge Joseph W. Williams, who was fond of harsh sentences. Singleton's lawyer quickly filed for a change of venue, but Dillinger was stuck with Williams, who gave him 10 to 20 years at the Pendleton Reformatory in Indiana. It was a tough blow. Even the deputy sheriff who transported Dillinger to prison called it a "raw deal."

But those 10 years (actually, 9) were the best thing that could have happened to an aspiring heister like John Dillinger—and the worst thing that could have happened to American banks. At Pendleton, Dillinger met two men who would have a profound influence on his life: Harry Pierpont, a handsome bank robber and ladies' man, and Homer Van Meter, a court jester who would throw himself around like a paraplegic to amuse his fellow inmates. When Pierpont and Van Meter were transferred to the state prison at Michigan City, Dillinger applied for a transfer, too, using his skill on the prison baseball team as a ruse. "Why do you want to go to Michigan City?" a parole board member asked.

"Because they have a real team up there," said Dillinger.

But he wasn't talking about baseball. "Here [in Michigan City] there were experienced forgers, holdup men, confidence men, and even several gangs of bank robbers," writes John Toland in his classic *Dillinger Days*. "The beginners in crime from the reformatory could, if accepted by these 'older heads,' get an education available nowhere else." In the summer of 1929 Dillinger learned that his wife Beryl had filed for divorce, but it didn't matter: He was sent to join his buddies at Michigan City and soon met other bank-robbing pros. There was John Hamilton, a tough, quiet convict who was nicknamed "Three-Fingered Jack" for the lost index and middle fingers on his right hand. Charles Makley was known for being able to bluff his way out of any situation and his ability to impersonate well-to-do businessmen or bank presidents. Russell Lee Clark was a stocky, violent man who repeatedly tried to escape, and then attempted to kill prison guards when the escapes inevitably went wrong. But perhaps the most influential pro behind the bars at Michigan City was a man named Walter Dietrich, who had worked with the legendary Herman "The Baron" Lamm (see "Herman 'the Barron' Lamm") and knew the "Lamm Technique." Dietrich promised to teach Pierpont and others the famous three-step process (case the joint, rehearse the heist, plan the getaway route) in exchange for being cut into future capers.

But first, Pierpont and his cronies needed out of Michigan City. And that's where their young apprentice, John Dillinger, came in handy. Dillinger was up for parole first. If Dillinger could start knocking over some easy jugs, he could raise enough cash to engineer a prison break. And if the prison break worked, Dillinger was promised a job as a wheelman (driver) for the new gang. With Dietrich serving as professor and Pierpont and the others acting as adjunct faculty, Dillinger enrolled in a virtual Master's program in bank robbery: the techniques, the tricks, and a list of banks that were ripe for the picking. Dillinger graduated on May 22, 1933, when he was paroled from Michigan City.

Stopping home, Dillinger arrived one hour after his stepmother had passed away. At her funeral, Dillinger told the pastor: "You will never know how much good that sermon has done me."

Two weeks later, Dillinger had gathered an impromptu gang and started hitting small stores and companies. Then, choosing a name from Pierpont's list, Dillinger struck his first bank. When the bookkeeper at the New Carlisle National Bank in Ohio opened up on June 10, 1933, he had a surprise waiting for him: three men holding guns and wearing handkerchiefs around their faces.

"All right, buddy," Dillinger said. "Open the safe."

But the bookkeeper fumbled with the combination, and one of Dillinger's gang members was getting antsy. "Let me drill him," he said. "The guy's stalling."

Dillinger ignored him and told the bookkeeper to take his time. It was worth the wait: The safe yielded $10,600, a nice chunk of change for a small-town bank during the Depression. Dillinger had come a long way since he mugged that elderly grocer. But he didn't have his technique down pat quite yet; for that matter, neither did his mentors. Many of the banks on Pierpont's "ripe" list had closed thanks to the Depression, and Dillinger would show up with his team only to find an empty building, forcing him to knock over grocery stores and small shops. By mid-July, Dillinger had targeted his second bank, the Commercial Bank in Daleville, Indiana. But on the planned day of the heist, cops pinched his two accomplices in front of their apartment. By sheer luck, Dillinger was around the back parking his car. When he saw the police, he threw the car in reverse and rocketed backward down an alley.

Two days later, Dillinger had pulled together a new accomplice, Harry Copeland—a name plucked from yet another handy Pierpont list—and took the Daleville Bank anyway. When he walked into the building, the sole bank employee was the teller, Margaret Good. Dillinger walked up to her and asked if the bank president was available. Good told him that he wasn't and that the cashier was out to lunch.

"Well, honey, this is a hold-up," Dillinger said, showing her his pistol.

Instead of letting himself in the open door to Good's cage, Dillinger lifted his leg, rested his foot on the six-foot cage ledge, then vaulted himself over in one athletic sweep. Good was amazed. She had been held up twice, and no one ever did anything like that before.

The Daleville heist earned Dillinger two things: $3,500 in cash and a sworn enemy for life. Captain Matt Leach, head of the Indiana State Police, heard about this "Leaping Bandit" and tied him to other robberies in the Indiana-Ohio area. Soon, the Leaper had a name: "Dan Dillinger," which is the alias that Dillinger used after leaving Michigan City. The papers dubbed him "Desperate Dan."

Dillinger was anything but desperate. He had two fairly nice pro heists under his belt, and he'd achieved a bit of local notoriety. After Daleville, he took a break and visited the World's Fair in Chicago with Mary Longnaker, the sister of one of Dillinger's Michigan City friends who was in on the escape plan. Longnaker wasn't all that crazy about Dillinger, but she was fiercely loyal to her brother, and any man who could help spring him from prison was worth keeping happy. Dillinger, however, was head over heels, and wrote Longnaker whenever they were apart. "Honey, I miss you like nobody's business and I don't mean maybe," wrote "Johnnie" in one of his mash notes. "Baby, I fell for you in a big way and if you'll be on the level, I'll give everybody the go by for you and that isn't a lot of hooey, either."

Maybe he wasn't the world's sweetest talker, but as the summer of 1933 came to a close, John Dillinger became awfully good at robbing banks. On August 4, along with Copeland and another accomplice, Dillinger walked into the Montpelier National Bank in Indiana. "This is a stick-up," he announced, once again vaulting over the teller's cages and scooping up $6,700.

Word of the Leaping Bandit's third strike found its way to Captain Leach, who within a few days found an address believed to be Dillinger's apartment. But while Leach's men were busy raiding it on August 14, Dillinger himself was busy robbing another bank, this time in Bluffton, Ohio. "Stand back!" he cautioned the cashier, Roscoe Lingler. "This is a stick-up!" After a few moments, the bank alarm went off, and Dillinger scooped up whatever he could—$6,000—and hightailed it out of there. The Bluffton Bank hired the Pinkertons to catch the bandit, and soon they had an interesting lead: the address of the Leaping Bandit's girlfriend, Mary Longnaker. Soon, the Dayton police was staked out in the apartment across the hall, waiting for their man to show up.

On September 6, Dillinger and Copeland had another "soft" bank lined up: the Massachusetts Avenue State Bank in Indianapolis. A bank manager was on the phone when he heard someone say, "This is a stick-up." He ignored it, thinking someone was making a joke. "Get away from that damned telephone," the voice said. When the manager looked up, he saw John Dillinger sitting on top of the seven-foot teller cages, his legs crossed. The Massachusetts Avenue State Bank turned out to be soft and highly lucrative; Dillinger and his men happened upon the bank on payroll day and walked away with $24,800.

At long last, there was enough money to bankroll the Pierpont Gang's escape from Michigan City. First, Dillinger tried tossing loaded guns wrapped in newspapers over the wall into the prison baseball field. But the wrong convicts found them, and promptly turned them over to the warden. Then, Dillinger used a hefty piece of his bankroll to bribe a foreman in a thread company. Loaded guns were placed in a barrel destined for the shirt shop, where Pierpont could recover them. Dillinger had the foreman mark the barrel with a crayon X. Now Dillinger could relax and wait for his boys to come busting out of the joint. On September 22 he drove to Dayton, Ohio, to finally spend quality time with his sweetheart. At about the same time, the stakeout crew across from Mary Longnaker's apartment decided to throw in the towel. But hours later, Longnaker's landlady called the police, frantic. "He's here!"

"Who's here?" the desk sergeant asked, munching on a sandwich.

"John Dillinger, you dumb flatfoot!"

At 1:30 A.M., two Dayton detectives with shotguns cornered Dillinger in the apartment. For the first time in weeks, someone was telling *him* to put his hands in the air. "Stick 'em up, John," one of the detectives ordered. "We're cops."

Dillinger's hand fluttered, and one of the cops thought it meant he was going for a gun.

"Do it, John, and I'll kill you on the spot."

Dillinger did nothing, and was taken into custody.

It was a tough break to be sure, but it couldn't have come at a better time. As Dillinger was cooling his heels in the Lima, Ohio, jail, his old buddies—Harry Pierpont, Charles Makley, Russell Lee Clark, John Hamilton, and six others—were crashing out of Michigan City. They knew who to thank for their freedom and exactly how to thank him.

On October 12, Pierpont, Makley, Clark, and another associate named Ed Shouse drove to the Lima jail and walked up the front steps at 6:20 P.M. "We're officers from Michigan City," announced Pierpont. "We want to see John Dillinger."

The sheriff, Jess Sarber, had just finished a pork chop dinner with his wife. "Let me see your credentials," Sarber said.

"Here's our credentials," Pierpont replied, and showed the man a pistol.

Sarber reached for a desk drawer. In a panic, Pierpont blasted away at the sheriff, striking him twice. The other men quickly snatched up the keys and freed Dillinger, who had heard the commotion and calmly readied himself to leave. When he passed Sheriff Sarber, who lay bleeding on the floor, Dillinger kneeled down to take a closer look. He didn't know why the lawman had to be shot, but he wasn't about to question his liberators, either. He left without a word. Sheriff Sarber died an hour and a half later.

Now that the gang was in place, the real work was about to begin. The boys holed up in an Indianapolis apartment, where Pierpont had been kind enough to prestash a girl for Dillinger Evelyn: "Billie" Frechette, a raven-haired beauty who'd been born on an Indian reservation in Wisconsin. On October 14, Pierpont's "Terror Gang" raided a police station in Auburn, Indiana, and a police armory in Peru six days later. The take: several machine guns, bulletproof vests, a dozen rifles and pistols, two sawed-off shotguns, and thousands of rounds of ammunition. "My God, what are you going to start—a small army?" asked Pierpont's girlfriend, Mary Kinder.

Around the same time, Captain Leach decided to play mind games with Harry Pierpont. He knew Pierpont was a proud man, and it would probably drive him nuts to see the credit for his heists go to his young protégé, John Dillinger. So Leach made secret deals with several Indiana newspapermen to play up Dillinger as the gang leader in their stories.

It didn't work. Pierpont ignored the clippings, and Dillinger took them as cues to dress and act more conservatively. Still, Dillinger couldn't resist his trademark move during the gang's next robbery at the Central National Bank in Greencastle, Indiana: Dillinger leaped over the chest-high bank counter and helped gather up $74,782. They had followed the Lamm Technique to the letter, with Dillinger and Hamilton "jugmarking" the bank ahead of time and taking detailed notes of the layout. The only snag: an elderly Asian woman who refused to stay put during the robbery. "I go to Penney's and you go to hell," she pronounced. Pierpont let her go.

The day before Halloween 1933, the paper reported that Dillinger had phoned Matt Leach. "This is John Dillinger," he said. "How are you, you stuttering bastard?" The taunts—whether they came from Dillinger or the overimaginative reporters—didn't bother Leach. Besides, he already had plans in motion to nail the counter-leaping bastard.

So did Lieutenant John Howe, head of Chicago's "Scotland Yard," a group of 40 undercover crime fighters. Both Leach and Howe, independent of each other, had recruited stoolies on the periphery of the Pierpont gang. Howe's guy pinpointed Dillinger's location one night, and officers surrounded the bandit, ready to pounce, but Howe decided to stand down and wait until they could nab both Dillinger and Pierpont at the same time. Again, a classic case of that Dillinger luck.

Then a new tip came in via both stoolies: On November 15, John Dillinger would be visiting a skin doctor to treat a case of ringworm he'd picked up in prison. This was too good to pass up, so Howe and Leach joined forces and met in the afternoon to get the plan straight. The original plan: Wait until Dillinger stepped out of the office, then blow him away with shotguns. One cop even cut a hole in his jacket to hide his gun. But then they decided that it would be better to let Dillinger drive away, then offer pursuit and box him in with cars, only shooting him if it became necessary.

That night, Dillinger stepped out of the doctor's office and rubbed his hands together. It was the bitterest winter night in recent memory. Then he looked up and noticed something odd: parked cars, facing the wrong direction on the street. Alarm bells went off in his head. He walked cautiously to his car, then got in and turned the ignition key. Dillinger's girlfriend Billie Frechette had been waiting in the passenger seat. "Hang on," he whispered to her.

Dillinger threw the car in reverse, then hammered the gas pedal, shot out backward onto a busy street, spun the wheel, threw it into first, and slammed his foot into the pedal again.

A quick peek in the rear-view mirror revealed one car, tearing after him. "Hunch down," he told Billie. "Quick!" He heard a shotgun blast, then a bullet nicked his driver's-side door frame.

Down the street, two trolleys were about to cross each other on a pair of tracks. Dillinger gunned his engine and somehow managed to squeeze through the narrow space before the trolleys crossed, leaving his pursuer to swerve wildly to avoid a nasty smash-up. Another car raced after the bandit, but halfway down the street, Dillinger pounded the brakes. His pursuer rocketed past. Dillinger reversed and escaped into the night. "That bird sure can drive," lamented one of the officers. As amazing as the chase had been, newspapers found ways to embellish the event. Some writers had Dillinger exchange shots with his pursuers; other claimed he drove a bulletproof car, complete with pop-up submachine gun port.

Not quite, but Dillinger was now a full-fledged pro. Only five days later, the gang tapped their next jug: the American Bank & Trust in Racine, Wisconsin, north of Chicago. Pierpont walked in the front door and proceeded to tape a huge Red Cross poster in the bank's front window. Tellers looked up, curious, then resumed their work. Then Dillinger, Makley, and Hamilton entered the bank; Clark waited out back with a getaway car. Makley pulled a gun on the head teller, Harold Graham, and told him: "Stick 'em up."

"Go to another window, please," said Graham, wearily. He was tired of these stick-up jokes already.

"I said, stick 'em up!" yelled Makley.

Graham turned and jolted, and that's when Makley panicked and pulled the trigger. The bullet punched through Graham's arm, and on the way to the floor Graham kept enough of his wits to slap the silent alarm, which summoned a squad car. When the first officer entered, Pierpont told him to "Stick 'em up" and tried to grab the cop's gun from his holster. A second cop entered with a machine gun. "Get him!" screamed Pierpont. Makley opened fire, hitting the second cop with two bullets, but merely wounding him.

Meanwhile, Dillinger and Hamilton had been busy on cage and vault detail. "I've got all of it," said Dillinger. The gang split, taking three female bank employees, the remaining cop, and the bank president hostage. Good thing. A pair of detectives, who had been across the street in a pool hall, had been summoned when the shots rang out, and now they were on the scene with their guns drawn. A half-hearted gun battle erupted, since cops are typically leery of gunning down innocent people. The gang piled into the getaway car, and Dillinger took off, with Hamilton reading the predetermined getaway route from a small notebook. The total haul: $27,789. Once again, the Lamm Technique had worked beautifully.

But even Lamm himself couldn't prepare a contingency plan for the bad luck of gang members. On December 14, John Hamilton found himself recognized by an anonymous tipster in Chicago and was almost nabbed at a garage; he had to shoot a cop to escape. This prompted the Chicago Police to form a special "Dillinger Squad" with only one directive: Shoot first, and shoot to kill. Panicked, Dillinger, Pierpont, and the rest of the gang dyed their hair and split up, only to rejoin for the holidays in Daytona Beach, Florida. The idea: Lay low and enjoy some of their ill-gotten gains. Christmas Day was a strange scene; Dillinger kicked Billie Frechette out of the house, followed by the gang members and their girlfriends exchanging presents. (What do you buy a pro heister for Christmas, anyway? A bulletproof scarf and mittens?) New Year's Eve was even stranger. When Dillinger heard fireworks popping up and down the beach, he took one of his machine guns out and started blasting the night sky. One of the gang members' girlfriend asked if she could try it out, and Dillinger handed her the weapon. But the gun started blasting almost as soon as the girl touched it, and nearly cut Dillinger in half. "Goddamn it, Margaret," he cried. "What are you trying to do, kill me?"

Next, the gang decided to travel to Tucson, Arizona. Everyone split up in separate cars except for Hamilton and Dillinger, who wanted to cash some stolen bonds in Chicago—audaciously enough, in the very backyard of the Dillinger Squad. On January 15, Dillinger decided to take a bank for the hell of it. The duo chose the First National Bank of East Chicago, Indiana. Dillinger removed a submachine gun from a trombone case and leveled it at the bank's vice president. "This is a hold-up." Dillinger noticed a customer backing away from a stack of cash he'd received. "Is that your money or the bank's?" he asked.

"Mine," the customer meekly replied.

"Go ahead and take it then," said Dillinger. "We don't want your money. We want the bank's money."

Patrolman Hobart Wilgus entered the bank, but Dillinger quickly disarmed him as Hamilton gathered up the money. When they emerged from the bank, they were surrounded by a human shield of hostages. Three more plainclothes cops were waiting for them. "Wilgus! Wilgus!" one cried. Wilgus ducked out of the way, leaving

Dillinger wide open. A gun fired, and bullets smacked into Dillinger's chest.

Once again, freakish luck was with John Dillinger. His bulletproof vest deflected the slugs, and he was able to return fire, shooting Patrolman William Patrick O'Malley through the heart. Hamilton, meanwhile, was also shot, his vest failing to protect him. Dillinger scooped him up, along with the $20,376 in cash, and struggled to the getaway car. After dropping Hamilton off at an underworld surgeon, Dillinger learned he was a murderer: The radio was reporting that Patrolman O'Malley had died at the scene. Dillinger sped away from Indiana, thankful to be putting miles between himself and the Dillinger Squad.

But as it turned out, he was no safer in Tucson. On January 23, a freak fire broke out in the hotel where Makley and Clark had been staying. Realizing that two suitcases full of expensive weapons were trapped in a burning building, both men asked two firemen to recover them and tipped them generously when they succeeded. It would have been better to let them burn. One of the firemen, an avid reader of *True Detective Monthly,* recognized Makley and Clark. Within days, the entire gang—Makley, Clark, Pierpont, and Dillinger—were rounded up by the Tucson police. Dillinger Squad, Schmillinger Squad: A small Southwest police force had rounded up the baddest bank-robbing gang in America. After three states fought bitterly over extradition rights, Clark, Makley, and Pierpont were sent to Ohio for the murder of Sheriff Sarber, while Dillinger was returned to Indiana to face the music for killing Patrolman O'Malley.

"MEEK DILLINGER IS JAILED," read the lead headline of the *Chicago Daily Tribune* on January 31. "HELD IN INDIANA AFTER AIRPLANE HOP TO CHICAGO." "John Dillinger, notorious criminal whose banditry and other depredations caused the state of Indiana to mobilize its National Guard several months ago," read the article, "was locked tight behind the bars of the Lake County jail at Crown Point last night." Rolling out the red carpet were some 120 cops, wearing bulletproof vests and packing rifles, shotguns, machine guns, and pistols. "If any effort is made to raid the caravan and release Dillinger," ordered Chicago police captain John Stege, "or if he makes a break at escape, kill him at once."

*My pal, John Dillinger: At the Crown Point jail in Indiana, Dillinger (in vest) touched off a political scandal when he draped a friendly arm over the shoulder of prosecuting attorney Robert G. Estell.*

The capture made Dillinger a national celebrity. Instead of fearing for his life, Dillinger started basking in the glory. He joshed with newspaper reporters; he smiled and put his arm around the prosecutor who vowed to stick him in the electric chair. And he was about to pull off the most stunning escape of his life.

Dillinger was being housed in the Crown Point jail, which was considered escape-proof. Between Dillinger and freedom were 6 steel doors, 50 armed guards, and dozens of roaming men with shotguns, courtesy of the Farmers' Protective Association and the National Guard. Spotlights bathed the jail at night. People joked that even Houdini couldn't squeeze himself out of Crown Point. But on March 3—using either a gun smuggled by Billie Frechette or a wooden gun blackened with shoe polish—Dillinger took control of the first guard he encountered, which in turn gave him the leverage to seize another and yet another. Before long, he had stolen the sheriff's car and had taken two prison guards as hostages. Dillinger let them out of the car in Illinois. "I'll remember you at Christmas," he told them, then drove off.

"In escaping from the Crown Point jail in Indiana," writes Courtney Ryley Cooper, unofficial Hoover PR man and author of the 1935 classic *Ten Thousand Public Enemies*, "[Dillinger] stole an automobile belonging to the sheriff and transported it across the state line into Illinois, thus violating the National Motor Vehicle Theft Act. The Division of Investigation thereupon took up the task of running him down and killing him, which it did with much celerity."

Thus the FBI, and its notorious director, J. Edgar Hoover, joined in the hunt for John Dillinger.

Dillinger's first order of business was fundraising. He found his old buddy Hamilton and even older buddy Homer Van Meter (from his Pendleton days), who quickly recruited another heister named Lester Gillis, otherwise known as "Baby Face" Nelson. (For more on him, see "'Baby Face' Nelson.") The newly formed gang headed toward St. Paul on March 4, merely a day after Dillinger busted out of Crown Point. There, Nelson hooked them up with a reliable jugmarker (heist planner) named Eddie Green and a tough gunman named Tommy Carroll.

This new team was far more volatile than the old one, which is understandable; Pierpont and the fellows had spent years in prison together, while this new gang had a matter of hours to get its act together. Baby Face Nelson made matters even worse: He disagreed with Dillinger's bank-robbery schemes and threatened to pummel Van Meter for making fun of him.

Still, by March 6, the new, if not exactly improved, Dillinger Gang was ready to rob their first bank. The mark, Securities National Bank and Trust, was in Sioux Falls, North Dakota, as far west as Dillinger would ever work. When the six men piled out of the car, a bank teller put his finger on the alarm—these guys didn't look right. When one of them burst into the bank yelling, "This is a hold-up! Lay on the floor!" the teller pressed the button. Alarm bells started clanging. This didn't bother Dillinger; he knew he had a certain amount of time before the law showed up and quickly began to gather up cash. But Baby Face Nelson was *outraged* that someone would have the nerve to press an alarm on him. He shoved his gun in a random teller's face. "I'm going to kill the bastard who hit that alarm, and I know you did it!"

"Forget it and grab the money," Dillinger calmly advised.

But when the first squad car appeared on the scene, Baby Face really went nuts. He leaped onto the counter and started spraying the front plate glass windows—and the cops behind them—with bullets. "I got one of 'em! I got one of 'em!" he exclaimed.

By the time the Dillinger Gang emerged with $49,000 and 10 hostages, a huge crowd had gathered around the bank. Most of them smiled, as if they were watching a particularly entertaining performance. That's because they thought they were, thanks to Homer Van Meter. He had scouted the place the day before and told everyone he was a movie producer.

The gang holed up in Minneapolis and divided the loot. Dillinger took his cut and sent it to his lawyer, in hopes that he could get Pierpont and the boys out of their legal mess. Then he dispatched Green and Van Meter to Mason City, Iowa, to case out their next job: the proverbial big score that would let them acquire whatever gear they needed and whatever politician they wanted in their pocket. On the night of March 12, Green came knocking at the home of the First National Bank's assistant cashier, Harry Fisher. "Is this 1228 North President?" Fisher pointed him in the right direction, and thought little of it until he saw the man again the next day, charging into the bank with friends and guns.

Green, Hamilton, and Van Meter immediately went after the bank president, who had barricaded himself inside his office. A guard in a bulletproof cage fired a tear gas shell at the robbers, and it pounded into Green's back. Hamilton returned fire and jammed the tear gas gun. A short while later, a woman escaped through the smoke where she practically ran into a short, stocky guy in the alley. "Hey you! Get to work and notify somebody. This bank is being robbed!"

Baby Face Nelson turned to her and smiled. "Lady, you're telling me?"

Dillinger, meanwhile, was working crowd control. He started lining up people along the sidewalk in front of the bank to discourage cops—who were sure to be there any minute—from taking any shots at them. But three floors up in the First National Bank building, an elderly judge named John C. Shipley had a clear shot at Dillinger: straight down. He found his old pistol, lined up his shot, then yanked back the trigger. A bullet sliced into Dillinger's shoulder from above.

Dillinger spun his machine upward and started spraying the side of the building, but the judge had already retreated.

Time was of the essence now. Wounded, Dillinger called his men to pull out. But Hamilton, who had only collected $32,000 from the tellers' cages, wanted to raid the vaults before leaving. That's where, according to Green's research, over $200,000 sat. Hamilton forced Harry Fisher—the same cashier Green had visited the night before—toward the vault, but the man stalled and then tricked his way between the barred doors and the main vault, with Hamilton on the outside. "All I can do is pass you the money," he said. Which Fisher did, ones and fives first. Time ticked by slowly. Flowers wilted and faded away. Fisher calmly passed through another thick packet of ones and fives.

"Give me the big bills or I'll kill you!" screamed Hamilton.

But by now, Dillinger had given urgent word: We're out. *Now.* It killed Hamilton to leave over 200 grand in that vault. But it hurt Hamilton even worse when he stepped outside and received a bullet in his shoulder—courtesy, once again, of John C. Shipley, still holding his own on the third floor. Dillinger's men piled into the getaway car, then surrounded themselves with hostages on the car's running boards. They drove away and released their cold, frightened guests 13 miles outside Mason City. Police pursued them for a while, but there was nothing they could do with innocent people in the way of a clean shot. The total take was one of Dillinger's largest, $49,500, but it wasn't quite the score they'd been dreaming of.

Dillinger and Hamilton had their wounds dressed by a doctor in St. Paul, then Dillinger and Billie Frechette moved to an apartment in the same town as Mr. and Mrs. Carl T. Hellman. A neighbor got suspicious, and on March 31 the FBI converged on the scene. They knocked, and "Mrs. Hellman" answered.

"We want to speak with Mr. Hellman," said one special agent.

"Wait a moment," said Frechette, who closed the door and ran to warn Dillinger, who dressed and grabbed a machine gun.

Homer Van Meter would provide an unwitting distraction when he came walking up the steps. "Who are you?" an agent asked. Van Meter stalled by explaining he was a salesman, then pulled a gun, which started a chase. Meanwhile, Dillinger and Frechette slipped through the now empty hallway and down a flight of back stairs. Dillinger sprayed his machine gun behind him to discourage pursuers. It didn't work, and Dillinger was shot in the leg as he made his escape. Another near-miss, another piece of Dillinger luck.

After a brief stop at Mooresville to visit his family, Dillinger drove Frechette back to Chicago. The next day she visited a taproom alone and was almost immediately picked up by the FBI; somebody had ratted her out. Dillinger sent money to his lawyer to defend her, then joined Hamilton for a retreat. Running and getting plugged was taking a toll on the 30-year-old bank robber. Dillinger chose Little Bohemia Lodge, a resort in northern Wisconsin. There, Dillinger, Baby Face Nelson, Homer Van Meter, Tommy Carroll, John Hamilton, and assorted gang girlfriends gathered to kick back, have a few laughs, and plan the next heist. But lodge owner Emil Wanatka noticed something odd about one of his off-season guests: the automatic pistols strapped to his chest, beneath his coat.

When Wanatka checked out a Chicago newspaper, he realized the identity of his guest. John Dillinger.

"You're not afraid, are you?" asked Dillinger when confronted by the owner.

"No," replied Wanatka. "But I've got everything tied up in this place. I don't want the joint shot up."

"Relax, Emil," said Dillinger. "We're just here to eat and rest for a few days. There's not going to be any trouble."

Wanatka said he understood, but was frightened enough to have his brother-in-law drive several miles to tip off the FBI. Within hours dozens of G-men, led by head Chicago agent Melvin Purvis, were speeding through the Wisconsin woods toward Little Bohemia. In the resulting gun battle, Dillinger and his men escaped through a back window, while the attacking agent mistakenly killed an innocent man and injured two others who had been staying at the lodge. Thinking the Dillinger Gang was still hiding inside, the agents unleashed bullets and tear gas at the lodge throughout the night.

Meanwhile, a distress call came from a neighboring resort two miles away. When two agents approached, they found a maniacal Baby Face Nelson cornered with his wife Helen and trying to steal a car. "I know you bastards wear bulletproof vests," snarled Nelson, "so I'm going to give it to you high and low." One agent caught a slug in the throat and died; another caught bullets in his arm, lungs, liver, and ankle but would recover from his wounds. Nelson stole the agents' Ford and sped toward Chicago.

When the gunsmoke and tear gas cleared the next morning, the FBI realized they had a public relations nightmare on their hands. There were two dead men—one civilian, one agent—and zero Dillinger Gang members in custody. (One bullet had found its way into John Hamilton's back, eventually killing him, but the Bureau wouldn't realize that until weeks later.) The public was outraged and, oddly enough, sympathized with Dillinger and his men. This prompted President Roosevelt to denounce the public's tendency to "romanticize crime" and encourage "gangster extermination."

Dillinger, reading the headlines from a safe apartment in Chicago, must have realized that they weren't going to let him quietly slip away.

In late May, Dillinger found an underworld sawbones and subjected himself to plastic surgery. For $5,000, his cheeks and eyebrows were resculpted, and his fingertips were carved up to erase prints. Dillinger wasn't exactly thrilled with the results. "It looks like I've been in a dogfight," he complained. But it would have to do, for it was time to fade. He talked about going to Mexico.

But Dillinger had other needs to address first. "Dillinger was torn between two desires," writes Cooper in *Ten Thousand Public Enemies.* "One was to evade the law, the other was to gain the pleasures which a long term in prison had denied him. He was mad about motion pictures; even during the hottest of the chase, he could not fight against the desire to see one." There was another pleasure that had been denied Dillinger: women. In early July he visited a Chicago brothel run by Anna Sage, a Rumanian madam who had been busted twice and faced deportation. Dillinger didn't know that part; he only knew Sage could find him a real honey, which she did. Polly Hamilton Keele was a curvy, 26-year-old redhead, and for two weeks Dillinger and Polly couldn't be pried apart with a crowbar.

On the night of July 22, Sage suggested the three of them catch a movie, *Manhattan Melodrama,* at the nearby Biograph Theater. The day before, Sage had cut herself a deal with the U.S. government: She would deliver John Dillinger in exchange for the $5,000 reward and the promise that she could remain in the country. So when the three exited the theater, Purvis and his agents were ready.

"Stick 'em up, Johnny," Purvis said.

Dillinger looked up, and saw that Sage and Keele had stopped walking with him. He reached for his pistol, then started to rocket down an alley. Shots rang out. One bullet struck the back of Dillinger's neck before he had a chance to unholster his weapon. Dillinger fell face down in the alley and died at the scene.

Dillinger drew a huge crowd at the scene of his death—women dipped handkerchiefs in pools of his blood. Crowds also jammed the mortuary, where his body was shown to the press, and at his burial in Crown Hill Cemetery in Indianapolis, Indiana. Some criticized the FBI for blasting away without first trying to arrest the man peaceably. But Hoover and his Bureau dismissed those who felt bad for John Dillinger. "If the efforts of sob sisters count for anything," writes Cooper in *Ten Thousand Public Enemies,* "Dillinger will some day be another Jesse James. Whereupon Jesse probably will put in an application to be allowed to turn over in his grave."

That is, if Jesse James is really in his grave. Or Dillinger in his.

## Cool Fact from the Vault

Most people pronounce "Dillinger" with a soft g, as in "derringer," the famous pistol. But John's family pronounced it with a hard g: "Dilling-GRR." (Rhymes with "killing-GRR.")

## DILLINGER'S FINAL ESCAPE PLAN

*Like Jesse James before him, John Dillinger is believed to have engineered his own shooting in front of the Biograph. Here's a look at a conspiracy theory:*

The official story is that Dillinger died at the hands of the FBI outside the Biograph Theater in Chicago. But then why did Dillinger's corpse have brown eyes, when the man himself had blue-gray? And why were prescription eyeglasses found on the corpse, when Dillinger had perfect vision? And what about that appendectomy scar—an operation Dillinger never had? The corpse also had a full set of teeth. Photographs and newsreels of Dillinger taken during 1934 clearly show that he was missing his right front incisor.

In 1970, Jay Robert Nash wrote *Dillinger: Dead or Alive* and made no secret that he thought Dillinger was the latter. Nash points to an elaborate conspiracy between the FBI, Anna Sage, lawyer Louis Piquette and Dillinger himself in which a dupe named Jimmy

Lawrence was led to the slaughter outside the Biograph. Fingerprints were planted; facial differences were explained by the plastic surgery Dillinger had weeks before. That way, the FBI could claim to have finally nailed the most wanted man in America, and Dillinger would be allowed to slip into obscurity with $70,000 in cash and the chance at a new life. That, or the FBI itself was duped, and forced to cover up the error. Nash even later found a robber named James "Blackie" Audett who claimed to have robbed banks with Dillinger before and long after July 1934 and produced alleged photographs of the aging outlaw in 1948. According to Audett, he last saw Dillinger in 1979.

Of course, most criminal historians discount the idea that Dillinger survived, and they scoff at Audett's testimony. Only a DNA test could prove that the wrong body was buried in Dillinger's grave, but there are currently no plans to start digging now. Perhaps it's best to let Dillinger lie … or at least continue his bridge game with Elvis in peace.

**Real name:** Charles Arthur Floyd

**Accomplices:** Fred "the Sheik" Hilderbrand, Jack Bradley, Nellie Maxwell, Nathan King, George Birdwell, and Adam Richetti

**Number of banks robbed:** More than 30

**Estimated lifetime take:** $100,000 to half a million

**Claim to fame:** Floyd was Robin Hood to his friends and neighbors, but a "dirty rat" to J. Edgar Hoover

## "NO OFFENSE. BUT HELL, I'M SURE YOU WOULDN'T MIND MAKING A LITTLE CONTRIBUTION TO THE COMMUNITY."

In 1931, 51 banks were robbed in the state of Oklahoma. Charles "Pretty Boy" Floyd was thought to be responsible for about half of them. On January 14, 1932, bank insurance rates were doubled, with rates even higher for banks in small towns with a population under 5,000—Floyd's preferred targets. Bank managers clamored for the governor to call out the National Guard to hunt the expensive bastard down. One newspaper at the time ran the headline: "Pretty Boy Pretty Bad."

Bad to some, a saint to others. A self-styled American Robin Hood, "Pretty Boy" Floyd was beloved by neighbors who liked that the bank robber destroyed mortgage records, gave heist money to the poor, and was utterly loathed by J. Edgar Hoover, who allegedly ordered his top man, Melvin Purvis, to *not* bring Floyd back alive. Some researchers claim he was a more successful bank robber than his contemporary, John Dillinger. Estimates of his total takes range from $100,000 to nearly half a million. He was also a great deal tougher. Contrary to his handle, "Pretty Boy" wasn't some wilting male model-type; he was a broad, chunky man with dark hair, gray eyes, and a face that could take a punch. Not to mention a steel vest that could take a bullet.

But before he was "Pretty Boy," Charles Arthur Floyd was known around the Cookson Hills of Oklahoma—home of famous outlaw Henry Starr (see "Henry Starr")—as "Chock" Floyd, because of his fondness for Chocktaw Beer, a local Indian brew. No one's completely sure of the origins of the "Pretty Boy" handle; some say his childhood pals called him that because of his meticulous grooming habits. Others say a whorehouse madam gave him the nickname: "I want you for myself, pretty boy." Still others claim the nickname stuck when police in Ohio mistook him for another outlaw, "Pretty Boy" Smith. No matter the origin, Floyd hated to be called "Pretty Boy." He much rather preferred "Chock."

Floyd's first crime was the heist of a box of cookies from J. H. Harkrider's Grocery in Sallisaw, Oklahoma. (The 14-year-old Floyd confessed and was given a stern talking-to.) His next theft wasn't all that spectacular, either—$3.50 in dimes left on the counter of a post office. But it did qualify as a federal offense, since it took place in a post office. Floyd got off the hook when witnesses felt sorry for the young hellraiser and failed to show up at his trial. By 1924, Floyd tried the straight life, marrying a 16-year-old raven-haired beauty named Ruby Hargraves and fathering a boy, Charles Dempsey Floyd, named after Floyd's boxing hero, Jack Dempsey. Floyd barely supported his young family by picking cotton, a brutal gig that left his hands callused and bleeding after only a few hours of labor. There had to be something better than this, Floyd thought.

Floyd found it when he befriended a 19-year-old co-worker named Fred Hilderbrand, who claimed he was a pro heister who went by the handle "the Sheik." Why spend all day picking cotton burrs from your paws, when instead you could be plucking big money from businesses? Together, Floyd and "the Sheik" robbed a series of grocery stores in late summer 1925, followed by their big score: a payroll robbery at Kroger's Food Store headquarters on September 11. "Don't scream, or we'll have to kill somebody!" cried the Sheik after barging into the cashier's office in the middle of the day. "All we want is the money." The boys walked away with $11,784. Unfortunately, they didn't walk for long: Days later they were nabbed in their brand-new Studebaker by suspicious cops. Floyd was sentenced to five years at the Missouri State Penitentiary.

But prison was simply finishing school for the fledgling robber. At Missouri, Floyd met Alfred "Red" Lovett, an experienced bank robber who said that Kansas City, Missouri, was where he could find some real action. On March 7, 1929, Floyd was released from jail and headed straight for Kansas City. (It wasn't as if Floyd had a family to return to; Ruby had divorced him shortly before his release.) Kansas City was great, Lovett told him, because it had a thriving underworld and a corrupt government that was very tolerant of outlaws. However, that was only true if the outlaws had money to grease the greedy palms of crooked cops and politicians. Floyd enjoyed various K.C. brothels—including one where he may have picked up his "Pretty Boy" tag—but was continually hounded by cops. Disgusted, Floyd left town with three heisters he'd met through Lovett: Jack Bradley, Nellie Maxwell, and Nathan King. The foursome lammed out for northern Ohio, where they started working their way through a list of ripe banks. "Pretty Boy" had found his calling.

The Bradley Gang's most lucrative score was the February 5, 1930, robbery of the Farmers' & Merchants' Bank in Sylvania, Ohio. They got $2,000 but could have had 10 times more if not for the quick thinking of a cashier who stashed most of the bank's loot in a timelock vault the moment the robbers showed up. A little over a month later, after another successful knockover, the Bradley Gang was arrested when two Akron, Ohio, cops spotted Bradley and King and rounded the gang up. Floyd, facing more time, decided that he'd had enough finishing school. En route to prison, Floyd smashed through the window of a moving train. He not only survived the fall and the spinning glass but eluded the manhunt that followed.

Thus began one of the longest bank-robbing runs in American history. Running back to Kansas City, Floyd teamed up with Bill "the Killer" Miller, a bank robber and part-time hired killer for Ohio gangs who had been arrested 28 times (and who had two wives). It was a weird, short-lived pairing. After robbing three small-town banks—one in Earlsboro, Oklahoma, for $3,000; the Mount Zion Trust Company in Kentucky for $4,000; and the Whitehouse Bank near Toledo, Ohio, for $1,800—a trio of cops recognized Floyd and Miller walking with their girlfriends on a street in Bowling Green. The cops swerved their car to the side of the road and leaped out, guns in hand.

"Put up your hands!" one of the cops cried.

Floyd and Miller didn't hesitate. They reached into their jackets, spun around simultaneously and opened fire.

Miller felt a bullet chop away half of his throat; he was dead by the time he collapsed to the sidewalk. (Both of Miller's wives would show up to claim the body.) One of the boys' girlfriend got clipped in the back of the head. Floyd fired back until his gun was clicking empty, then took off like a jackrabbit between houses. He'd managed to hit one of the cops, Patrolman Ralph Castner, who later died of his wounds. But by that time, Floyd was long gone.

In May 1931, Floyd was paying protection money to his Kansas City associates and hiding out above a flower shop on Independence Avenue. But on July 30, U.S. Prohibition agents raided the joint, since it also doubled as a bootlegger hideout. They were surprised to discover Floyd in bed, with a .45 caliber revolver in his belt. "He's got a gun!" someone cried.

Agent Curtis C. Burks took the gun away but didn't see Floyd reaching for the other one he had stashed. Floyd shot Burks, then fired away at three more cops as he raced down a hallway and out of the building. When agents returned fire, they accidentally shot a male passerby in the head. When the smoke cleared, Burks was dead, the passerby was dead, and three other cops were wounded. Now Floyd had the blood of two lawmen on his hands, and he fled back to the only place on Earth he felt safe: the Cookson Hills of Oklahoma.

It was here that Floyd teamed with George Birdwell, a former traveling preacher who lost his faith somewhere deep in a bottle of booze, and the duo proceeded to give nearly every banker in the state of Oklahoma a king-sized migraine. It was another weird partnership, but this time Floyd was in his element. He and Birdwell could easily hide among the sympathetic people of the Cookson Hills, who liked that Floyd was generous to whoever helped him out—especially poor folks. Even the sheriff of his hometown, Sallisaw, was cowed by Floyd, who once wrote him a letter: "I'm coming to see my mother. If you're smart, you won't try to stop me." The sheriff didn't even dare.

The fun began August 4 with the knockover of a bank in Shamrock for $400, followed a month later by a $1,745.30 robbery at the Morris State Bank near Okmulgee. Twenty-one days later, it was $3,849.28 from the Maud Bank. On December 12, 1931, Floyd repeated the success of the Newton Boys and robbed two banks in the same day, in Paden and Castle. The Floyd-Birdwell team would rob at least 20 more banks, all of them in Oklahoma, and all of them using the same basic strategy: Steal a car, leave it running outside, cover employees with a submachine gun, force one to open the vault, and gather the loot, then run, one hand on the money, one hand on a weapon. Sometimes, a hostage would be taken, especially if someone tripped a bank alarm. Then Floyd and Birdwell would race back to their hideouts.

Floyd even had the guts to rob the bank in Sallisaw and warned friends and family in advance. They came out to watch as if it were dinner theater. "No offense," Floyd told the teller inside. "But hell, I'm sure you wouldn't mind making a little contribution to the community."

Meanwhile, Floyd had reunited with his ex-wife Ruby and son Dempsey and moved them, under the alias of "the Douglases," to Fort Smith, Arkansas. There, Floyd spent a lot of quality time with his family—cooking, playing T-ball, and generally goofing off. He especially loved taking Dempsey to Universal horror movies like *Frankenstein* and *Dracula*. "I was only six," recalled Dempsey years later, "and [they] scared me. But my father kept holding me, telling me there was nothing to be afraid of." But Floyd also found plenty of time to rob Oklahoma banks with Birdwell. Somehow, Floyd had mastered the art of balancing career and family.

That is, until the career got the best of him. In early 1932, Floyd moved his family to Tulsa under the alias "Jack Hamilton," but his new neighbors got suspicious. He looked an awful lot like that Pretty Boy fella whose picture was hanging in the downtown courthouse. On February 11, Tulsa police spotted Birdwell visiting "Hamilton" and promptly raided the house. Floyd and Birdwell barely escaped, and they fled back to the Cookson Hills to hide. Ruby and little Dempsey were retained for questioning, but Ruby refused to admit anything. All little Dempsey knew was that his daddy "always had plenty of money and we have lots to eat and a radio."

Later that year, Birdwell grew sick of Floyd getting all of the press, which described Birdwell as a mere lackey. Birdwell set off on his own and mere weeks later was gunned down in a hold-up he'd organized. Meanwhile, Floyd had found a new—and as it would turn out, final—partner: Adam Richetti. The two successfully robbed banks in Oklahoma and Missouri until June 17, 1933, when both of their lives would change forever.

That was the day of the Kansas City Massacre, which is still a point of debate among 1930s crime-wave enthusiasts. The story is fairly simple: Kansas City underworld figures paid three gunmen to liberate Frank "Jelly" Nash, who had been recaptured after busting out of Leavenworth back in 1930. (Some say those underworld figures hired gunmen to kill Nash, but let's give them the benefit of the doubt.) At about 7:20 A.M., the gunmen approached Nash and the seven lawmen—three of them FBI agents, the others local police—who were escorting him.

"Put 'em up! Up! Up!" one of the gunmen shouted.

One of the cops drew his gun and fired back.

"Let the bastards have it!" yelled another gunman, and a blistering firefight ensued, leaving Nash, FBI Agent R. J. Caffrey, and three Kansas City cops dead.

The entire nation was stunned; it had been the worst mass slaying since the St. Valentine's Day Massacre in 1929. J. Edgar Hoover immediately announced the names of the killers: Pretty Boy Floyd, Adam Richetti, and Verne Miller. "No time, money or labor will be spared toward bringing about the individuals responsible for this cowardly, despicable act."

Meanwhile, Floyd, who happened to be in Kansas City that day, swore he didn't do it. He even sent a postcard to the police:

*Dear Sirs—*

*I—Charles Floyd want it made known that I did not participate in the massacre of officers at Kansas City.*

*Charles Floyd*

Floyd immediately moved his family under another alias—"Mr. and Mrs. Sanders"—far away to Buffalo, New York, and tried like hell to stay anonymous. Richetti also fled to Buffalo with his girlfriend, where they lived as "Mr. and Mrs. Brennan." But Floyd worried that even Buffalo wasn't far enough away; his name was plastered on wanted posters all over the country as a "Public Enemy." And the FBI seemed to be making short work of their Public Enemies: first Bonnie and Clyde in May 1934, then Dillinger in July. Floyd and Richetti decided they'd be safest in Mexico, beyond the reach of even J. Edgar Hoover.

But he made the tragic mistake of driving back to Oklahoma to say good-bye to the family. On October 22, 1934, Floyd was trapped in Ohio and gunned down by FBI agents while trying to make a run to the nearby woods. Hoover's star agent, Melvin Purvis, approached the bleeding man and asked him about the Kansas City Massacre. "I didn't do it," Floyd insisted for the last time.

Then, changing gears, Floyd propped himself up on an elbow and asked Purvis, "Who the hell tipped you off? You've got me this time."

Pretty Boy Floyd died a short while later. Richetti was caught and executed on October 17, 1938. Most historians today believe Floyd and Richetti had nothing to do with the Kansas City Massacre.

## Cool Fact from the Vault

Floyd was featured in John Steinbeck's masterpiece, *The Grapes of Wrath,* which paints "Pretty Boy" as a cornered dog turned mean. "He done a little bad thing an' they hurt 'im, caught 'im and hurt 'im so he was mad, an' the next bad thing he done was mad, an' they hurt 'im again. An' purty soon he was mean-mad."

# 21 "BABY FACE" NELSON

**Real name:** Lester Gillis

**Number of banks robbed:** At least half a dozen

**Estimated lifetime take:** At least $100,000

**Claim to fame:** Nelson was arguably the most bloodthirsty, trigger-happy bank robber in history (Can you say "Napoleon Complex"?)

## "I WANT YOU ALL TO KNOW THAT I DON'T TAKE NO ORDERS; I WALK INTO A BANK, OPEN FIRE, KILL ANYTHING THAT MOVES, GRAB THE MONEY, AND I'M OUTTA THERE!"

George Nelson compensated for his elfin stature (5 feet, 4 inches) with a trigger-happy bloodlust. It seems he wasn't happy unless he was pumping bullets into something or somebody. Nelson even scared John Dillinger. The day after Nelson and Dillinger teamed up for their first heist, they were driving through the streets of St. Paul. Nelson was driving like a nut, jabbering on, trying to impress Dillinger. That's when he smacked into another car. When the angry driver raced up to Nelson's window and started to yell, Nelson took his .45 from his jacket and pumped a bullet into the guy's face. Nelson pounded the gas and pulled away, leaving the driver's corpse to tumble from the running board.

"You didn't have to do that!" yelled Dillinger.

"Hell, why not?" said Nelson.

Such a psychotic worldview is not born overnight. Lester Gillis was born in the tough streets of Chicago in December 1908, where other kids routinely kicked the stuffings out of him because he was a pugnacious little shrimp. Looking to prove himself, Gillis turned to crime. Before he was 15 years old, Gillis was stealing cars and bootlegging liquor, and within five years he was running his own protection racket. In 1928 he married a petite Woolworth's salesgirl named Helen Wawzynak, but she wasn't exactly the best influence on the budding bandit. Later, Helen would make a point of telling George how handsome he looked holding a machine gun.

Gillis worked for a while busting heads for Al Capone's mob, but soon his brutality made even the racketeers wince, and they let him go. (Even mobsters have their standards. Years later, when Gillis, then known nationally as "Baby Face" Nelson, needed a place to hide, the Las Vegas mob gave him the cold shoulder. "Do us a favor," they said. "Die.") Needing money, Gillis started holding up jewelry stores but got pinched after a January 1931 heist and was sent to the Illinois State Penitentiary.

After a forceful escape during a prison transport a little over a year later, Gillis moved Helen to California and found work with a bootlegging mobster operating in Sausalito. There, he toughened up his name to "George Nelson" after a boxing hero, and he befriended John Paul Chase, an admirer who would be a long-time partner. By 1933, Nelson, nicknamed "Baby Face" by his bootlegger boss, decided he wanted to go into business for himself. But not running booze. No, Nelson drove back to the Midwest to recruit his own bank-robbing gang.

The gang, which included Chase, planning whiz Eddie Green, and gunman Tommy Carroll, started hitting small-town banks in Wisconsin, Iowa, and Nebraska. Nelson's method was simple: Bust into a joint, start pumping the ceiling full of bullets, bark commands, corral the employees, bag the cash, and split. It was a successful formula. But Nelson soon became upset when an upstart named John Dillinger began to steal all of the good ink; some Nelson heists were even falsely attributed to Dillinger. According to author Jay Robert Nash, Nelson approached Dillinger associate Homer Van Meter and asked about joining the gang. Van Meter shook his head. "We don't know you, Nelson," he said. "And we don't trust you." Months later, however, when Dillinger was about to escape the Crown Point jail, the roles were reversed: Van Meter ate crow and asked Nelson for help. "Do you have any big action for us?" he asked.

"Yeah," Nelson replied, and proceeded to list the banks Eddie Green had cased. "But can Dillinger take orders?"

"Why, you little …"

"They're my men and my jobs," said Nelson. And of course, Dillinger would team up with Nelson, Green, and Carroll for two bank robberies. (For more, see "John Dillinger.") Nelson tried to make it clear that he called his own shots. "I want you all to know that I don't take no orders," he once told Dillinger and the others. "I walk into a bank, open fire, kill anything that moves, grab the money, and I'm outta there!"

After nearly getting nabbed at Little Bohemia and Dillinger's bloody death in front of the Biograph Theater in Chicago, Nelson went into hiding and started planning his own capers. Even though Dillinger's death meant that Nelson had inherited the title of Public Enemy Number One, Nelson was still jealous of his one-time partner. Why had Dillinger's reward offer been $10,000, while Nelson's was only $5,000? Soon, Nelson came up with a way to make the world forget about John Dillinger. Nelson was going to rob a bank a day for an entire month.

The only problem was that the law was breaking up that old gang of his. As 1934 wore on, it became increasingly clear that Hoover's FBI was winning the war on the so-called Ten Thousand Public Enemies. Dillinger's cronies were picked off one by one, and on November 27, 1934, the end came for Baby Face Nelson. He had been traveling with his wife Helen and John Paul Chase when two FBI agents, William Ryan and Thomas McDade, spotted their car. (The exact specs of Nelson's car, down to the current license plate— Illinois 639578—had been spread to FBI officers throughout the area.) The G-men cut a U-turn and rocketed after Nelson. "Heat!" Nelson cried.

Nelson spun the wheel and pulled a U-turn himself, then sped past the FBI agents to take a cold hard look at them. Then he U-turned yet again and raced up to the car. "Let him have it!" Nelson cried to Chase. A fury of gunfire exploded between the two moving vehicles, but somehow, none of the bullets found a target—except for one bullet in the radiator of the G-men's car and one bullet in the water pump of Nelson's car.

Ryan and McDade were out of commission, but by that time two additional FBI agents, Sam Cowley and Herman Hollis, were on the scene, ready to take up the chase. Nelson decided he couldn't outrun them, so he swerved his steaming car to a stop near the entrance to the North Side Park. Nelson emerged with a machine gun in his hands; John Paul Chase did the same. When the FBI men skidded to a stop, Nelson and Chase started blasting away at the car, which rocked on its suspension from the impacts.

The agents tumbled out of the car, Hollis taking up a position behind the car with a shotgun, and Cowley scurrying for cover with a submachine gun in a nearby ditch. Both agents returned fire. Nearby highway workers couldn't believe their eyes. "It was just like Edward G. Robinson," one worker would later recall. "I've never seen nothing like it."

Finally, Nelson got tired of trading shots back and forth. Chase's jaw dropped as he watched his partner rise to his feet. "Les, what are you doing?" Chase yelled.

"I've had enough of this cat-and-mouse," spat Nelson. "I'm going down there to kill them!"

Nelson marched forward, spraying his gun from the hip at the trapped G-men. Cowley unleashed his own bursts from his machine gun, and Hollis with his shotgun. Bullets ripped into Nelson's arms, legs, and chest, but that didn't stop him or throw off his aim. He continued marching and shooting like an unstoppable machine. Cowley was soon overcome with gunfire, the ditch offering him little protection. Hollis ran out of shotgun shells and made a run for a nearby telegraph pole, popping bullets at Nelson as he ran. But Nelson swung his fire toward Hollis, cutting him down. As the two agents lay dying, Nelson finally dropped his gun and collapsed.

Helen and Chase rushed to Nelson's side, then dragged him up to Hollis and Cowley's car. "You'll have to drive," Nelson said. "I've been hit."

Seventeen times, to be exact. Nelson died hours later, and his wife and best friend unceremoniously dumped his naked body in a ditch. After all, the longer it took to identify the body, the longer Helen and Chase had a chance of escaping the law. (It didn't work. Helen surrendered days later, and Chase was arrested exactly a month later.) With the gruesome death of "Baby Face" Nelson, Bloody 1934 was officially over.

But there were still more public enemies at large.

## Cool Fact from the Vault

While everyone called the cherubic little psychopath "Baby Face," Nelson tried to get his own nickname going: "Big George Nelson." (It was wishful thinking.)

# 22 "MACHINE GUN" KELLY

**Real name:** George Kelly Barnes; later shortened to George Kelly

**Number of banks robbed:** At least 5

**Estimated lifetime take:** Technically $265,000, but most of that was made tagging along with Harvey Bailey; Kelly's cut was much smaller

**Claim to fame:** This swaggering, tough-as-nails bank robber was all talk, and his wife helped him fake it

## "I AM SPENDING YOUR MONEY TO HAVE YOU AND YOUR FAMILY KILLED—NICE, EH?"

Clyde had Bonnie; George Kelly had Kathryn. But where Clyde was a fully formed robber by the time he hooked up with Bonnie, Kelly was just another doughy, blue-eyed, blowhard bootlegger when he met Kathryn Thorne in a Fort Worth speakeasy in 1927. "The coppers will never take me alive," he'd snarl out of the corner of his mouth, bragging about being wanted in 12 states for murder and bank robbery. Truth was, Kelly had never so much as carried a gun, let alone robbed a bank with one. He just liked impersonating big-shot mobsters. He thought it was funny.

Kathryn could tell that Kelly was full of suds but still thought he had potential. Kelly was a big, tough-looking guy. Some people even seemed to be afraid of him. The wheels started spinning in Kathryn's mind.

Kathryn was no stranger to reinvention: She had been born Cleo Brooks in Saltillo, Mississippi, but changed her name to "Kathryn" at 15 because it sounded more romantic. She had been married three times by the age of 23. Her last husband, Charlie Thorne, was a Texas bootlegger who made the mistake of cheating on Kathryn. Cops found a suicide note next to Thorne, who had a bullet in his left temple. The note read:

> I can't live with her or without her, hence I am departing this life.

Friends noted that Thorne wouldn't know how to spell "hence," let alone use it in a suicide note. A local gas station attendant noted how he'd seen Kathryn the night before, fuming that she was going to "kill that goddamned Charlie Thorne." Kathryn swore she had nothing to do with it, and the law believed her.

Now Kathryn had her sights on Kelly, and she convinced him to run away with her to her mother's farm in Paradise, Texas. There, the training began. Kathryn was going to teach Kelly to be a tough bank robber and earn big money if it killed him.

First, Kathryn handed Kelly a Thompson submachine gun and made him practice with it. She lined up walnuts along a fence and ordered Kelly to blast them off. Within a few months, Kelly could nail quite a few of them. Then came phase two: public relations. Kathryn would pass out the spent cartridges to friends and relatives, bragging that "Machine Gun" Kelly could sign his name on a wall with bullets. Kelly learned to wield his Thompson chopper, Kathryn explained, in World War I. (Somebody forgot to tell Kathryn that Thompson submachine guns weren't used in that war.)

But it wasn't Kathryn's endless training and promotion work that would land her boyfriend in the big leagues. It was Kelly's small-time bootlegging. On January 13, 1928, Prohibition agents caught Kelly trying to sneak liquor into an Indian reservation, and he was sentenced to three years in prison. On the outside, Kathryn told people her boyfriend was off robbing countless banks in Kentucky. But inside Leavenworth, Kelly met real-life bank robbers Charlie Harmon, Frank "Jelly" Nash, Francis Keating, and Thomas Holden. And this is where

Kathryn's ceaseless drilling might have paid off. His new pro friends seemed to buy the tough-guy act and allowed him to join their robbing gang upon their release from jail. (Keating and Holden weren't exactly *released*; they used forged passes to escape. And Kelly and Harmon were believed to have helped them, since both worked with photographs in the prison's records room.)

Upon his parole in 1930, Kelly promptly became Kathryn's fourth husband and then joined his prison buddies on July 15 to rob the Bank of Willmar in Minnesota. Kelly must have been impressed with himself, since the take was fat—$70,000—and the gig was masterminded by genius bank robber Harvey Bailey. The same team stole $40,000 from a bank in Ottumwa, Iowa, a few months later and another $40,000 from the Central State Bank in Sherman, Texas, the following April. Kathryn had finally gotten her wish: Big ol' George Kelly was a real-life professional bank robber.

But the takes weren't quite what she imagined, and Kathryn's wheels started spinning again. The newspapers at the time, the spring of 1933, were full of accounts of high-profile kidnappings, and Kathryn thought that was the secret to making the really big money. She now decided that George Kelly would become a master kidnapper. Their first attempt didn't work out: The banker's son they grabbed, Howard Woolverton, convinced the Kellys that his family didn't have the $50,000 they demanded. But he promised to raise it upon his release, so they let Woolverton go. Of course, he never paid up, despite several angry collection calls from Machine Gun himself.

While working out the kinks of this new kidnapping racket, Kelly hooked up with a trio of veteran heisters for more bank robberies. Along with Albert Bates, Eddie Doll, and Eddie Bentz, Kelly robbed the First Trust and Savings Bank in Colfax, Washington, on September 21, 1932. The take was $77,000. Two months later, the same team—minus Bentz, who had been nabbed in Dallas and later jumped bail—robbed the Citizens' State Bank in Tupelo, Mississippi, and took $38,000. For some reason, Kelly wielded a .38 pistol during this robbery, which kind of ruined the whole "Machine Gun" thing he had going. In fact, Tupelo police at first thought it had been the work of "Pretty Boy" Floyd.

Flush with money, the Kellys returned to Texas and started to plan their second kidnapping. But Kathryn spilled the plans to a pair of Fort Worth detectives, thinking they had agreed to be in on the caper. They hadn't. So when it came time to nab oil heir Guy Waggoner, the Kellys were shocked to see their target under heavy police surveillance. Somebody had tipped off the coppers, but Kathryn couldn't figure out who. The plan was nixed.

Finally, the Kellys pulled off a real kidnapping when they grabbed oilman Charles F. Urschel from his porch in Oklahoma City. "Keep quiet or we'll blow your heads off!" growled Kelly to the two couples who were sitting in the open air, playing bridge. Another gunman stood next to him, covering his back.

But once he set foot on the porch, Kelly wasn't sure which of the two men was his quarry. "Which of you is Urschel?"

Nobody said a word.

"Well, we'll take both of them, then," Kelly said to his accomplice.

The kidnappers forced both into a car at gunpoint. A couple of miles and one wallet check later, and Kelly knew which bird he wanted. The other, family friend Walter Jarrett, was released, but not until Kelly filched $51 from his wallet.

As it turned out, Machine Gun Kelly should have stuck with bank robbery. His captive was no dummy. Urschel carefully listened for audio clues (planes flying overhead), baited his captors for hints about the area, and planted his fingerprints on whatever surface he could. Once the $200,000 in demand money was delivered and Urschel was released, the millionaire immediately gave the FBI a detailed description of where he had been held. When agents swooped down upon Kathryn Kelly's mother's farm in Paradise, Texas, they didn't find the kidnappers, but they did find Harvey Bailey, who had chosen the worst possible moment to call on Kelly for an old favor. The Kellys, meanwhile, were running helter-skelter across the Midwest. From the road, Machine Gun couldn't resist doing his tough-guy routine one last time. He wrote Urschel a threatening letter, promising payback for siccing J. Edgar Hoover on his tail:

*Ignorant Charles—*

*In the event of my arrest I've already formed an outfit to take care of and destroy you and yours the same as if I was there. I am spending your money to have you and your family killed—nice, eh? You are bucking people who have cash—planes, bombs and unlimited connections both here and abroad. If my brain was no larger than yours, the Government would have had me long ago, as it is I am drinking good beer and will yet see you and your family like I should have left you at first, stone head. Now, sap—it is up to you ... Adios, smart one.*

*Your worst enemy,*

*Geo. R. Kelly*

On September 26, 1933, the FBI raided the Kellys' Memphis, Tennessee, hideout and took him without a fight. Popular legend has it that Machine Gun Kelly cowered in a corner and pleaded, "Don't shoot, G-men!" But in reality, Kelly looked down at the rifle poking his belly and calmly dropped his own gun. "I've been waiting for you all night," he said, with a friendly smile. Kathryn was in bed next to him. On the floor sat the remnants of six quarts of gin. Both outlaws were hungover as hell and now the property of the U.S. government.

Years later, deep into a life sentence at Alcatraz, Kelly wasn't slinging the tough-guy talk around any more. He remorsefully said that five words were burned on the wall of his cell: "Nothing can be worth this." He died there, of a heart attack, on July 17, 1954.

His mentor, Kathryn, also received life in prison, but was released in June 1958. The last anyone heard of her, Kathryn Thorne Kelly worked as a bookkeeper at a nursing home in Oklahoma.

*Out of bullets: G-men escort George "Machine Gun" Kelly out of a Memphis jail.*

## Cool Fact from the Vault

Kelly is the only one of the depression-era bank robbers who attended college. But he flunked out miserably after a few months; his highest grade was a C+ (and that was in Physical Hygiene).

# 23  EDDIE BENTZ

**Full name:** Edward Wilhelm Bentz

**Number of banks robbed:** Anywhere between 50 and 100, as Bentz once boasted to the FBI

**Estimated lifetime take:** At least $5 million in bonds

**Claim to fame:** Thanks to his expert planning skills, Bentz had millions in stolen bonds—but he died in prison before he had a chance to spend it

## "I DECIDED TO BECOME A YEGG—YOU KNOW, A BANK ROBBER. THEY'RE THE ARISTOCRACY OF THE CRIMINAL PROFESSION."

The unsung heroes of the bank-robbing profession are the "juggers"—the detail men who case bank jobs and then sell the plans to an enterprising team of heisters. They're not usually flashy and don't have a dozen shoot-out stories to tell their buddies. They simply dedicate themselves to planning and ironing out every possible wrinkle in a heist, carefully, slowly, methodically.

Perhaps this is why history has forgotten Eddie Bentz, who had one of the most lucrative bank robbery runs in history. At a young age, Bentz knew he was destined for career in crime. "I decided to become a yegg—you know, a bank robber. They're the aristocracy of the criminal profession." Unlike some juggers, Bentz did go out personally on jobs. He started out as a nighttime safecracker, apprenticed with a pair of Chicago bank robbers nicknamed the "Gold Dust Twins," once accompanied "Machine Gun" Kelly on a gig, and is said to have planned and helped execute the huge $2 million Lincoln National Bank heist in Nebraska in 1930. But by the early 1930s, Bentz had made enough money to retire from the stick-up life and spent most of his energies planning capers for other gangs. Jay Robert Nash dubbed Bentz "America's Master Bank Robber" in his *Almanac of World Crime.* "Bentz was an unusual pioneer of high crime whose penchant for detail and obscurity has undoubtedly become the credo of the modern bank robber," wrote Nash.

What made him so good at jugmarking? Bentz developed an amazing technique that allowed him to pinpoint the ripest banks. First, he would visit the target town, introducing himself as an investor. He had the personality for it. "I'm a big farmerish-looking sort of fellow," explained Bentz, "sort of easygoing, like to laugh and talk and be chummy with people, and that doesn't match up with ideas about criminals. People think crooks hide in cellars." Next, Bentz would make a trip to the nearest public library and scour the local newspaper, going back several months, if need be. He was keeping an eye out for bank ads, which invariably gave clues to assets and liabilities. Bentz would also use his phony investor status as an excuse to visit a bank and ask for detailed statements. He kept an eye on the news, looking specifically for events that might influence cash flow. It was painstaking work, but it enabled Bentz to predict how much money a particular bank had on a specific date. Bentz became so good at it, he was often able to nail the figure within $1,000.

Once Bentz had done his job, the messy work of the actual robbery would be left to a team of professionals, and Bentz would receive a cut of the proceeds, usually in stocks and bonds. Most heisters didn't want the paper, anyway; it was too difficult to cash in. But Bentz had developed a financial network that earned him up to 70 cents on the dollar. The Master Robber had thought of everything ... everything, except how to discourage tipsters. One led the FBI to his apartment in Brooklyn, where he was arrested in 1936.

"On the upside," thought Bentz, "I'll eventually get out and unearth the $5 million in bonds I've hidden."

On the downside, Bentz died in prison.

## Cool Fact from the Vault
Bentz was a bookworm and when he traveled abroad (which was often), he always lugged trunks full of first editions of literary classics.

# 24 THE BARKER-KARPIS GANG

**Core gang members:** Arizona Kate Donnie Clark "Ma" Barker, Arthur "Dock" Barker, Fred Barker, and Alvin Karpis

**Other family members:** Herman Barker and Lloyd Barker

**Associate gang members:** Lawrence DeVol, Bill Weaver, Earl Christman, and Freddie Hunter

**Number of banks robbed:** At least 12

**Estimated lifetime take:** More than $800,000

**Claim to fame:** The Barker-Karpis Gang brought whole new meaning to the term "crime family"

## "THE COPS HERE WON'T EVER STOP PERSECUTING MY BOYS."

Was "Ma" Barker the first lady of depression-era crime, as J. Edgar Hoover and his G-men would have it? "She became a monument to parental indulgence," wrote Hoover, who claimed she trained her sons in the ways of crime. Others, most notably Barker Gang member Alvin Karpis, dispute Ma's role in planning Barker Gang heists: "The most ridiculous story in the annals of crime is that Ma Barker was the mastermind," Karpis wrote in his autobiography. "That legend only grew up after her death to justify how she was slaughtered by the FBI." Adds Harvey Bailey: "Plan a heist? That woman couldn't plan breakfast."

Whether or not Arizona Kate Donnie Clark Barker ever planned anything, one can't deny that something weird was going on with her boys. Four out of four turned to a life of violent crime. From the beginning, their loving Ma would defend or outright hide them from accusing fingers. "The cops here won't ever stop persecuting my boys," said Ma after eldest son Herman got nailed for a robbery in Joplin, Missouri, in 1915. Never mind that Herman was clearly guilty.

Perhaps Ma turned a blind, loving eye to her outlaw offspring because she had admired bank robbers since she was a little girl. She was born in 1872 near Springfield, Missouri, and when she was 10 years old, "Arrie" Barker was crushed to hear that her hero, Jesse James, had been gunned down by that yellow-bellied Bob Ford. (According to Lew Louderback's *The Bad Ones*, little Arrie and her schoolyard friends used to chant: "The dirty little coward that shot Mr. Howard has laid Jesse James in his grave!") By the time she was 20, she was mourning the loss of those nice Dalton Boys, who met their grisly end in the town of Coffeyville, Kansas. That same year, she married a laborer named George Barker, who was by all accounts an upstanding, law-abiding citizen, and moved to Aurora, Missouri, where she gave birth to four boys: Herman in 1894, Lloyd in 1896, Arthur (later known as "Dock") in 1899, and baby Freddie in 1902.

By 1910, the three older boys would be mixed up in crime—Herman and Lloyd organizing a teen gang dedicated to pulling petty robberies, and 11-year-old Dock racking up juvvie violations left and right. Five years later, the whole family would get into the act after 13-year-old Freddie paid a visit to Herb Farmer, who specialized in hiding outlaws in his Joplin, Missouri, home, and invited outlaws to crash his Ma's new place in Tulsa, Oklahoma. Pro heisters like Al Spencer, Frank Nash, Ray Terrill, Earl Thayer, Francis Keating, and Thomas Holden were quick to take Freddie up on his offer. This became the Barker family business for years, and it gave young Freddie and his brothers an education in the business of crime.

Unfortunately, the Barker Boys didn't master their studies. In 1922, Lloyd tried to rob a post office in Oklahoma but was caught at the scene and given 25 years at Leavenworth. That same year, Dock was sent up the river for murder—a crime he swore he didn't commit. (It appears he was telling the truth; years later, a California thief would confess to the crime.) In 1926, Freddie cracked his first bank in

Winfield, Kansas, but was soon caught and sent to Kansas State Penitentiary at Lansing. The following year, Herman was busy robbing banks with the Kimes-Terrill Gang but caught a bullet racing past a police roadblock. Herman, who had killed a police officer during his getaway, decided to end his suffering quickly and wrapped his mouth around the barrel of his Luger.

If Ma Barker had been hoping to raise a family full of professional criminals, she was probably feeling quite sorry for herself in 1927.

But hope came in 1931, when a freshly paroled Freddie showed up at Ma's Tulsa home with a prison buddy named Alvin Karpis. Karpis, who would eventually be dubbed the "Last Public Enemy," was born in 1908 with the unwieldy handle Alvin Karpowicz; a grade school teacher shortened it. His criminal career started at age 10, when he helped an 18-year-old thug break into a grocery store. His teenaged years were full of this "penny ante stuff," says Karpis in his autobiography, *The Alvin Karpis Story*. He met Freddie at Kansas State after taking a fall for a warehouse burglary. The two became fast friends and agreed to form a gang together.

Ma quickly took a shine to young Karpis and invited him to move in with the family—which by this point only consisted of Ma, Freddie, and Ma's new boyfriend, Albert Dunlop. (Freddie's dad had split years before.) Dunlop was a bit of a dope, but that was okay. He knew to keep his mouth shut and didn't get in the way when Freddie and Karpis hooked up with other guys and started robbing jewelry and clothing stores in Kansas and Missouri. By the fall of 1931, Freddie announced he had something grander in mind.

"I know a bank in Mountain View, Missouri," Freddie said.

"If we're going to make money, I'm interested," replied Karpis, "I'm sick of beating boxes for a few bucks. I'm for the bank."

Karpis and another ex-con broke into the Mountain View Bank at 3 A.M., then hunkered down and waited for the first employees to show. When they heard keys in the front door, both lifted handkerchiefs over their noses and took out their pistols. A beautiful young teller was the first to enter.

"Don't move!" Karpis shouted. "We're robbing this place!"

As employees arrived, they were herded together at gunpoint, until an employee who knew how to open the vault arrived. Karpis scooped up $7,000, then ran outside to where Freddie was waiting with a getaway car. Two-inch roof tacks were scattered in their wake, to discourage pursuing vehicles. "My first daylight job," later wrote Karpis, "and not a hitch in the whole operation."

Next came a move to the big leagues: St. Paul, Minnesota. Like Hot Springs, Arkansas, and Joplin, Missouri, St. Paul was known as a "friendly town" in the criminal underworld. As long as they didn't stir up trouble within city limits, the political bosses were more than happy to have gangsters spend their cash on their turf. Toward the end of 1931, Freddie and Karpis started doing minor tasks for a fixer named Jack Peifer, including cracking safes and hijacking whiskey and cigarettes. Ma Barker and her boyfriend Dunlop also moved to St. Paul so Ma could be near her boys. (Some still insist that Ma was the mastermind who hooked her boys up with the St. Paul underworld— brokering deals, casing banks, supplying plans.)

Shortly after New Year's 1932, Freddie and Karpis organized their first major bank score: The Northwestern National Bank in Minneapolis. They were joined by Tommy Holden, Phil Courtney, and an old Karpis buddy named Lawrence DeVol. The job was a stunning success—$75,000 in cash, $6,500 in coins, and $185,000 in bonds. Karpis's only complaint? "Courtney was doing a lot of gab-bing with the pretty switchboard operator." That, and the fact that a bank employee pulled a mini-caper of his own, stuffing $10,000 in cash into his own pockets during the stick-up.

From there, the new Barker-Karpis Gang—usually consisting of the two titular leaders, DeVol, and other men from the St. Paul scene— ripped through banks all over the Midwest. Picture a red line, zigzag-ging across the middle of the United States: Beloit, Wisconsin, to Flandreau, South Dakota, to Redwood Falls, Minnesota. "We made a lot of money," said Karpis, "but we worked hard for it. Every score had its special problems and each its special surprises." Once, while speeding away from the Wahpeton, North Dakota, bank, police winged one of the gang's female hostages, who was riding on the car's running boards. (So much for the human shield theory.) The screaming girl distracted the driver, who ended up running into a ditch and bursting tires. Karpis and DeVol ran to a nearby farm to steal another car.

"We just robbed the Wahpeton Bank," he explained to the farmer, "and we need a car to take us out of here fast. We're taking yours and leaving ours and we'll give you some money to square it."

DeVol produced some bills to underscore the point.

"You robbed a bank, you say?" replied the farmer. "Well, I don't care. All the banks ever do is foreclose on us farmers."

Another "special problem" turned out to be Ma's boyfriend, Arthur Dunlop. Some of Freddie Barker's St. Paul friends overheard Dunlop blabbering on about all of the bank heists. A short while later, Dunlop's lead-ridden body popped up along Lake Freasted in Wisconsin. "Jack Peifer's boys did it as a favor to us," recalled Karpis. And apparently, Ma wasn't all that upset to be single again.

After a $47,000 Fort Scott, Kansas, caper with pro Harvey Bailey and an amazing quarter million dollar heist at the Cloud County Bank in Concordia, Kansas, the Barker-Karpis gang was joined by another Barker. Dock had been paroled from prison by the governor of Oklahoma after the real murderer confessed, and he quickly joined the gang. But Dock turned out to be a jinx. During the $112,000 stick-up of the Third Northwestern Bank in Minneapolis, the gang shot and killed two cops and wounded an innocent bystander. (Curiously enough, Karpis in his autobiography claimed he was tending to a sick Ma Barker during this heist-gone-bad.) In the aftermath, DeVol was arrested and caught with his $17,000 share of the heist. The law took the cash and, in return, gave him life at Minnesota State Penitentiary. Freddie, Dock, Ma, and Karpis fled to Reno for a vacation. It had been a busy year.

The gang returned in April 1933, with a strong $151,359 heist in Fairbury, Nebraska, but the bank guard surprised the gang with a pistol and shot sometime member Earl Christman. Then, the entire town seemed to show up with rifles, à la Coffeyville in 1892, when someone cried, "Bank robbers! Bank robbers!" The Barkers and Karpis shot their way out of town, and were convinced they would read about dozens of dead citizens in the newspapers the next day. When they checked, eight had been shot, but miraculously, all had survived.

Maybe the violence spooked them—or, once again, maybe criminal supergenius Ma Barker had a brainstorm—but after the Fairbury job, the Barker-Karpis Gang changed gears and got into the kidnapping business. The first target was St. Paul brewer William A. Hamm Jr., and the operation was a success: Hamm was released unharmed, and the Barker-Karpis Gang was suddenly $100,000 richer. Their next kidnapping in 1934 didn't end as smoothly. After releasing banker Edward G. Bremer for $200,000, Dock Barker made the mistake of dropping a gasoline canister he had touched. The FBI dusted it, and soon the Barker-Karpis Gang were national public enemies.

Feeling the eyes of America upon them, Freddie and Karpis immediately reported to underworld plastic surgeon Dr. Joseph P. Moran, who kept an office on Irving Park Boulevard in Chicago. Moran wasn't as skilled as they'd thought. "The fingerprint operation was damned painful," wrote Karpis. "Moran looped elastic bands tight around my fingers at the first joints. Next, he froze my fingertips with an injection of cocaine in each one. Finally, he started the scraping, sharpening the ends of my fingers like a pencil." Karpis's was $750 face job wasn't all that great, either. The fact was, Freddie and Karpis didn't look all that different after going under the knife.

But Doc Moran's worst mistake wasn't made in his operating room, but in a bar. According to FBI files, Moran was at the Casino Club in Toledo, Ohio, hitting the booze hard with Dock Barker and other gang members. "I have you guys in the palms of my hands," he boasted. That drunken remark would cost him big. Moran was last seen leaving the club with Freddie and Karpis. Freddie later cracked, "Doc will do no more operating. The fishes have probably eaten him up by now."

But it was also true that Dock and Freddie Barker would do no more robbing. Dock was caught by FBI star agent Melvin Purvis on the streets of Chicago. "Where's your gun?" asked Purvis.

"Home," replied Dock. "Ain't that a hell of a place for it?"

In Dock's apartment, the FBI found a map of Freddie and Ma's hideout in Florida, where the two were taking their usual winter break. On January 16, 1935, agents stormed the Barker's cottage on Lake Weir. "Freddie Barker!" one agent yelled. "Come out with your hands up!" Someone—most likely Freddie—started shooting, and the G-men let him and his Ma have it. And whether or not Ma had planned the Barker heists all along, she decided to pick up a gun in the end. Next to her bullet-ridden body was a .300 gas-operated rifle, with nearly half of its rounds expelled.

Karpis was also in Florida, off on a fishing trip. He had been set to join up with Freddie and Ma the next day. But now it was time to bolt. "I was torn up that Ma and Freddie were dead," he wrote. "Freddie was my best friend. Ma was like a mother. But I was scared, too." Now that Dillinger, Floyd, Nelson, Kelly, and the Barkers were either dead or out of circulation, Alvin Karpis became branded the last public enemy. And J. Edgar Hoover, who had been catching heat for his heavy-handed methods, also came under fire for never personally arresting a criminal. How could the top cop in the country have risen so high without never once slapping the cuffs on a perp?

That changed on May 1, 1936, when J. Edgar Hoover slapped a meaty paw on Karpis's upper arm as he sat in his car in front of his New Orleans apartment. Karpis had been going for his rifle. "Put the cuffs on him, boys!" Hoover said triumphantly.

Well, maybe it didn't quite happen that way. Karpis swears that other agents pounced on him first, took his rifle away, then shouted for the FBI Director to come out of his hiding spot to do the honors. Either way, there's no denying that Hoover's career soared after the capture of Karpis. "I made that son of a bitch," wrote Karpis.

Karpis was sentenced to life at Alcatraz. As for the other surviving Barkers, Dock was shot and killed trying to break out of Alcatraz in 1939. Lloyd, the forgotten Barker boy, was released from prison in 1947, only to be killed by his wife two years later. In 1969, Karpis was paroled and deported to Canada, his birth country. He lived long enough to dictate his memoir and participate in a CBS special about his life in 1979, but died later that same year after taking an overdose of sleeping pills.

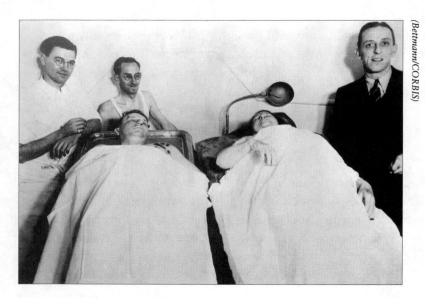

*(Bettmann/CORBIS)*

*Mother and child reunion: Ma Barker and her son Freddie Barker in morgue of Iklawaha, Florida, after they were ambushed by the FBI.*

## Cool Fact from the Vault

According to Karpis, Ma Barker loved to do crossword puzzles and listen to hillbilly songs on the radio. (That is, when she wasn't polishing guns, hobnobbing with St. Paul gangsters, and casing banks throughout the Midwest.)

# 25  WILLIE SUTTON

**Nicknames:** "The Actor," "the Gentleman"

**Accomplices**: Eddie Wilson, Jack Bassett, Joe Pelango, and Tommy Kling

**Number of banks robbed:** 20

**Estimated lifetime take:** More than $2 million

**Claim to fame:** "The Actor" could skillfully impersonate anyone—mailman, cop, Western Union man, medieval knight—but was a master bank robber at his core

## "DO I LOOK LIKE A BANK ROBBER TO YOU?"

Willie Sutton's quip about robbing banks—"Because that's where the money is"—has appeared in hundreds of articles about banks. But Sutton never said it. He later admitted that the quip came from a snarky newspaper man, and Sutton never thought to dispute ownership. "If anyone had asked me, I would have said it. Anyone would have said it."

Sutton always knew where the money was; at first, the problem was getting to it. The first bank Willie Sutton tried to rob, Ozone Park National Bank in Queens, was an unmitigated disaster. Sutton and his partner, Eddie Wilson, took all night to chop through a concrete floor to gain access to the vault, and by the time they did, there was only 15 minutes left to burn through the vault before the bank opened up in the morning. Sutton was forced to abandon his expensive tools and the robbery. To make matters worse, an oxygen tank—the kind used for safe-burning torches—was traced to Wilson two weeks later. Sutton was tied to Wilson, and on April 5, 1926, he was found guilty of burglary in the third degree and attempted grand larceny. Sutton was headed to Sing Sing.

After winning parole in 1929, Sutton found himself with a new bride and tried to make an honest living on the eve of the Great Depression. Then, Sutton was laid off from his landscaping job a week after his wife told him she was pregnant. "Right there, I began to think about making money the way I knew best," wrote Sutton.

Sutton started kicking around the shortcomings of the Ozone Park heist and remembered the two employees lingering outside, ready to open the bank. Why chop through inches of concrete and steel, Sutton thought, when the waiting employees could be forced to open the vault at gunpoint? Hell, why not *be* the employees? "That is the answer," wrote Sutton. "A uniform provided automatic entrée. Ring the bell and you could walk right in." Willie "the Actor" was born. Sutton used theatrical-costume houses to outfit himself with enough disguises—cop, mailman, fireman, security guard—to make The Village People jealous.

Next, Sutton went looking for a partner and found one in Jack Bassett, a trustworthy prison buddy who had been sprung from Dannemora and was looking for work. Now it was time to test-run the Actor Method. On October 28, 1930, Sutton disguised himself as a Western Union delivery man and knocked over the M. Rosenthal and Sons jewelry store, which was on Broadway between 50th and 51st Street—in the heart of Times Square. He bagged $150,000 worth of gems and jewelry, which he fenced through the infamous Dutch Schultz, who was running most of the rackets in the city. "I doubt very much that there could be a recital of crime so daring in New York," a judge would later say.

Sutton and Bassett considered themselves ready for a bank. Sutton had been eyeing one in Jamaica, Queens, and he set himself to study it more closely, specifically the comings and goings of its employees. Sutton called the bank and asked for the name of the manager. He sent himself a Western Union telegram just to get the envelope, and typed up a phony telegram to the bank manager. Presto—a key prop was ready. "I was beginning to think of this as a drama, with myself as director and main actor," Sutton recalled. Together with Bassett, Sutton carefully rehearsed their roles.

The morning of the robbery, Sutton whipped out his makeup box and spent time flattening his nose and lightening his complexion. He donned a Western Union uniform and paid the bank a visit an hour before it was set to open. After the guard entered, Sutton waited a minute, then knocked on the door. It opened a cautious inch or two, but when the guard saw the uniform, he opened it all the way.

"I got a telegram for the boss," Sutton cheerfully announced.

When the guard took Sutton's offered clipboard and pencil, Sutton reached down and took the guard's gun. Jack Bassett appeared with another gun and closed the bank door behind him. The show had begun.

Thirty minutes later, the first bank employee arrived, exactly as Sutton had expected. "It's a wonderful day, Fred," he called to the guard.

"That's what you think," replied the guard.

When the manager arrived, Sutton approached him with the gun. "All I want you to do is open the vault. It would be very silly to refuse."

Apparently, the manager agreed with Sutton's logic. He opened the vault without complaint. Sutton helped himself to $48,000 in crisp new bills, then told the frightened employees that a third man was waiting outside. If anyone bolted after them, they'd get shot. Of course, employees could use the phone to call the cops, but that didn't bother Sutton, because he knew it would take the first squad car at least 10 minutes to respond. Sutton and Bassett would be long gone by then. The drama was an amazing success, with Sutton giving himself rave reviews. "This," Sutton decided, "would be my technique from now on."

Willie the Actor, along with Bassett, used a variety of ruses and disguises—postal worker, cop, window cleaner with sponge—on at least a dozen more banks. It became fun to spot some of the code signals bank guards and managers used to warn each other in case of trouble. For instance, window blinds might be pulled halfway up until the bank guard pulled them up all the way, giving the signal that all was clear. Once, Sutton told a bank guard to turn the calendar in the front window up. "I thought he was going to fall right through the floor," recalled Sutton.

The technique was wonderful, but trouble came from the best supporting actor. Bassett, flush with money for the first time in a long time, felt rich enough to start cheating on his wife. When the wife got wise to his tomcatting, she turned both Bassett and Sutton in to the cops. "Me? A rob-ber?" Sutton protested, trying to play the part of the innocent rube. "I'm not a rob-ber." But fingerprints matched; Sutton was indeed the rob-ber they were looking for. Sutton was sent back to Sing Sing in June 1931, five years after he'd left it. A year and a half later, Sutton made his first prison escape when he fit two nine-foot ladders together and scaled the wall.

Eager to resume the drama, Sutton hooked up with his old pal Eddie Wilson and a new robber named Joe Perlango to rob the Corn Exchange Bank, on 110th Street between Amsterdam and Broadway, which netted the trio $30,000. Not the take of a lifetime, but it was enough to move to another city and make a new start for himself.

New York City cops were too wise to the Sutton technique, so after New Year's 1933, Sutton moved to West Philadelphia, where he found an apartment for himself and his new girlfriend, Olga. (Sutton's wife Louise had already left him.) Eddie Wilson would bring his girlfriend down to visit, and the foursome would watch football games at nearby Franklin Field on the University of Pennsylvania campus. But all the while Sutton was casing his new city for a juicy target, and found one at the Corn Exchange Bank at 60th and Market, not far from a busy elevated train station. "We'd been lucky with one Corn Exchange," Sutton reasoned, "we might be lucky with another."

Sutton noticed that the bank's mail slot was fairly small, so he rented a postal worker's uniform and made up a phony package that couldn't possibly fit it. On January 15, 1934, Sutton took his package in a leather pouch to the bank an hour before it opened. A tired-looking guard peeked through the glass and decided to let him in. Sutton pulled his gun, and his two partners—Wilson and Pelango—entered behind him. As bank employees entered, the three would round them up and tell them to behave or risk a bullet. When the manager finally arrived, Sutton forced him to open the vault and put $160,000 in cash into his leather pouch. As they were about to make their getaway, Sutton was surprised to see that customers had already begun to line up outside. Sutton sent Wilson and Pelango outside to their getaway car and told the customers it'd only be a few more minutes. When he heard the car start up, he exited the bank, locking the door behind him. "Just another minute," he told the puzzled customers, who were probably wondering: *Who is this guy?*

The next day, the newspaper would supply the answer: Law enforcement officials branded the Corn Exchange Bank heist a Willie Sutton job. "They recognized my technique, all right," recalled Sutton, "and according to newspapers, police of both cities were searching intensively for me." However, the law found Wilson and Pelango first and engaged them in a brief shootout in New York City, which would leave Wilson blinded by a bullet to the head. The squeeze was put on Pelango, who told them exactly where to find Willie the Actor.

A 15-man team of New York City and Philly cops armed with tommy guns stormed Sutton's West Philly apartment and arrested him on February 5, 1934. He was sentenced to 25 to 50 at Eastern State Penitentiary, an old prison known for keeping inmates in solitary confinement. "From its birth the Eastern State Pen had a bad name," wrote Sutton, who would be a guest of the prison for over a decade. Entering during the height of the Depression, Sutton would pop out, quite literally, at the tail end of World War II.

On April 3, 1945, Sutton and 11 other convicts performed a daring escape from the prison, tunneling under the huge walls and right up onto Fairmount Avenue, a busy city thoroughfare. Unfortunately for Sutton, two beat cops happened to be walking by across the street and rounded up the escapees. Sutton was given a life term and transferred to another tough Philly jail: Holmesburg Prison. On February 10, 1947, Willie Sutton and four other prisoners stole a set of guard uniforms and marched across the yard with two huge ladders.

Spotlights swung in their direction. Sutton cried out, "It's okay!"

The bluff was lame, but it bought Sutton and his friends enough time to scale the wall, hijack an early morning milk truck, and race toward downtown Philadelphia. The group split up, and hours later Sutton ducked out of the cold snow and hitched a ride from a kindly man who was headed to Princeton, New Jersey. The man had a late-edition paper on the seat next to him. Sutton glanced over and saw his own face staring back at him.

"I hear they got all of 'em by now," the driver said cheerfully.

"I'm glad of that," Sutton said.

After getting dropped off in Princeton, Sutton wandered in the snowy dark all night, thinking the cops would find his frozen corpse in the middle of New Jersey. Luckily, another driver gave him a lift all the way to the Bronx, and soon Sutton set himself up with a new alias—"Eddie Lynch"—and a new job as an orderly at a hospital for the infirm on Staten Island. The job left him with enough time to take trains and wander odd corners of New York City, and before long, Sutton was getting that old feeling again.

On a walk through Sunnyside, Queens, Sutton passed the Manufacturers' Trust Company. "Almost unconsciously my mind photographed the bank entrance, the condition of its roof, the depth of the plot on which it was situated, and the number of people who were going in and out of the establishment," recalled Sutton.

On March 9, 1950, the Manufacturers' Trust Company in Sunnyside, Queens, was hit, and the three bandits got away with $63,933.

On weekdays, "Eddie Lynch" would clean hospital halls with a mop; on weekends, Willie Sutton and some bank-robbing buddies would mop up at small banks in New York and New Jersey. It was the perfect cover. Once, a nurse saw Willie Sutton's photograph in the *New York Daily News* after he had landed on the FBI's Ten Most Wanted List, and confronted him. "Hello, Willie Sutton."

"What did you call me?" Sutton asked.

"I'm calling you Willie Sutton. Here's your picture in the paper."

"You kidding me?" Sutton laughed. "You think I'd be working in this dump at $90 a month if I was this person?"

Of course he would.

In late February 1952, Sutton was riding the BMT subway when he noticed a young guy giving him strange looks. Sutton's eyes darted down to the guy's shoes: they were black suede. No cop—even a plainclothes man—would be caught dead in black suede "hepcat" shoes. He shrugged off the incident as paranoia. When he left the station, Sutton walked to his car and discovered his battery had died. He started to change it himself when two cops approached and asked if he needed help.

"This damn battery's gone sour," Sutton said.

"Let's see your owner's license."

The bank robber handed over the papers, which seemed to satisfy the officers. Sutton continued to fiddle with the battery.

Unbeknownst to Sutton, that young man with the black suede shoes had trailed Sutton as he emerged from the BMT and tipped off the two cops who had approached him. They promptly ran to the station to grab a detective, and before long Sutton heard a voice behind him.

"You'd better come to the station house with us."

Sutton turned. One of the original cops was standing there, along with a detective. "Why?"

"You look like Willie Sutton."

"Do I look like a bank robber to you?" Sutton replied.

"That's the point. Come on."

Once in custody, and after a fingerprint check, Sutton admitted who he was.

The tipster was 24-year-old Arnold Shuster, who had seen Willie the Actor's mug on an FBI Ten Most Wanted poster. Shuster was immediately famous, which would be the worst thing that could have happened to him. A local mob chieftain named Albert Anastasia watched a TV report featuring Shuster and immediately launched into a blind rage. He didn't know Sutton, nor did he particularly care that he had been captured. Something else bugged him. "I hate squealers!" he reportedly screamed. "Hit that guy!" Apparently, one of his underlings took the request seriously, and on March 8, 1952, an unknown gunman pumped four bullets into Shuster's head and two into his stomach. Shuster was only 10 steps away from his own front door. The primary suspect: Frederick J. Tenuto, who had been along with Sutton for both his Eastern State breakout attempt and the Holmesburg escape.

(Bettmann/CORBIS)

*Curtain call: Willie "the Actor" Sutton, after his arrest in February 1952. "Do I look like a bank robber to you?" Sutton asked his arresting officers.*

Nevertheless, Sutton insisted that he had nothing to do with Shuster's murder. There was good reason to believe him; he had never so much as laid a finger on bank employees during any of his heists. Then again, there was that tricky matter of the Sutton-Tenuto connection. A loyal criminal buddy might have felt it a matter of honor to ice Shuster—and an opportunity to make a little cash from the Anastasia contract. It was a dead-end proposition for Tenuto either way; he was later believed to be gunned down by fellow mobsters, who thought that killing a civilian betrayed their own code of ethics. His body has never been found.

Willie Sutton was sentenced to 30 years in prison, and there would be no more escapes—the kind that required a shovel or ladder, anyway. Sutton, suffering from emphysema and clogged leg arteries, was shown mercy and released from Attica on Christmas Eve 1969. A year later, he was paid to appear in a TV commercial promoting the New Britain, Connecticut, Bank and Trust Company's credit cards, and later wrote the more candid of his two biographies, 1976's *Where the Money Was*. (The first one, *I, Willie Sutton*, was co-written by Quentin Reynolds and published in 1953.) The Actor took his final bow in Spring Hill, Florida, on November 2, 1980.

## Cool Fact from the Vault

Open a medical textbook, and there's a good chance you'll find "Sutton's Law," which was inspired by the bank robber. In short, it means that it's never a bad idea to look at the simplest answer when diagnosing a patient. The term originated with a doctor from Yale who used the alleged Sutton quip—"Because that's where the money is"— with medical interns who were overlooking the obvious.

## BIG WILLIE STYLE

The following are the costume and makeup techniques of Willie Sutton. Kids, don't try these at home—or in your local bank branch, for that matter.

1. **Put a cork in it.** You can change the appearance of your nose without going to an expensive Long Island plastic surgeon. Simply take a piece of cork, hollow it out until you have a ring

shape, then stick it up your schnoz. Sutton had a whole set of different cork shapes, so that he'd have a different nose shape for each bank job.

2. **Do your hair.** For each different heist, Sutton would dye his hair a different color. He would also use fake moustaches, some grown, some false. "If I really wanted to look distinguished," wrote Sutton, "I'd grow a Vandyke." As for eyebrows, Sutton used to give them false heft by intertwining separate strands of hair. "Also my eyelids," he added.

3. **Accent your language.** Sutton would also fake the slightest bit of foreign accent and change it up from job to job. "Never anything really conspicuous," wrote Sutton, "just enough to give the victims something to focus on."

4. **Become the role.** The key to any successful impersonation, of course, is mentally becoming your subject. Sutton did this to perfection. Once, while disguised as a cop in Philadelphia, a police captain drove by and chastised him for having a button loose on his uniform collar. Sutton felt horrible—but not because he was impersonating a cop and about to rob a bank. No, he felt as if he'd neglected his duty as Philadelphia police officer. "I was a very conscientious cop," Sutton wrote, "right up to the time I stopped being a cop and started being a thief."

# 26  WILLIAM LIEBSCHER JR.

**Number of banks robbed:** 14

**Estimated lifetime take:** $28,455

**Claim to fame:** Liebscher sold used cars, lived in the suburbs, acted in local theater productions, and robbed banks

## "BE CALM AND I WON'T SHOOT. GIVE ME YOUR TWENTIES, TENS, AND FIVES."

They might have called Willie Sutton "the Actor," but William Liebscher was the real thing: an amateur in his local community theater. He was also a used-car salesman who lived with his wife, Jan, in a swank suburb in Marion County, California.

In the mid-1950s, however, the suburban dream wasn't quite what Liebscher had hoped for. His debts were piling up, and sales at the car dealership were sluggish. To supplement his income, Liebscher decided to use his acting techniques to rob banks. He used makeup to draw crows' feet, worry lines, and a moustache on his face, then took a prop pistol and wrapped it in a cloth. He also prepared a printed note so there was no chance that he would bungle his lines. The note which he used in all of his stick-ups, read: "Be calm and I won't shoot. Give me your twenties, tens, and fives."

Liebscher debuted on February 3, 1956, and his one-man bank-robbing show ran for 18 boffo months at banks up and down the California coast: San Francisco, Napa City, Fairfield, and Daly City. His box office receipts weren't spectacular—anywhere from $700 to $2,500 per performance. But he was a definite crowd pleaser: Not one teller could resist Liebscher's skillful impression of an aging, violent bank robber.

However, the curtains were destined to fall. During one robbery in Daly City on July 18, 1956, Liebscher forgot to take back his trademark demand note, and FBI agents eventually used it, along with a fragment of a license plate one witness happened to catch, to trace the actor back to his dealership a year later. Jay Robert Nash described Liebscher's capture in *Bloodletters and Badmen*. When approached, the 39-year-old used-car salesman didn't try to lie or run for it. He simply said: "I'm sorry, gentlemen, for all the trouble I've caused you."

According to Nash, Liebscher was given his one phone call upon arrest and decided to let his wife know what he'd been up to. "I won't be home for a long time," he told Jan, who had just put a roast in the oven. "I'm in trouble. I'm with the FBI. I hate to tell you this, but I've been robbing banks for a year and a half." Later, FBI agents stopped by the Liebscher home to pick up his toothbrush and razor.

Liebscher received 15 years in prison and promised the judge he'd never launch a revival act.

## Cool Fact from the Vault

Liebscher was also known as the "Friday Afternoon Bandit," because he always hit banks on Fridays just before closing time.

# 27  BOBBY WILCOXSON AND AL NUSSBAUM

**Nicknames:** Wilcoxson was also known as "One-Eye"; Nussbaum liked to be called "Bumpy"

**Number of banks robbed:** 8

**Estimated lifetime take:** $236,253

**Claim to fame:** Wilcoxson was famous for keeping his remaining eye—he lost the other one as a child—squarely on the money. His partner, Nussbaum, armed himself with hand grenades and anti-tank guns and routinely taunted J. Edgar Hoover by mail.

## "YOU DUMMY—YOU HAVE ALL OF THESE COLLEGE-EDUCATED AGENTS. WHY CAN'T YOU CATCH ME?"

Like so many great crime teams, Bobby Wilcoxson and Al Nussbaum met in prison—the federal reformatory in Chillicothe, Ohio, to be exact. Wilcoxson was serving a hitch for buying a car with a rubber check and then driving it across state lines; Nussbaum was in for possessing and transporting a Thompson machine gun.

The future partners couldn't have been more different. Wilcoxson was a tough, leathery thug who could barely read and had a glass right eye thanks to a childhood accident. Nussbaum was a bookworm who loved biographies and novels about bank robberies, as well as chemistry, firearms, and explosives textbooks. Wilcoxson liked betting on the ponies and flashing greenbacks at the track; Nussbaum was a master chess player who entered a correspondence tournament while in prison. God knows how the two hit it off at Chillicothe, but they did, and agreed to go into business together upon their release. The business? The one Nussbaum loved reading about.

In mid-September 1960, the two met up at Nussbaum's Buffalo home to plot their first jobs. The first order of business was funding: Nussbaum told Wilcoxson it was important to have seed money to buy guns and rent cars so they could outshoot and outrun any pursuing cops. A few local burglaries later, the pair had enough of an operating budget to take their first bank.

Wilcoxson and Nussbaum, Inc., made its debut on December 5, 1960. The duo stormed into the First Federal Savings and Loan Association in Schiller Park, New York, with a handgun and a sawed-off shotgun. Nussbaum had the pistol and wore a gauze mask. Wilcoxson didn't bother with a disguise, and one witness later told the police that one of the gunmen had "something unusual about his right eye—it didn't focus." Wilcoxson and Nussbaum fled in a rented car with $18,979. On January 12, 1961, they struck again, this time at the Manufacturers' and Traders' Trust Company in Buffalo. Another witness commented on Wilcoxson's bum eye. The take: $87,288.

Then—precisely according to Nussbaum's plan—the partners separated, each of them setting up legitimate businesses with their ill-gotten gains. For Wilcoxson, that meant buying a stake in a jewelry store, lettuce farm, and car dealership in Florida. For the gun-loving Nussbaum, it meant opening up a weapons shop in Buffalo.

Nussbaum wouldn't demonstrate his true bank-robbing genius until the following summer. In June 1961, the citizens of Washington, D.C., were besieged by a mad bomber who had been blasting city trash cans and mailboxes at random. Phone calls from a rabid white supremacist promised more explosions. Little did anyone know that the white supremacist was Nussbaum and that the threats were merely meant to distract police from the real target: a bank. On June 30, while police were busy with a bomb found in an office building, Nussbaum and Wilcoxson raided the Bank of Commerce and stole $19,862.

Weeks later, Nussbaum and Wilcoxson hit the Trust Company in Rochester, New York, after an armored car made a delivery of fresh cash. The two walked away with $57,197—somehow missing an additional $81,700 that was sitting behind a counter, already bagged. Meanwhile, an acquaintance from Chillicothe named Peter C. Curry had been released and put out the word that he was looking for work. Wilcoxson and Nussbaum welcomed Curry into the fold and prepared for their next knockover.

In mid-December 1962, Wilcoxson walked into the Lafayette National Bank in Brooklyn and joked to 53-year-old guard Henry Kraus that he was going to rob it. Kraus laughed. Wilcoxson then asked Kraus what he would do if someone *did* hold up the bank. Kraus's laughter died down, and he told Wilcoxson that if someone tried to knock over the bank, then he guess he'd have to shoot it out.

Kraus should have given a different answer. Two weeks later, on December 15, Wilcoxson and Curry stormed the Lafayette National, while Nussbaum sat outside in the getaway car. Curry leaped over the four-foot guard rail and shouted, "Everyone get down! Flat on the floor!" When Henry Kraus reached for his revolver—just like he said he would—Wilcoxson sprayed him with submachine gun fire. Kraus got four bullets in the chest and only had time to cry "Oh!" before slumping to the floor.

"Don't move or I'll kill you!" shouted Curry, who started scooping packs of money into his canvas bag. At each cage, he would stop to press his revolver to the head of each employee and repeat: "Don't move, or you'll get what the guard got!"

In the confusion, three customers managed to slip out of the bank. They summoned the first cop they saw—foot patrolman Salvatore Accardi. Nussbaum, outside in the getaway car, saw the cop approaching and calmly spoke into a radio unit, which carried his words to a receiver in Wilcoxson's ear. The machine gunner spun around to see Accardi outside the bank doors, drawing his .38 service revolver. Wilcoxson blasted away through glass, and the bullets grazed Accardi's leg.

The cop fell to his knees, yet somehow kept his wits together and returned fire. But Accardi's .38 slugs couldn't penetrate the glass. Wilcoxson's submachine gun had no such problem. His bullets shattered the remaining glass and forced the cop back onto the sidewalk, knocking him out. Miraculously, the only bullet that hit the cop found his badge, saving him from death. One minute later, Nussbaum peeled away with Wilcoxson, Curry, and a sweet $32,763 score.

But the Lafayette heist was the turning point for the mad genius and the brutal killer. Their getaway car was quickly discovered, as was the submachine gun used to kill Kraus. A trace of the serial numbers led FBI agents to Nussbaum's gun shop in Buffalo. When the FBI raided the joint, they didn't find their suspect, but they did find a large collection of machine guns with matching clips and magazines, 60 hand grenades, bulletproof vests, 14 automatic pistols, two Lahti antitank guns, and thousands upon thousands of rounds of ammunition. Making matters worse, one-time partner Pete Curry was captured by agents the day before Valentine's Day 1962 and immediately began to fink on his ex-partners.

In June, Wilcoxson and Nussbaum robbed a Philadelphia savings and loan but only netted $160. Next was a Pittsburgh bank that offered a bigger take—$4,373—but again, Nussbaum and Wilcoxson somehow missed over $10,000 sitting in the bank. The following month, their faces were all over *Reader's Digest* in a feature article suggested by J. Edgar Hoover himself. The previous year, an FBI Ten Most Wanted fugitive named Joseph Corbett had been captured thanks to eagle-eyed *Digest* readers, and Hoover thought lightning might strike twice with Wilcoxson and Nussbaum. The magazine even offered a $10,000 reward for information leading to their arrest.

The heat was starting to burn away the partnership. Nussbaum and Wilcoxson agreed to pull the proverbial "last job" together: the September 19, 1962, robbery of a Pennsylvania bank. But Nussbaum insisted on driving the getaway car, and nothing more. Wilcoxson couldn't believe it. After cracking the bank and bagging $28,901, Wilcoxson handed Nussbaum a paltry $500. "Your cut for driving," Wilcoxson explained. Nussbaum was furious beyond words and stormed away. Alone and on the run, Nussbaum—most likely in reaction to the *Reader's Digest* feature—sent taunting letters to J. Edgar

Hoover. Retired FBI agent Andrew Soltys paraphrased Nussbaum's letters to a reporter from APB News Online: "You dummy—you have all of these college-educated agents. Why can't you catch me?"

But those college-educated agents would catch Nussbaum, with help from the bank robber's own wife. Alicia Nussbaum was staying with her parents when her husband called her, desperate to see her and their 19-month-old daughter. When Alicia told her mother about it, Mrs. Macjchorowicz called the feds. They set up an early morning sting at the Statler Hilton Hotel in downtown Buffalo, New York. On November 4, 1962, Nussbaum pulled up in his light-blue 1962 Chevy sedan. Alicia waved from the front doors. It was a signal. Thirty unmarked cars full of FBI agents and Buffalo cops sprung into action.

Nussbaum saw what was happening, hammered the gas pedal, and squealed away. The law offered pursuit, but Nussbaum knew his hometown streets cold and was able to negotiate tight turns at 100 mph. No one could get a clear shot at his tires. About two miles away from the hotel, a K-9 cop heard the sirens and steered his dog wagon out into the middle of the street to see what was going on. Nussbaum's Chevy smacked into the wagon but still managed to squeeze past. A few blocks later, Nussbaum swerved to the side of the road, turned off the ignition, then flattened himself to the bottom of the car. He was hoping that the G-men would zoom right by and miss him.

They didn't. Seconds later, Nussbaum looked up and found himself staring down the barrel of an agent's rifle.

The arresting officers found two live hand grenades in the bank robber's jacket pockets and a .22 caliber rifle on the back seat. While Nussbaum declined to shoot it out—that was more Wilcoxson's style, anyway—he did swallow a handful of Seconal tablets in an attempt at suicide. The FBI rushed Nussbaum to nearby Columbus Hospital to have his stomach pumped. Afterward, Nussbaum remained silent, especially when asked about the whereabouts of his partner.

Ultimately, it didn't matter. Five days later, FBI agents surrounded Wilcoxson's hideout in Baltimore, waiting until he emerged from the house with his girlfriend Jacqueline Rose and carrying Rose's infant son, Kenny. Wilcoxson surrendered peacefully. The man that *Reader's Digest* had dubbed "The Most Wanted Criminal Since Dillinger" was in custody. Wilcoxson and Curry, with the blood of guard Henry Kraus on their hands, were sentenced to life in prison. Nussbaum received 40 years for his multiple bank robberies.

Years later, after winning parole, Nussbaum would find a legitimate outlet for his intellectual curiosity and love of planning capers: He became a mystery novelist. Nussbaum's works include *Gypsy* and *How to Be Sneaky, Underhanded, Vile and Contemptible for Fun and Profit*, along with dozens of short stories that appeared in digests such as *Alfred Hitchcock's Mystery Magazine*. Nussbaum died in 1995 after a lengthy illness, but his fiction lives on the Internet. You can sample one of his short stories, "Collision," at Lady M's Mystery International website (www.mysteryinternational.com/manscrpts/AN/An1.htm).

## Cool Fact from the Vault

In July, 1962, writer Dan J. Marlowe opened up a fan letter from a guy named Carl Fischer who praised Marlowe's novel, *The Name of the Game Is Death*. The book was about Earl Drake, an unrepentant bank robber who struggles to survive after a heist goes wrong. Fischer said he loved the book, and asked Marlowe how he learned key pieces of information. Marlowe answered the letter, spelling out some of his research techniques. Four months later, on November 6, two FBI agents showed up on Marlowe's doorstep, wanting to know more about this "Carl Fischer." As it turns out, Fischer was Al Nussbaum.

# 28 PATTY HEARST

**Accomplices:** The Symbionese Liberation Army, including Donald DeFreeze, Bill and Emily Harris

**Number of banks robbed:** 1

**Estimated lifetime take:** $10,900

**Claim to fame:** Hearst was the heiress who says she was brainwashed into packing a submachine gun and knocking over a bank. She went by the name "Tania."

## "IT'S A HOLD-UP! DOWN ON THE FLOOR! ON YOUR FACES, YOU MOTHERF......!"

One of the weirdest heists in bank-robbing history went down at 9:40 A.M. on April 15, 1974. Four white women and one black man stormed into the Hibernia Bank at 1450 Noriega Street in San Francisco, holding automatic weapons and shouting: "It's a hold-up! Down on the floor! On your faces, you motherf......!" The entire hold-up took no more than four minutes, but it left bullets in two innocent bank customers, and left the Hibernia Bank $10,900 short. A female hold-up gang was surprising enough, but police got an even bigger surprise when they rolled back the surveillance camera tape. One of the women was Patricia Campbell Hearst, the publishing heiress who had been kidnapped two months earlier.

To fully appreciate the shock value of the bank robbery, you have to go back to February 4, 1974, when Patty Hearst was kidnapped from the Berkeley apartment she shared with fiancé Stephen Weed. Two men forced their way in, sprayed cyanide-tipped bullets everywhere, and severely beat Weed. "They knock on the door, and the next thing I know, there is a kidnapping," Hearst recalled on *Larry King Live*. "People are being beat up, and you know, gunshots." The kidnappers stuffed Hearst into their trunk, then fired automatic weapons in the air to discourage any rescue attempts and sped off into the night. There was no bigger story in early 1974 than the Hearst kidnapping. (Imagine the headlines today if someone grabbed Ivanka Trump or Paris Hilton.) Her abductors took full advantage of that fact.

The kidnappers soon revealed themselves to be the radical leftist "Symbionese Liberation Army." Don't bother looking for "Symbionia" on a map—it's not a country. The word comes from *symbiosis* and refers to different organisms living together in peace and harmony. The group's alleged goal: Incite a revolution of poor people to overthrow their capitalist pig rulers. The SLA proclaimed that if Hearst's parents ever wanted to see her alive again, they had to give millions of dollars worth of food directly to the poorest people in California. The Hearsts did dole out $2 million worth of food, but part of it was stolen by greedy profiteers and never ended up in the hands of the people who needed it.

Next, the SLA released a videotape of Patty Hearst in which she was dressed in military gear and holding a submachine gun. Behind her was the evil emblem of the SLA: a seven-headed cobra. It was a surreal moment, made more surreal when Hearst claimed to be a willing member of the SLA. "I have been given the choice of one, being released in a safe area, or two, joining forces of the Symbionese Liberation Army and fighting for my freedom and the freedom of all oppressed people. I have chosen to stay and fight." She also renounced her birth name and now wanted to be known as "Tania."

That was the last anyone heard from Patty Hearst until the Hibernia robbery, during which security cameras clearly showed her pointing her submachine gun at customers and barking angry commands. The images, broadcast on the nightly news, shocked Americans everywhere.

The robbery itself was no surprise; revolutionary groups had been knocking over banks since the late 1960s and would continue to do so until the early 1980s—including the infamous 1981 "Big Dance" armored-car heist masterminded by Mulutu Shakur and the Black Liberation Army. The surprise was Patty Hearst herself. Had she been mesmerized by the SLA and unable to control her actions? Or had she truly gone over to the dark side and become an active, violent participant in the heist, as some eyewitnesses claimed?

Forty-eight hours after the Hibernia robbery, another communication came in from the SLA. It was a tape of Hearst, claiming that she was fully aware of what she was doing in the bank. "My gun was loaded," she said, "and at no time did any of my comrades intentionally point their guns at me. As for being brainwashed, the idea is ridiculous to the point of being beyond belief. I am a soldier of the people's army."

A month later, it looked as if Hearst had indeed gone SLA all the way. On May 16, she laid down a fusillade of submachine gun fire to help SLA members Bill and Emily Harris escape custody in a sporting goods store after Bill was caught shoplifting tube socks. The van peeled away, but a parking ticket left behind led the FBI to the SLA hideout. In the battle that followed the next day, DeFreeze and six other SLA members died in a firestorm of flames and bullets. Meanwhile, Hearst and the Harrises—all that remained of the mighty SLA—fled to a motel near Disneyland and stayed on the lam for over a year, moving through New York, Pennsylvania, and finally California. Hearst was on hand for two more bank robberies, including one at a Crocker National Bank branch near Sacramento on April 21, 1975, which resulted in the shooting death of bank customer Myrna Opsahl. (Amazingly, the four SLA members thought responsible for the stick-up—not including Hearst—wouldn't be charged with this crime until early 2002. Why the delay? The forensic technology needed to tie the bullets to an SLA shotgun wasn't developed until just a few years ago.) The FBI finally cornered Hearst and the Harrises in San Francisco on September 18, 1975, and the nation waited for answers.

In some ways, the nation is still waiting. Some believe that Hearst cooked up a phony kidnapping in order to join the SLA and gain notoriety from the group. But Hearst maintains that she had been brainwashed during her captivity, the result of being locked in a closet for 57 days and repeatedly beaten, raped, and then deprived of all sensory input for hours upon end. As a result, she doesn't remember much about the Hibernia robbery. "I said my name, because I was supposed to say my name and make a speech, but it's all pretty unclear," Hearst told Larry King. "Then Donald DeFreeze shot someone, and then everything went blank. My next memory is sitting in the car leaving the bank."

Despite this, and famed lawyer F. Lee Bailey taking up Hearst's defense during the so-called "Trial of the Century" in early 1976, Hearst was found guilty of two counts of armed robbery and was given seven years in jail. She served two before President Jimmy Carter commuted her sentence in 1979. Two months after her release, Hearst married her bodyguard, Bernard Shaw. In 2000, President Bill Clinton gave her a full pardon.

Over the years, Hearst carved out an offbeat career for herself, co-writing a mystery novel about her own grandfather's California estate called *Murder at San Simeon* and appearing in four John Waters movies—*Cry Baby, Serial Mom, Pecker,* and *Cecil B. Demented.* In the last one, Hearst played the mother of an indie filmmaker who kidnaps a movie star and forces her to be in his underground flick. Maybe Patty Hearst wasn't kidding about the sensory deprivation, after all.

## Cool Fact from the Vault

In the late 1970s, Stephen King once started to write a *roman à clef* novel about the Patty Hearst story called *The House on Value Street.* "It seemed to me to be a highly potent subject," recalled King in *Danse Macabre,* "and it seemed to me that only a novel might really succeed in explaining all of the contradictions." But King abandoned *Value Street* in favor of his epic *The Stand,* whose main villain, Randall Flagg, was partly inspired by Donald DeFreeze.

# 29 STANLEY RIFKIN

**Number of banks robbed:** 1

**Estimated lifetime take:** $10.2 million

**Claim to fame:** Rifkin stole millions from Security Pacific Bank in Los Angeles—the first (and largest) electronic bank heist in American history

## "THIS IS MIKE HANSEN FROM INTERNATIONAL."

On October 25, 1978, a bank robber walked through the lobby of the Security Pacific National Bank in Los Angeles. He was wearing a three-piece suit and carrying a briefcase. The bank robber stepped into the elevator, rode up with a car full of bank employees, then calmly made his way to the wire transfer room. He approached a young man hunched over a computer at a corner cubicle.

"Hi there," the bank robber said. "I'm here to help out with your wire transfer problems. The Federal Reserve sent me."

The employee seemed glad to see the bank robber. He'd been hearing complaints about the system for days now and started ticking them off one by one. The bank robber nodded, scribbling the complaints on a notepad. When the employee turned his head, the bank robber took a quick glance at a series of numbers posted on the wall and scribbled those down, too.

The bank robber looked at his watch and explained that he'd better get going. It was 10 minutes until closing time. When employees would be in the biggest rush to get home. The bank robber left the room, found a pay phone downstairs, then dialed the number to the wire room. "This is Mike Hansen from International," he said. "International" meant Security Pacific's international division.

"Okay," replied the wire room clerk. "And the office number?"

"286."

"286. Okay. What's the code?"

"4739," the bank robber said.

There was silence for a few moments. "Okay."

The bank robber then ordered the clerk to send $10.2 million from the Irving Trust in New York City to the Wozchod Bank in Zurich, Switzerland. The clerk began the transaction but seemed to be having a problem. She transferred the bank robber to another clerk, a male. "Okay," the new clerk said. "What's the interoffice settlement number?"

As calmly as he could, the bank robber started to read off the nine-digit sequence he'd copied down minutes before. "10613 ..."

"I'm sorry," the clerk said. "We need a 109 or a 107 number."

The bank robber read the number again, wondering if he'd miscopied it. But still, no luck. The clerk helpfully told him to try back later when he had the right number and ask for "Lupe."

This was not good. The bank robber realized he must have copied down the wrong code for an international transfer of funds. His clammy hand hung the phone on the hook, then picked it up again. What the hell. He called the wire transfer room, asked for Lupe, and read the same code again—only this time substituting a "109" for the 106.

Amazingly, it worked. A few keystrokes later, the Security Pacific National Bank was robbed.

There were no silent alarms triggered, no frantic calls to the police or insurance companies. In fact, Security Pacific had no idea that they had been robbed until November 2, when the FBI told them they might want to check their books. The heist—the first of its kind—had been masterminded by Stanley Mark Rifkin, a 32-year-old short, doughy, balding computer consultant who once worked a consulting job for Security Pacific. Rifkin realized that while tangible assets were guarded by armed men and steel vaults, electronic assets were protected by only a few simple digits. Without so much as scribbling a demand note, Rifkin had managed to steal more money than the James Gang, John Dillinger, Bonnie and Clyde, and all the other depression-era heisters combined.

According to writers Marvin J. Wolf and Katherine Mader in *Fallen Angels: Chronicles of L.A. Crime and Mystery,* Rifkin first got the idea during his consulting gig at Security Pacific. He noticed that he could walk in and out of the wire transfer room all day without anyone raising an eyebrow. After the first day, he'd simply become part of the landscape. Why not capitalize on that? Rifkin told his best friend his idea, and the man—who happened to be an auditor for the Internal Revenue Service—laughed until his ribs hurt. Of course, the auditor thought Rifkin was messing around. Rifkin wasn't.

After the $10.2 million transfer went through, Rifkin took the elevator back down through the building and drove to the airport. Now it was time for his getaway plan, which he'd prepared weeks before: First, Rifkin had established a bogus identity as "Mike Hansen," complete with phony passport, driver's license, Social Security card and, most importantly, a bank account at Irving Trust Company in New York. But "Mike Hansen" couldn't show up at the bank and ask for his $10 million. So Rifkin had contacted a legit diamond broker to help arrange the purchase of 115,000 perfectly cut diamonds from Russia. All "Mike Hansen" needed to do was wire the $8,145,000 purchase price to a bank in Zurich.

At the airport, Rifkin hopped a plane to Switzerland, where he picked up his diamonds (five pounds worth), and smuggled them back into the United States, where he planned to sell them a few rocks at a time. But Rifkin, who had grown up a fat nerdy kid, was bursting at the seams. He needed to tell someone—*anyone*—about the audacious heist he'd pulled off. Rifkin thought about it and settled on his attorney, Gary Goodgame. Weren't lawyers bound to keep secrets through attorney-client privilege, or something?

Not this attorney, apparently. Goodgame marched straight to the FBI, who had a hard time believing the story until Goodgame produced three of the diamonds that Rifkin had given him as a present. The FBI went to Security Pacific, who also had a hard time believing the story. But when they checked their records, they were horrified to discover that Goodgame was right.

Word of the heist spread quick, and Rifkin—hiding out in a Rochester, New York, hotel room surrounded by bottles of champagne and chomping on a caviar omelet—saw himself on TV. He jumped around hotels in New York, then flew to San Diego to hole up at a friend's apartment. That's where the FBI finally nabbed him, after tracing his new address through a rented post office box.

*(Bettmann/CORBIS)*

*Collect call: Stanley Rifkin in the custody of U.S. Marshals after stealing $10.2 million from a bank using only a telephone.*

The FBI's case, however, was flawed thanks to a technicality: Someone forgot to include Goodgame's name on the warrant. While Rifkin's attorney started the legal wrangling, Rifkin started planning his next transfer theft. Once free on $200,000 bail, Rifkin immediately made contact with a shifty banker named Joe McAfee who he'd heard had been looking for someone to help plan a wire heist. But Joe McAfee was the alias of FBI agent Joseph Sheehan, who helped make the tape of their meeting. Flawed case or not, the FBI had Stanley Rifkin by the mainframe.

Rifkin agreed to plead guilty to two of the original four charges and was given eight years in prison. He was out after serving only three and a half years and later would land computer consulting jobs to help companies prevent guys like him from stealing money electronically.

And Security Pacific? They were only able to recover $6.4 million of their money after selling the diamonds at auction. (The diamonds, having been in Rifkin's beefy paws for days on end, were seen as slightly flawed.) And from that point on, there were no telephone transfers of money. Computers would handle that function.

Which, of course, set the stage for a new kind of bank robber.

## Cool Fact from the Vault

On Mother's Day 1980, a California department store offered a special sale of jewelry made from the Rifkin-purchased diamonds. (Because nothing says "I love you, Mom" like a piece of booty from an international electronic bank heist/Russian diamond caper.)

# 30  THE COPS WHO WERE ROBBERS

**Gang members:** Gerald W. Clemente, Thomas K. Doherty, Joseph P. Bangs (the cops), Kenneth Holmes, Francis X. O'Leary, and Arthur "Bucky" Barrett (the robbers)

**Number of banks robbed:** 1

**Estimated lifetime take:** $1.5 million, not to mention $18 million in jewelry

**Claim to fame:** The six men who knocked over a Medford, Massachusetts, bank were different from all heist gangs that had come before: Three of them were police officers

## "DON'T PUT YOUR MONEY IN THE BANK NO MORE, LITTLE GIRL. PUT IT UNDER YOUR PILLOW."

Some bank robbers like to justify their line of work by claiming that they're not stealing innocent people's money; banks and their insurance companies are the ones that take it on the chin.

But that wasn't the case on Memorial Day weekend 1980, when the Depositors' Trust Bank in Medford, Massachusetts, was robbed of $1.5 million in cash and an estimated $18 million in jewels. The loot didn't come from the bank vault. It came from 714 safety deposit boxes, which, unlike savings and checking accounts, aren't federally insured. "I had $5,150 in there," one elderly depositor told the *Boston Globe* days after the heist. "I've had two heart attacks and can't get insurance, so $2,550 of it was in cash like an insurance policy to pay for my burial." Some lost their life savings. One woman lost her priceless collection of Russian spoons dating back to the czars. Another woman said she lost $50,000. As she stood in line to make her claim to the bank, she heard another depositor telling her six-year-old daughter: "Don't put your money in the bank no more, little girl. Put it under your pillow."

To make matters worse, it eventually was revealed that three of the six men responsible for the Depositors' Trust job were police officers.

The heist—the largest in Massachusetts history—started the Saturday of Memorial Day weekend. Six men slipped into Burns Optical and Hearing Aid Center, then proceeded to drill through four inches of concrete into the adjoining bank. The resulting hole was perfect: It was two feet wide and situated directly above the bank's vault. Then, the men used their quiet high-speed drills to cut down through the vault ceiling: 18 inches of concrete. All that remained were reinforced steel rods, which were melted away with an acetylene torch. No alarms sounded; the men had disabled the system by splicing the power supply to battery packs, thereby transferring the current without signaling police headquarters. The gang spent an estimated 12 hours in the vault, busting into and rooting through safe deposit boxes, taking what they wanted, abandoning objects they didn't— such as black pearls and silver dollars. By Monday night, the crew had taken their loot and ran.

The next morning, bank officials opened the vault and found the area "looking like something from a bombed-out German city," one official told a *Boston Magazine* reporter. They were left with the sorry task of informing their customers about what had happened.

But it wasn't only Ma and Pa Sixpack who got upset over the robbery: Half a dozen of the safe deposit boxes were owned by reputed organized crime figures. The *Boston Globe* reported that the stolen loot may have included up to $2.2 million in laundered mob money; the *Boston Herald American* reported that local gangsters knew the thieves responsible "and are upset because some of their friends [depositors] got hurt in the robbery." Did the heisters make the blunder of a lifetime, or did they know who they were hitting? And did they care?

At first, the police thought the Depositors' Trust job might have been the work of the Canada-based Kingston Gang. This team had been slipping into America to pull bank heists throughout the 1970s, and a wire used to short-circuit the alarm system was Canadian. Some even speculated that the perps might have been government spooks, who broke in for the sole purpose of gathering mob evidence.

But the truth turned out to be more shocking than either of those possibilities. One week after the break-in, two separate informants pointed the finger at two Boston-area cops: Gerald W. Clemente, a captain with the Metropolitan District Commission, and Thomas K. Doherty, a sergeant in the Medford Police Department.

Doherty denied it. "Someone," he said, "is looking to break my balls." But the evidence was damning. Doherty was an expert lock-smith and had kept his own box at Depositors' Trust for over a decade—plenty of time to case the joint. And on the night of Memorial Day, a local shopkeeper named John Boniface had to restrain his barking dog when he seemed to want to lunge in the direction of the Depositors' Trust. Five minutes later, a cop—Sgt. Doherty—showed up at the Boniface's ice-cream shop, asking questions. "He wanted to know who I was, what I was doing there, and how long I was going to be," Boniface told *Boston Magazine*. Only later did investigators realize that what made Boniface's dog go nuts was the high-pitched whine of a drill.

Once the media outed the two cops as suspects, an angry public started taking revenge. Clemente reported that people had started throwing rocks at his house, and Doherty had to change his phone number 16 times after receiving calls from people demanding their jewelry back.

Such treatment of public servants would have been tragic, except for the fact that both men were guilty. The truth wouldn't come out until October 16, 1984, when a crooked cop named Arthur Bangs came in from the cold and told the FBI that another dirty cop had been trying to kill him over cocaine money and a woman. That cop was Thomas K. Doherty. Soon, Bangs admitted his role in the Depositors' Trust heist back in 1980 and told FBI agents how it came together.

As it turns out, it was a relatively spontaneous heist, considering the magnitude of the theft. Bangs had originally enlisted some thugs—Francis X. O'Leary and Arthur "Bucky" Barrett—to rob a local television store. When Bangs told his superior and friend, Gerald Clemente, about the plan, Clemente instead suggested they team up to rob a bank. Enter Thomas Doherty, who had blueprints for the Depositors' Trust. The team was complete when Barrett told the men he knew an ace safecracker named Kenneth Holmes.

Bangs sang in the nick of time; the federal statute of limitations had run out, and the Massachusetts statute would be up in less than a year. After a 1986 trial, Clemente was given 30 to 40 years in state prison; Doherty received 18 to 20 on top of 18 to 20 he received for the attempted murder of Bangs. "I have prosecuted murder, rape, and other crimes, but until today I had never seen a situation where someone had perverted his sworn duty," said the First Assistant D.A. while prosecuting Clemente. "His idea of a night shift was a license to steal."

Clemente, who would write a book about the incident, *The Cops Are Robbers,* won parole in 1999. In Boston, dozens of people are still waiting for the return of their jewelry; most of it has never been recovered.

## Cool Fact from the Vault

At the optics shop next to the bank, cops found various candy-bar and Twinkie wrappers; the robbers had snacked on sweets as they drilled through to the bank. (An empty doughnut box would have been too obvious.)

# 31  THE BOYS

**Gang members:** David Lee Grandstaff, Douglas Wayne Brown, Douglas Bruce Fennimore, John Anthony Oliver

**Number of banks robbed:** More than 30

**Estimated lifetime take:** $12 million

**Claim to fame:** In 1981, Grandstaff and his crew stole $3.3 million from the Valley National Bank in Tucson, Arizona, which would remain the largest heist in U.S. history for over a decade

## "ALL RIGHT, DAVID GET ON UP OFF OF THERE AND DON'T DO ANYTHING STUPID. THIS IS A ROUTINE HOLD-UP. NOBODY HAS TO GET HURT."

The three men did the money dance in a motel room outside San Diego. Each would circle the tower of money and take turns snatching a packet of money, over and over again. When they began, the stack of greenbacks was 4 feet tall, 3 feet wide, 5 feet long, and approximately 350 pounds. When they were finished three hours later, the tower would be gone, and the individual takes securely packed into shoe boxes to be mailed out across the country.

The tower of money was the $3.3 million in cash stolen from the Valley National Bank in Tucson, Arizona. The alleged mastermind: David Grandstaff, a poor kid from Des Moines who grew up to lead some schoolyard buddies in some of the biggest heists in American history. Author Debra Weyermann, who profiled Grandstaff and his alleged exploits in *The Gang They Couldn't Catch*, writes that the gang often said "please," "thank you," and "yes, ma'am" during a hold-up, and even once returned a gun (unloaded, of course) to a bank guard after realizing it was a precious souvenir from World

War II. Weyermann asserts that the Boys were basically good blue-collar boys with decent values who were "left out of the party"—in other words, too poor to enjoy the middle-class life they so desperately wanted.

As Grandstaff grew up, petty crimes (cracking vending machines) gave way to adult offenses (sticking up gas stations and grocery stores), which led to prison terms, which instead of discouraging the budding bandit, gave him the contacts and info he needed to launch more sophisticated crimes. Two bank heists in the mid-1960s landed Grandstaff in the U.S. penitentiary at Leavenworth until 1975, but upon release he supposedly started right where he had left off: hooking up with buddies from Des Moines and robbing grocery stores, jewelry stores and, eventually, armored cars. In 1978, an armored car at a Coca-Cola plant yielded $300,000 alone. A 1980 jewelry store heist in Phoenix resulted in a $1.5 million retail take. A Mid-States' Bank in Denver gave up $100,000 in 1981.

But the Valley National job was definitely the Boys' greatest hit. Valley National wasn't your usual bank; it was basically a money warehouse, where stacks of unmarked bills sat waiting to be transported to various branches. Amazingly, there appeared to be very little security. Grandstaff had stumbled onto it one day, writes Weyermann in *The Gang They Couldn't Catch,* and after casing the building for three months, Grandstaff decided that it was time to strike. The three-man team—Grandstaff, along with Bruce Fennimore and Doug Brown—woke up at 3 A.M., assembled their weapons, wiped down the getaway vehicles, and applied Krazy Glue to their fingertips to avoid leaving any prints. But as they pulled up to the building at the corner of Broadway and Country Club, something spooked Fennimore, the driver. The heist was called off. Same thing happened the second time. And the third. And fourth. Fifth. Sixth ....

Finally, on April 22, 1981, their ninth time making a run at it, Grandstaff decided it was now or never. "This time, we go," he said, as they all climbed into the van.

Fennimore looked uneasy about that.

"I don't care if the Pope is having a parade," said Grandstaff. "We've got to get out of here."

The Boys had planned a simple Willie Sutton–style takeover: Keep employees under control at gunpoint until a manager arrives, force him to open the vault, and then make your escape. At Valley National, the first employee they subdued was a janitor, Charlie Virgil, who all of sudden found himself in the back of a van with a gun in his mouth. Two men in masks stared down at him. "Charlie," one of them said, "don't move or I'll blow your f...... brains out."

Virgil nodded.

"Now, Charlie," the man in the mask continued, "this is just a routine bank robbery. It's got nothin' to do with you. Do you understand?"

Virgil understood, and wondered how this stranger knew his name.

But the Boys knew all the necessary names: Virgil, the janitor, Bud Grainger, the depository manager, and David Harris, the assistant manager. They also knew how to talk to their hostages, according to Weyermann. "Listen to me, Charlie," the man in the mask said after they moved inside the depository. "We've been kicked in our asses all our lives, just like you. We ain't never had nothin', either. We ain't out to hurt nobody. We're just out to even things up a little bit. These bankers wouldn't never give you nothing but a boot in the ass anyway. Why should you risk your life for them?"

When depository manager Grainger showed up, he was similarly subdued at gunpoint, and with a disarming bit of personal info: "If you want Betty to have another birthday like she did last night, you'll do what I say," one of the men told him. Betty was Grainger's wife. Same thing happened to assistant manager Harris, who entered the building and found himself flung to the ground. "All right, David," one of the robbers said. "Get on up off of there and don't do anything stupid. This is a routine hold-up. Nobody has to get hurt."

Despite Grainger giving the robbers a hard time—at one point even faking a heart attack—Grandstaff and his partners loaded $3.3 million cash into the back of their van and drove away. Hours later, the Boys would gather at a motel near San Diego to get their first real look at the loot and move around it in a circle while dividing it up. But a month later, Fennimore, who had been so nervous about pulling the trigger on the Valley National job, suddenly became reckless with his money, and an informant ratted him out to the FBI, which in turn convinced Fennimore to rat out his partners. Grandstaff and Brown were arrested in Denver without a fight.

Grandstaff's case didn't go to trial until 1998, and when it did, the jury came back with a verdict of "not guilty." (The jury thought the FBI cut corners in pressing its case, hated Fennimore the snitch, and even considered the bankers from Valley National "unlikable.") Grandstaff served time for the 1980 Phoenix jewelry heist but, for all intent and purposes, got away scot-free for his alleged Valley National job. Much of the money has never been recovered.

Grandstaff never admitted his role in the Valley National job to anyone, including author Weyermann, even though the two had become close friends during the writing of her book. (It was her assertion, however, that Grandstaff was responsible.) When the book was published in 1994, Weyermann caught flack for romanticizing Grandstaff and his crimes. "I'm telling a story as it happened, and if people think he's romantic, well then, maybe he is," Weyermann told a reporter from the *Arizona Republic*. "We do have a history in this country of liking outlaws when they seem to be doing it for reasons other than murder and mayhem."

## Cool Fact from the Vault

After the Boys allegedly knocked over Valley National, some enterprising students from the University of Arizona printed up T-shirts that read "I Yanked Hank's Bank." The shirts were extremely popular.

## 32  DOUGHERTY AND CONNER

**Full names:** Joseph Dougherty, Terry Lee Conner

**Number of banks robbed:** At least 6

**Estimated lifetime take:** More than $1.5 million

**Claim to fame:** Dougherty and Conner perfected the sleepover bank heist

## "I DON'T WANT YOUR MONEY. I WANT THE BANK'S MONEY."

Raymond and Verona Deering had a car for sale in their driveway and were very happy when two men came knocking the night of June 30, 1986. Raymond and the men haggled for a while, at which point the two buyers pulled out .45 caliber pistols from their jackets and put a small submachine gun on a chair next to the dining-room table.

"Okay," blurted Thomas, the Deerings' 19-year-old son. "You can have the car."

But the two men, Joseph Dougherty and Terry Lee Conner, weren't in the market for new wheels.

"Sit down," Dougherty said.

Raymond Deering said, "I don't have any money."

"I don't want your money," Dougherty. "I want the bank's money."

At the time, Deering was assistant manager and assistant vice president at a 1st Independent Bank branch in Hazel Dell, Washington. Dougherty and Conner had perfected a novel way of knocking over banks: Hold a bank employee and his family hostage the night before, show up at the bank the next morning bright and early, and have their hostage open the vault for them. It had worked before—that past September, when the two held a Wisconsin bank manager hostage and helped themselves to $574,119 at his workplace the next day. (They forced their way into the manager's house with FBI badges, and when he asked to see ID, one of them said, "We're not here to display badges. We're here to rob banks.") And back in 1982, a similar hostage stunt worked in Oklahoma City, netting the duo $706,000.

That 1982 job ended badly for Conner. He was arrested and received a 25-year jail term. Dougherty kept up the good work, knocking over banks in Phoenix, Salt Lake City, and Reno before his own arrest. But you can't keep a successful partnership down for long. On June 19, 1985, the two found themselves on the same prisoner transport bus. Conner spit out a handcuff key he'd hidden in his mouth, followed by a razor blade. In a scene right out of *The Fugitive,* Conner used to key to free himself, then held the blade to a deputy U.S. Marshal, commandeered the transport bus and forced it to make an early stop. Dougherty and Conner stole their captors' badges, handcuffed them to a tree, and made their escape in a stolen truck. Later, they used their new badges to force their way into a house, where they helped themselves to new clothes.

The boys, who both sported matching tattoos of purple roses with green leaves on their upper arms, were back in business. They knocked over a St. Louis bank for $27,000 and soon after pulled the Wisconsin hostage job. Dougherty was named to the FBI's Ten Most Wanted List that following November. The FBI would have liked to have included his buddy Conner, but there weren't any other spots open at the time.

Dougherty, in fact, bragged to the Deerings about being a wanted man. "We can leave our prints everywhere, and within 20 minutes, they will know who we are." Interestingly, the Deerings came to sympathize with their captors, according to interviews with *The Oregonian* after the incident. "I felt sorry for them," said Thomas Deering. "They were unable to have a normal family life." Added Verona: "I told them they didn't seem like criminal types. They said they were victims of circumstances, and were just playing out roles."

Dougherty and Conner played their roles well. They suited up in business attire—over bulletproof vests—and forced Raymond Deering to open the vault at 7:05 A.M. and took $225,000. The Deerings, along with six other bank employees, were locked in a storage room as their captors made their escape.

One week after the crime duo forced the Deering family to help them rob the Hazel Dell, Washington, bank, Conner finally earned his own place on the FBI's Ten Most Wanted. The FBI focused part of their search on Chicago, where Conner was believed to have friends and family—and, word had it, a big bank caper was in the works, involving hostages and explosives. An anonymous phone tip directed agents to a Red Roof Inn in suburban Arlington Heights, Illinois, and Conner was picked up after he left his room to find a cup of coffee. He surrendered without a fight. At the time, G-men and U.S. Marshals thought his partner in crime might be nearby. "They work together, but stay apart when planning to rob a bank," FBI spokesman Robert Long told the *Chicago Tribune*. Conner received life in prison for his crimes.

Ten days after Conner's capture, Dougherty was trapped by the FBI and U.S. Marshals after they started trailing one of his prison friends, Robert Butcher, and captured him as they met in a Laundromat in Antioch, California—possibly to plan another caper. More jail time was piled on Dougherty, who told a judge that he already had enough time to last until his 193rd birthday.

## Cool Fact from the Vault

In 2000, Dougherty and Conner would receive a doff of the hat from mega–best-selling author James Patterson in his novel *Roses Are Red,* which pits his series detective, Alex Cross, against a mad bank robber dubbed "the Mastermind." In one scene, Cross and some FBI agents are comparing the Mastermind's exploits with those of Dougherty and Conner. "There's a big difference, though," says one agent. "Dougherty and Conner never hurt a soul in any of the robberies. They weren't killers like the scum we're dealing with now."

# 33 PATRICK "PADDY" MITCHELL

**Accomplices:** Lionel Wright, Stephen Reid, Cecil Kinkaid, and Johnny Stuart

**Number of banks robbed:** More than 50

**Estimated lifetime take:** $12 million

**Claim to fame:** The Stopwatch Gang could rob a bank in five minutes or less—or your money back

## "THIS BANK, MY SISTER COULD HAVE ROBBED."

Patrick "Paddy" Mitchell's last heist on February 22, 1994, wasn't the score of a lifetime—the one he always hoped would be enough to let him and his buddies retire. It was just another random job: a small bank in sleepy Southaven, Mississippi, a suburb of Memphis. "This bank, my sister could have robbed," Mitchell told a reporter from the Associated Press. "It was an easy, easy bank. There was nothing to it, but I was too much in a hurry."

Mitchell was in a hurry because he had been featured on *America's Most Wanted*, and figured he'd better strike and split quick. So for the Southaven heist, Mitchell fell back on an oldie-but-goodie ploy: Call City Hall and threaten to blow the place to kingdom come, wait for every black-and-white in the area to scramble to City Hall, then hit the bank and be out before the cops had time to respond. (Bank robber Al Nussbaum pioneered this stunt in the 1960s; see "Bobby Wilcoxson and Al Nussbaum.") But the Southaven police chief was wise to the trick. When the bomb threat was called in, the chief sent a car to every bank. "There are only nine banks in town," said Mitchell. "I was out in about 45 seconds. I scooped up the money bags and left, but the police were waiting."

Until then, Mitchell's so-called "Stopwatch Gang" was grade-A Hollywood caper movie material: They were cool, polite professionals who prided themselves on being in and out of a bank in less than two minutes. Not even the waitstaff at Applebee's works that fast. They also were fond of wearing masks of ex-presidents, and they never fired a single shot during any caper. "I've never even had a bullet in the chamber," said Mitchell, who in his prime bore a resemblance to actor Tom Selleck. Even his dogged pursuers fell for his charm. "There is a rare quality to him," said U.S. Marshal David Crews. "He has a certain kind of old-style integrity, a criminal ethic you don't see much these days." America hadn't seen such a gentleman robber since Willie Sutton. In fact, Mitchell's only crime against innocent civilians was inspiring the 1991 Keanu Reeves/Patrick Swayze stinker, *Point Break*.

Mitchell's professional, polite attitude paid off. Between 1974 and his arrest in 1994, Mitchell estimates that he and his associates robbed 40 banks, with a tally reaching into the millions. The team started small. After getting laid off from his job as a delivery man for Pure Spring Bottling in Ottawa, Ontario, in the early 1970s, Mitchell received a call from an old friend named Lionel Wright. It seems that Wright, who had a foolproof method for tampering with seals and boosting goods from the trucking company where he worked, needed help moving the merchandise. "I have never done another day's work since that night Lionel called me," says Mitchell today. "Over the next couple of years, we stole everything from the company but the kitchen sink. Come to think of it, we did steal a load of plumbing supplies and, if I remember correctly, there were some kitchen sinks included."

But Mitchell dreamed of a big score that would let him retire, and cooked up a $750,000 gold heist—six 65-pound gold bars—at the Ottawa International Airport. Along for the gig were Wright and Stephen Reid, a Canadian bank robber who had escaped prison the year before. It was indeed a score to retire on, but Mitchell and Wright were caught in 1976 and sentenced to 17 years in prison, but not for the gold heist. Instead, Mitchell was convicted of conspiring to import cocaine—a crime Mitchell insists he didn't commit. (He claims he took the fall for a buddy.)

Three years later, Mitchell started gasping and clutching at his chest. Prison guards figured he was having a heart attack. An ambulance was summoned, and two attendants strapped him to a stretcher and rushed him away to a hospital.

Only Mitchell never quite made it to the hospital. Three men, dressed in hospital masks and carrying pistols, were waiting outside the hospital to take Mitchell away. One of those men was Stephen Reid, who had busted out of prison himself. (The other two have never been positively identified.)

Mitchell and Reid crossed the border into the United States, met up with Lionel Right, and started robbing dozens of banks with carefully timed, precision operations. Thus was born the Stopwatch Gang, which earned the nickname after Mitchell's habit of timing every heist. Mitchell and the boys eventually had enough money to lay low in a gorgeous cedar-and-glass home in Sedona in the Arizona mountains, where they all posed as eccentric rock-concert staging experts. Even the local sheriff bought the act and made the Stopwatch Gang his bridge partners.

But in 1980, time ran out for Reid and Wright. They were caught at their hideout and charged with the gang's latest hit, a $283,000 bank heist in San Diego, and each sentenced to 20 years in prison. Mitchell was now on his own—and without a hideout. He moved operations to Florida and started all over again. In his yet-to-be-published memoir, *This Bank Robber's Life,* Mitchell details his lone-wolf years, a life of fine restaurants and romantic encounters sandwiched between expertly timed robberies. In 1982, Mitchell visited a Florida honky-tonk bar and met a teenaged girl named Janet Rush who claimed to be 21. That was okay; the 40-year-old Mitchell had claimed he was only 31. The two hit it off over white wine and expensive marijuana, and eventually Rush confided to Mitchell that her last boyfriend had been carted away by the FBI when it turned out that he was a bank robber.

"When I saw you come in," Janet said, "I knew you were different from those other hayseeds." Then she added, half-joking: "I hope you're not a bank robber!"

Mitchell assured her he was no such thing. The next morning, he kissed her goodbye, then drove 60 miles to Ocala, Florida, to case a bank. "In my business, it wasn't wise to live and work in the same town."

Mitchell and Rush moved in together, all without Rush knowing what her new boyfriend did for a living. "I would venture to say that I was probably the happiest, most content man on the planet," writes Mitchell. "I had the prettiest lady in town, the greatest sex in the universe, and we never had an argument or cross words." But three months later, she came home from work to find the man she knew as "Richard John Baird" sitting on their couch in handcuffs.

"Do you know this man?" asked the FBI agent, who strangely enough, had been on hand to arrest Rush's previous bank robber boyfriend.

"Yes, I know him," Rush said, horror building on her face. "Now what the hell is going on here?"

"What's going on here, Janet," continued the agent, "is that this man is an escaped convict who is also wanted for robbing a couple dozen banks between here and California. This man is Patrick 'Paddy' Mitchell."

"It's all a mistake, Janet," explained Mitchell. "I'll get this cleared up and be back in time to cook you dinner."

"Yeah, you'll be back in time to cook her dinner alright," said the FBI agent. "In about 20 years."

Mitchell was indeed sent back to prison, but it didn't take 20 years for him to become a free man again. He escaped from Arizona State prison on May 9, 1986, by sawing through steel bars and crawling through an air-conditioning duct with two other inmates. (The duct ran straight above the warden's office.) Mitchell began another impressive run, robbing more banks with the two men he'd helped break out of Arizona State—Cecil Kinkaid and Johnny Stuart. "I don't believe there is a bank in the world that can't be robbed," wrote Mitchell. "All banks are creatures of habit and time schedules. On a Fourth of July weekend, I can get as much as $150,000 to $200,000. If I miss the Fourth of July weekend and hit the following week the amount I get is 50 percent less. I know my business!"

But by 1990, Mitchell had been named to the FBI's Ten Most Wanted list, so he moved to the Philippines under the alias "Gary Wayne Weber." There he remarried, sired a son, and tried to live a normal life. The FBI nearly nabbed him in a 1993 raid; a relative of his new wife had snitched after seeing *America's Most Wanted,* and Mitchell escaped only hours before agents broke down his front door. He flew back to the United States. He was down to his last $12,000. Next came the ill-fated Southaven heist, and the end of line for Mitchell.

Today, 59-year-old Mitchell is serving a 30-year-sentence at Leavenworth, and is currently editing his autobiography. Is Mitchell sorry for his crimes? "I ain't going to bullshit you," wrote Mitchell. "If I have any [regrets], it's not for robbing banks and stealing their money. The worst thieves in the world are banks. Everybody knows that. You want to know the greatest thrill in the world? It's being back at an apartment after a successful job, counting the money."

## Cool Fact from the Vault

Mitchell's prison terms were good for him—at least in terms of physical health. When sent to jail in 1976, he took up running. When sent to Arizona State in 1983, he became a vegetarian. "I didn't care for what they were doling out there," wrote Mitchell. "Maybe burro or rattlesnake."

# 34  VLADIMIR LEVIN

**Online handle:** Vova

**Number of banks robbed:** 1

**Estimated lifetime take:** $10 million or $400,000, depending on how you look at it

**Claim to fame:** Levin pulled off the most audacious American cybercrime of the 1990s with a refurbished 286 laptop in Russia

## "THE LESSON FROM THE CITIBANK CASE IS THAT THIS IS THE TIP OF THE ICEBERG."

The first great electronic bank heist involved a Russian diamond dealer (see "Stanley Rifkin"). Sixteen years later, the first computer bank heist involved a 24-year-old Russian graduate student.

Vladimir Levin was a biochemistry grad student at Tekhnologichesky University in St. Petersburg, Russia, who somehow figured out how to hack into the Citibank computers using only a modem and laptop computer. In August 1994, Levin transferred some $10 million to bank accounts opened by accomplices in the United States, Israel, Finland, Sweden, Germany, the Netherlands, and Switzerland. The plan: Scoop up as much money from those accounts as possible before anyone noticed. The plan unraveled when some Citibank customers noticed money missing, and called the bank in a panic. One Levin accomplice had been minutes away from withdrawing $30,000 from a San Francisco Citibank branch when a frantic call came in from headquarters: Drop the cash—those funds had been illegally transferred. The woman was arrested, and she eventually named Levin as the mastermind. But by that point, about $400,000 had already been cashed out.

How did Levin pull it off? Details of the case remain sketchy to this day, and that's because Citibank—and other major American banks—would prefer you didn't know about these kind of robberies. "The lesson from the Citibank case is that this is the tip of the iceberg," said computer security specialist Peter Norman in an interview with National Public Radio. "It's very hard to assess how many cases are unreported, but if you just listen to the inside stories that you pick up over the years, there are an awful lot of them."

Nonetheless, Timothy O'Brien, a reporter who broke the story at *The Wall Street Journal* in 1995, did manage to piece together some of the heist details. Levin would use his computer at AO Saturn, a small company where he worked, to dial up Citibank and pretend to be a corporate customer. "He pretended at one point that he was Invest Capital, a company based in Buenos Aires, Argentina, because he knew the passwords that identified the user at that particular company," O'Brien told NPR. O'Brien also believed Levin had inside information from a mole at Citibank, something that the bank vehemently denies.

Levin—who reportedly used an old 286 machine to pull the heist—was later arrested in London. He fought extradition for over two years but to no avail: He was brought to the United States for trial, then given three years in jail and was ordered to pay Citibank $240,015. Since then, Levin has been immortalized on the web in various Hacker Halls of Fame.

## Cool Fact from the Vault

Levin claimed that one of his U.S.-hired attorneys was an undercover FBI agent.

# 35 "HOLLYWOOD" SCURLOCK

**Real name:** William Scott Scurlock

**Accomplices:** Steve Meyers, Mark Biggins

**Vital stats:** Died in 1996

**Number of banks robbed:** 18

**Estimated lifetime take:** $2.25 million

**Claim to fame:** This 1990s Seattle-area robber went from rank amateur to respected heisting genius in a few short years—that is, until one final, ill-fated bank job the day before Thanksgiving 1996

## "THIS IS MR. WALKER. I THINK THAT BANK ROBBER MIGHT BE HIDING IN MY CAMPER IN THE BACK YARD."

In the 1990s, there was no better place to rob banks than Seattle. The sudden cash influx from newly minted tech barons resulted in such an explosion of bank branches that you could throw a rock in any direction and hit either a bank or a Starbucks. Fate conspired to place Scott Scurlock in Seattle in 1991, the same year he saw both the Kevin Costner movie *Robin Hood: Prince of Thieves* and the Keanu Reeves film *Point Break* and decided that he wanted to be a bank robber.

Scurlock was a body-proud daredevil who sold a key component of crystal meth to drug dealers throughout Washington State. He grew rich, lived rich, and even built an elaborate tree house—75 feet in the air, resting on seven cedars, and complete with a fireplace, electricity, hot and cold water, and a working bathroom—on his secluded 20-acre property. Then in the late 1980s, one of Scurlock's main distributors got a bullet in the head, and it spooked Scurlock out of the drug trade.

But it didn't scare Scurlock away from his expensive tastes. Without his meth sales, he needed money, and in a hurry. After watching both *Point Break* and *Robin Hood,* Scurlock decided that bank robbery was the answer. Longtime friend Wendy Scofield told CBS News that it was simply the next step for the thrill-seeking Scurlock. "He always wanted to get that bit higher," Scofield said. "Treehouse high, adrenaline high, crystal meth high, bank robbery high."

Scurlock used pointers from *Point Break* for his first knockover on June 25, 1992. He and a loyal college buddy, Mark Biggins, donned rubber masks and stormed into the Seafirst Bank on Madison Avenue in Seattle. But it wasn't as easy as Keanu made it look. A getaway car they stole from a bank employee wouldn't start; Biggins had flooded the engine. They made their getaway on foot, down an alley, past snapping dogs and through a golf course. Somehow, they made it out. Biggins announced he was out of the bank-robbing business; that had been too close a call. Scurlock decided to continue alone.

Fate was on Scurlock's side; most amateur bank robbers are busted before they have a chance to practice the craft. But Scurlock stayed at large long enough to completely perfect his technique. By his second bank job, which also went down at the same Seafirst branch he'd already hit, Scurlock had begun to use disguises: pancake makeup, a wig, and a false putty chin. The get-ups and theatrical leaps over the bank counters would eventually earn Scurlock the nickname "Hollywood" from FBI agents. By the end of 1992, Scurlock would have robbed a total of six banks and netted over $70,000. Not bad for a half a year's work. And no one had a clue he was behind any of the robberies.

For his seventh heist, Scurlock had recruited another loyal friend, Steve Meyers, who had a very specific job to do: listen to a police scanner outside in the getaway car. If an alarm call went out, Meyers would radio in to Scurlock, who would promptly leave. Then the two would exchange the first getaway car for another. This technique would help the pair rob the Seafirst Bank branch at Hawthorne Hills twice—once for $98,500, the other time for $114,000—and hit the U.S. Bank in Olympia for $15,800. Scurlock also relied on inside information, which he received by paying people to work in banks for the sole purpose of learning which banks had electronic tracers on their money. "The banks that didn't carry tracers were the ones we robbed," recalled Meyers to CBS News. At the end of 1995, Scurlock and Meyers had stolen close to $1 million.

By this time, "Hollywood" had two very obsessed lawmen looking for him: Seattle detective Mike Magan and FBI agent Shawn Johnson. Both knew they were dealing with a pro—he left virtually no clues and seemed to know how to handle his weapons and control a crowd. Detective Magan climbed onto bank rooftops, hoping he'd stumble across a clue. Meanwhile, Agent Johnson studied Hollywood's patterns, and soon discovered that the frequency of heists depended upon the cash take of the previous heist. If Hollywood scored big, he could afford to take more time off. Johnson even calculated that Hollywood burned through $20,000 a month, and if his number crunching was correct, he would need more money by the end of January 1996—on January 25, to be exact.

On January 25, 1996, Scurlock, Meyers, and Biggins—who had returned to the fold—robbed a First Interstate Bank branch and drove away with $114,000. Sadly for Agent Johnson, he'd picked the wrong bank to stake out. "I heard alert tones go out—bank robbery, First Interstate Bank, Wedgewood, which was about two miles from my location," Johnson recalled to CBS News. "I raced up there and I heard the description, and I said, 'Hollywood.'" By mid-1996, two more banks would be knocked over, bringing Hollywood's grand total up to 17.

Looking for the next high, Scurlock soon came up with an elaborate bank-robbery scheme that would put the double bank heists of the past to shame. Hollywood wanted to rob not three, not four, but *five* Seattle banks, all in the same two-hour period. "We'd had the mobile base station set up to white out the police frequencies in Seattle," explained Meyers. But when some of Scurlock's informants told him that the FBI had urged every bank in Seattle to use electronic tracers, he was forced to shelve the idea.

In its place, Scurlock began planning his great last heist, one that would allow him and his buddies to retire. In planning the five-bank heist, Scurlock had learned that the Lake City Seafirst Branch was supposed to have $3 to $4 million on a certain date. Despite the risk of electronic tracers, Hollywood decided to give the project a green light. But clearly, apprehension and fear were preying on him. At a family gathering, Scurlock's niece ran back to her mother, Suzanne, and told her: "Uncle Scott's only going to live till he's 42."

"What?" asked Suzanne, stunned.

"Yeah, he just told me that."

Suzanne marched back into the living room to confront her brother. "Uncle Scott, what are you telling her?"

The day before Thanksgiving 1996, Scurlock and Biggins stormed the bank, while Meyers took up his usual position by the scanners in the van. At 5:41 P.M., Meyers intercepted a scratchy police transmission: "We're currently receiving a silent hold-up alarm." Meyers radioed Scurlock and told him the time was up.

The men made it out of the bank with over $1 million and climbed into Meyers's van. Meyers hammered the gas pedal to peel away from the scene before the first squad car arrived, but there was the tricky matter of those electronic tracers. Scurlock and Biggins combed through the cash like mad, looking for them. Meyers then made the mistake of not taking an easy turn out of Seattle and ended up in a preholiday traffic snarl. The clock was ticking. Meyers was sure the electronic tracers were going to get them all busted.

But Detective Mike Magan didn't need the tracers. He heard the initial radio report, sped to the scene, then started to comb likely escape routes in the area surrounding the bank. Soon, Magan came across a white van that looked suspicious. "You could see flashlights going back and forth, in and out of the van." With five patrol cars behind him, Magan decided to stop the van.

What happened next is a matter of debate; Magan insists Hollywood leveled an assault rifle at them, which prompted Magan and his men to open fire. Meyers, however, insists that the law fired first. Either way, in the ensuing gun battle, Meyers and Biggins were hit but still managed to return 37 rounds of fire. Someone jumped behind the wheel of the van and started it moving again. The cops followed. The van stopped around a corner, and there was another shootout, with Scurlock hopping out of the van long enough to blast three shotgun rounds at his pursuers. Then the van started moving again, this time much faster.

Too fast, as it turned out; the white van crashed into a house. When cops surrounded the van and popped it open, they found the stolen $1 million scattered throughout the interior, along with guns, flashlights, clothes, makeup, and pools of blood. They also found Meyers and Biggins, wounded and ready to surrender. But no Hollywood. An impromptu manhunt failed to uncover him. The bank robber had somehow disappeared. Detective Magan couldn't believe it. "They searched high, they searched low. They searched north, south, east and west, and they couldn't find him."

The next day, Thanksgiving, an elderly man a few blocks from the crash site called the police. "This is Mr. Walker," he said calmly. "I think that bank robber might be hiding in my camper in the back yard."

Within minutes, three cops had arrived at the scene. "Seattle Police. Come out," a sergeant yelled. "If there's anyone inside, come out now."

Nothing.

As a precaution, the sergeant sprayed two full cans of pepper mace into the 10-foot camper, but still nothing. Probably just the old couple's imagination.

Then a shotgun blast sounded.

The three cops opened fire, then ran for cover. The stand-off lasted four hours, with repeated calls to surrender, followed by nothing but silence. Finally, after another round of tear gas, the cops entered the camper and found Scurlock. He was already dead. In fact, that first shotgun blast had been Hollywood's exit, stage left.

## Cool Fact from the Vault

Scurlock was always doing crazy things for money. Once, a friend dared him to jump from an outdoor patio restaurant into a body of water for $20. Scurlock did it without a second thought.

# 36  THE NORTH HOLLYWOOD GUNMEN

**Gang members:** Larry Eugene Phillips and Emil Matasareanu

**Number of banks robbed:** 3

**Estimated lifetime take:** More than $1.3 million

**Claim to fame:** Phillips and Matasareanu engaged the LAPD in the bloodiest getaway-gone-wrong since the Daltons rode into Coffeyville

## "REQUESTING ASSISTANCE. WE HAVE A POSSIBLE 211 IN PROGRESS AT THE BANK OF AMERICA ON LAUREL CANYON NORTH OF KITTRIDGE. WE HAVE SHOTS FIRED."

In the 1995 crime thriller *Heat*, a team of bank robbers led by Robert DeNiro use machine guns to blast their way out of a bank and up a crowded L.A. street. Bullets smack and pop and snick against every physical surface. It's a loud, exciting, and ultraviolent piece of film-making. It also prompted critics to ridicule the movie for being too unrealistic, too over the top.

Almost two years later, it happened for real. And it was worse than anyone—even director Michael Mann—could have imagined. On Friday February 28, 1997, two body-armor–clad bandits held off over 100 Los Angeles police officers for close to an hour in North Hollywood, using a series of high-powered submachine guns and rifles, more than 11,000 bullets, and an unbreakable determination to escape. The North Hollywood gun battle made the shootout from *Heat* look like a third-grade spitball fight.

On that bloody day at 9:15 A.M., two guys in black ski masks walked into the Bank of America on Laurel Canyon Boulevard and immediately issued demands. "Everybody down!" one of them shouted. "Cover your eyes!" Thirty-two customers and ten employees did as they were told. One man, who couldn't keep his four-month-old baby quiet, felt a gun butt pound the back of his head.

Then the robbers opened fire with their AK-47s, obliterating the Plexiglas barrier between the lobby and the back of the bank. The vault area was laid open for the looting. This wasn't merely a stick-up; this was a commando raid.

Meanwhile, an alarm had been tripped, and police began to arrive and surround the bank. When the two ski-masked robbers emerged minutes later with a cart full of money, they saw cops everywhere. But that was okay. They had the superior firepower to deal with the situation. "They had full black gear, with belts and ammo around their waists," said an appliance-store manager who witnessed the battle. "These guys were ready for war."

"When I first saw them coming out of the bank," said one L.A. cop, "My first thought was, 'Wow, these are monsters.'"

One of the robbers opened fire, and the fight began. It was a lop-sided battle from the start. The police were forced to plunk away using only 9mm handguns, while the robbers were able to unleash hundreds of rounds from their AK-47s with the mere press of a finger. The police were further handicapped by trying to protect innocent bystanders, who were literally everywhere. The robbers didn't seem to care who got plugged—cops, civilians, animals, vehicles, whatever. "I was laying down in my car, and the next thing I know, a cop is telling me, 'Get out, get out,'" recalled Crystal Ransome in the L.A. *Times.* (Ransome had left the Bank of America and passed the robbers on their way in.) "A cop ran me across the street. He was holding his gun drawn the entire time."

The LAPD were so tragically outgunned that a squad of cops were forced to run to a nearby gun shop to beef up on more powerful weapons. The gunfire was so intense that one kiosk—which cops used as a makeshift shield—absorbed over 150 bullets alone. The shootout was so shocking that it closed nine elementary schools and the Hollywood Freeway in both directions, and kept neighborhood residents barred behind their doors with instructions to call 911 if they had to leave their home for some reason.

After nearly 40 minutes of blistering gunfire—the majority of it broadcast live from TV news choppers at the scene—the robbers made a run for it. One hopped behind the wheel of their getaway car and started a slow crawl forward, while the other walked calmly beside the car, taking shots at anything that moved. Then, the two decided to split up. One walked down Archwood Street, around the corner from the bank, while the other drove past him into a residential neighborhood.

The walking robber kept blasting away, then crouched down behind a fence. When he stood up again, he placed a handgun to his own head and pulled the trigger. His head jerked to one side, and he collapsed to the sidewalk. At nearly the exact same moment, police sharpshooters also fired head shots. It's still unclear which bullet—the LAPD's or the bandit's—did the trick. Either way, the result was the same: one robber down, one to go.

The second robber, still heavily armed, had sped down Archwood Street, but police managed to shoot out his tires. Undaunted, he then fired his pistol at the driver of an approaching truck, and the gambit worked: The driver ran for safety, leaving his truck behind. The robber then started to transfer money and weapons to the truck, intending to resume his getaway.

That's when three SWAT officers in a patrol car sped up, jumped out, and opened fire on the robber. He fired back, then ducked for cover. One officer dove to the ground and fired at the robber's legs beneath the car. The robber flipped forward, and the other officers pounced, pinning and handcuffing him. He died minutes later, face still pressed against the asphalt.

The assault on North Hollywood was over. In the end, 11 officers, 5 civilians, and 1 dog would be injured, but none fatally.

Beneath the ski masks were two guys named Larry Phillips, 26, and Emil Matasareanu, 30. Phillips, the man who died beside his getaway car, later emerged as the mastermind behind the robbery, a self-styled criminal genius who wanted to be able to drive fancy cars and spend "$100 bills by the handful," according to his half-brother. By all accounts, Matasareanu, the suicidal robber, was a not-so-bright henchman who did whatever Phillips told him, and was driven not so much by the glamorous life but a desire to get his mother, a Romanian immigrant, out of debt. Larry Phillips' half-brother maintains that Larry controlled Matasareanu like a puppet. "Larry didn't bring anybody into his inner circle unless he had a plan for him," he told *L.A. Times* reporters.

The Bank of America job wasn't their first. Later, Phillips and Matasareanu were linked to possibly five other heists, including two in May 1995, which netted the pair an estimated $1.3 million. It was also revealed that the pair had been pulled over for speeding in 1993, and a search of the car turned up automatic weapons, ammo, and cans of gasoline. Both were arrested for illegal possession, but served only four months.

## Cool Fact from the Vault

According his half-brother, Phillips's biggest heroes were the accused racketeer and inside trader Michael Milken and Don Corleone of *The Godfather* movies.

# 37 THE TRENCH COAT ROBBERS

**Gang members:** William A. Kirkpatrick and Ray Bowman

**Number of banks robbed:** 28

**Estimated lifetime take:** $8 million

**Claim to fame:** Kirkpatrick and Bowman pulled the single largest bank robbery in U.S. history

## "LOOK AT ALL THAT MONEY."

The elusive Trench Coat Robbers combined the subtle art of bank burglary with the over-the-top action of a daylight stick-up. They would wait until a bank had closed or until it was about to open, then pick the locks on the door and take the employees by surprise. This was something new. In the past, robbers might have nabbed bank employees on their way to work, or even kidnapped bank bigwigs the night before. But no one had ever thought to make their play when employees thought themselves safest: inside a locked bank.

That's what the staff at the Seafirst Bank branch in Lakewood, Washington, were probably thinking on Monday February 10, 1997. The front doors had been locked and the tellers were busy storing their cash for the night. Time to wrap up, go home, pop open a beer, and watch some TV.

But suddenly the front doors swung open, and in stormed two guys holding pistols and wearing beige trench coats, baseball caps, and dark sunglasses. The three employees were ushered to the vault, grilled about the technical details of the alarm system, then bound with plastic handcuffs and told to close their eyes.

"If you don't cooperate, you'll be coming with us," said the shorter of the two men to Seafirst employee Rachel Johnson. "If you do what you're told, you'll go home tonight." The taller guy kept a pistol trained on the employees, while the short one busied himself with picking the locks on a cash cart in the vault.

Up until this point, it had been a trademark Trench Coat Robbers heist—no violence, no alarms, no delays, no resistance. The job was so perfect, people kept tapping the Seafirst ATM outside without a clue that something was wrong inside. But when one of the robbers opened the main vault box, it soon became apparent that this was no ordinary heist. "Look at all that money," he said.

Inside the vault was the staggering sum of $4,461,681—largely money from other banks, businesses, and a nearby casino. When the Trench Coat Robbers loaded the loot into their sacks, they entered the history books, having robbed the largest amount of money from a single bank in U.S. history.

The Seafirst knockover prompted FBI agent David M. Tubbs to proclaim the Trench Coat Robbers "the most efficient bank robbery gangs in the FBI's history of investigating bank robberies." For 15 years, the two had confounded the hell out of the agency. No security cameras had managed to capture their images; no real clues were ever found at any of the 28 robbed banks. All the FBI knew was that the bandits were white, male, middle-aged ... and of course, had this weird thing for trench coats.

The two didn't perfect their routine overnight. In fact, during their first robbery—a September 3, 1982, stick-up of a rural Missouri bank—the bandits wore ski masks and coveralls. "It happened in the morning, around nine o'clock, shortly after we opened the door," recalled one female employee in the *Kansas City Star*. "Then this big guy came to the door and held a sawed-off shotgun at our heads. I just stared him in the eye. I thought, 'If you're going to shoot me, you're going to shoot me looking me in the eye.' He stood there for an eternity, then just turned and walked away." Meanwhile, his shorter partner had scooped up more than $30,000, and the two immediately fled.

"I've tried to forget about it," the employee said. "But I can still see that sawed-off shotgun at my head."

Their next robbery, at a bank in Spring Lake Park, Minnesota, in January 1983, didn't go that smoothly. The bandits entered the bank right after it closed for the night and immediately tried to control the employees by herding them into the bank vault. One of the tellers, however, was claustrophobic and freaked out. One of the robbers shot her in the torso, and continued the heist as planned. (The employee would recover from her wounds.)

For the next eight years, however, the Trench Coat Robbers' heists were carefully planned, nonviolent, and highly lucrative. "These guys were slick," said one Des Moines, Iowa, police officer after the bandits struck a bank on his home turf in November 1987. "This wasn't their first job. They've been around the block before." In November 1991, the bandits ran into a little trouble at a bank outside Las Vegas. A teller managed to trip a silent alarm, and soon after, three lemons popped up: cops. The Trench Coats grabbed a female teller for a hostage and then sped away in their getaway car. The police pursued and exchanged gunfire, at least two of their bullets smacking into the getaway vehicle. The Trench Coats responded by whipping out automatic rifles and blasting away at the cops. Bullets made Swiss cheese of the squad car, nearly clipped three innocent bystanders and even found their way into the walls of a nearby medical office building. Later, the police found the hostage, shaken but alive, along with a mask that one of the bandits had worn.

As the Trench Coats got older, they got better. Soon they learned how to pluck a bank from the vine when it was ripe, like the Portland, Oregon, bank in 1994 that had just received its weekly shipment. (The haul: $233,026.) Or the West Carrollton, Ohio, bank eight months later, which had just received its weekly fix. (The haul: $362,259.)

After the record-breaking Seafirst job in 1997, the FBI created a special task force dubbed "Trenchrob" to snare the two workmanlike robbers. But without any hard clues, all the task force could do was hope for them to goof up somewhere along the line. Little did they know that one of them already had, and a series of stupid mistakes soon after would do them in.

A year before, a Minnesota couple bought a house and paid in cash. The woman, however, picked a fight with the builder, who promptly reported the cash transaction to an IRS agent. The agent got curious. On paper, this couple—one Donald Wilson and Myra J. Penney—didn't seem to be able to afford such a lavish purchase. An investigation began.

Flash-forward to May 1997, three months after the Seafirst robbery. A Missouri storage company noticed that one of its customers hadn't paid his bill, so they sent someone to clean out the locker. Inside were guns and cash. The locker belonged to one Ray Bowman.

A few months later, Nebraska state trooper Chris Bigsby pulled over a guy who had been driving seven miles per hour over the speed limit. The car was a rental and being driven by 56-year-old William A. Kirkpatrick. Something seemed hinky to Trooper Bigby, so he called for a drug-sniffing dog. The car's trunk was popped, and inside sat four guns and $1.8 million in cash. Kirkpatrick was thrown into the slammer.

Kirkpatrick's girlfriend, Myra J. Penney, took $100,000 in cash and drove to Nebraska to bail him out. She should have never bothered. By the time she arrived, a judge already deemed the search of Kirkpatrick's car illegal, and weapons charges were dismissed. But when Penney showed up with the bail money, it turned out to have markings from the Seafirst robbery.

Penney was arrested and soon turned government stoolie. She talked about Kirkpatrick's partner "Ray" from Kansas City, but she didn't have a last name. That was okay. The FBI was already onto Ray Bowman after guns and cash were found in his storage locker. Soon, several million in stolen loot was recovered from all over the country—some in Bowman's home, some in safe deposit boxes in Utah, Colorado, Nebraska, Iowa, and Missouri, some even from friends, who had been entrusted with cash in trunks and suitcases. Kirkpatrick confessed to his crimes in March 1999, and he and his partner were sentenced to at least 35 years in prison for robbery, conspiracy, and money laundering.

There was a silver lining for the Trench Coats: 20 of their 28 robberies were so old, they were past the statute of limitations. Kirkpatrick and Bowman got those free.

### Cool Fact from the Vault
$4,461,681 million in cash weighs approximately 335 pounds.

# 38 THE AVERAGE JOE BANDIT

**Real name:** Daniel Schwarberg

**Number of banks robbed:** At least 17

**Estimated lifetime take:** $60,000

**Claim to fame:** "Average Joe" eluded capture for two years by simply being a nobody

## "THIS IS A ROBBERY. I HAVE A GUN. I WANT $5,000. LARGE BILLS OK."

His robberies were unspectacular, to say the least. No Dillinger-style cage-jumping, no tough-guy theatrics, no wild gunwaving. Instead, the man who one Kentucky FBI agent would call "the Average Joe Bandit" worked a bland but highly effective routine: He would walk into a small branch, wearing a baseball cap, glasses, and a nondescript windbreaker. Then the robber would pass the teller a computer-generated note that read, "This is a robbery. I have a gun. I want $5,000. Large bills OK."

When the teller handed over the money, the robber would take back the note, leaving no fingerprints, then exit the bank, driving away in a car without a license plate. The transaction was usually so quiet, no one else in the bank knew it was being robbed. The robber sometimes asked for $3,000, but never more than $5,000. It was a smart figure: Small enough for the teller to gather up without much fuss, and small enough to fit into the pockets of a windbreaker. He struck roughly every six weeks, as if tapping an ATM whenever he needed more greenbacks.

Bank security cameras had captured his image, so authorities knew exactly what the robber looked like. But that was the problem.

"It seems like everybody knows someone who looks like him," said Northern Kentucky FBI agent Doug Warner, who came up with the "Average Joe" tag after two years of trying to discover the identity of the robber. Banks hung security cam-snaps of Joe around the employee lounge; the FBI put his mug up on their website; eventually, his plain old mug even made *America's Most Wanted*. Amazingly, no one recognized him. It drove Agent Warner a bit crazy. All he wanted was a name to go with that average face. "Joe has just about become my life," he told a *Cincinnati Enquirer* reporter in May 2000.

Average Joe's run began a little more than two years before that, on February 26, 1998, at a Star Bank branch in Crestview Hills, Kentucky. After his first successful robbery, he waited a little over three months before pouncing on a Huntington Bank in Florence, Kentucky, then a little over a month before hitting another Star Bank in Florence. His fourth robbery was nearly his undoing: A clever teller at a bank in Southern Ohio slipped him a dye pack, which exploded all over the bandit as he walked across the bank parking lot. Average Joe dropped all the money and ran for it. After that, he would look carefully for dye packs, and if he thought a teller was going for one, the Average Joe would calmly shake his head and make a "tut-tut-tut" sound.

His knockovers continued at banks up and down I-75 as far north as Dayton, Ohio, and as far south as Lexington, Kentucky, with some pit stops in Louisville along the way. No teller ever remembered seeing him show a weapon—although one thought she glimpsed a gun butt sticking out of his pants. Several theories about the Average Joe developed. Some thought he might be an unemployed loner. Others thought he lived in the neighboring state of Indiana, and was choosing only to rob banks in areas where nobody would recognize him. In

1998, the Average Joe robbed five banks; the following year, he knocked over nine. Bank tellers, who had been trained to comply with the wishes of robbers who threaten employees and customers, were helpless.

By March 2000, the Average Joe made *America's Most Wanted,* but it didn't seem to matter. A month later, he held up Fifth Third Bank in Lexington. And on May 19, he robbed a Key Bank Branch in Eastgate/Union Township in southern Ohio. Still, no solid leads. Who *was* this guy, anyway?

A month later, Agent Warner told a reporter from trade magazine *American Banker* that "Murphy's Law could kick in for this guy. He's been lucky ... but if he continues, he will be caught."

On July 11, Warner's prophecy came true. The Average Joe had held up a Bank One branch in Lexington when a cop pulled over the robber's getaway car—a 2000 Mitsubishi Mirage. The man driving quickly explained that he'd been driving around the neighborhood, looking for an apartment to rent. The cop hadn't asked him, which tipped him off, as did the Bank One money wrappers found inside the car. The Average Joe was finally under arrest.

When the baseball cap, glasses, and windbreaker were removed, the Average Joe was at last revealed to be ... Daniel Schwarberg, a 43-year-old factory supervisor from Verona, Kentucky. In other words, a nobody.

Schwarberg had done a little disguise work, though nothing on the level of Willie Sutton. Schwarberg ordinarily wore contact lenses; the glasses he wore during robberies were fakes. And he would often ditch the windbreaker and work attire he wore into the bank to change into casual clothes after making his getaway.

While it's true that Schwarberg had a sordid past, it wasn't exactly the stuff of supercriminals. He was behind on his child support payments, fending off three ex-wives, and dealing with a theft conviction, in which he had been convicted of taking money that belonged to his employer. (Instead of jail, he agreed to pay $15,000 in restitution.) He also had a girlfriend he wanted to make Wife Number Four and a beat-up house in dire need of repair. At the time of his arrest, he had been supervising ramp workers at a company called Comair. Not exactly the stuff of bank-robbing legend.

On October 30, 2000, Schwarberg pleaded guilty to his 11 robberies in Kentucky. He faced an average sentence of 20 years in prison.

## Cool Fact from the Vault

Months after the Average Joe's arrest, his graduating class at Oak Hills High School threw their twenty-fifth anniversary reunion. Naturally, Schwarberg was the buzz of the event. (Think anybody could remember what he looked like?)

# 39  PRITCHERT AND GUTHRIE

**Full names:** Craig Michael Pritchert and Nova Esther Guthrie

**Number of banks robbed:** At least 12

**Estimated lifetime take:** At least $500,000

**Claim to fame:** These bank-robbing lovers are a modern-day Bonnie and Clyde ... on snowboards

## "I CAN IMAGINE THEM HITTING THE SACK AFTER ONE OF THOSE ROBBERIES JUST LAUGHING THEIR HEADS OFF AND HAVING FUN."

Craig Pritchert had serious baseball dreams when he enrolled at Arizona State University in the early 1980s. He had married his high school sweetheart, started a family, and thought it wouldn't be long before the Major League scouts discovered him and signed him to a pro contract. Unfortunately, Pritchert played for the Arizona Sun Devils at the same time another young talented ball player: Barry Bonds. When Bonds started winning all the attention, Pritchert sulked and eventually dropped out of school.

Still, Pritchert lusted after the luxuries he thought a pro ball career would bring. He tried some get-rich-quick schemes, but none of them panned out, so he ditched his family and tried the ultimate American get-rich-quick scheme: robbing a bank. In 1991, Pritchert was nailed for sticking one up in Nevada, and was released in 1997.

But Pritchert, a lanky, sharp-featured guy, refused to let one strike throw the ball game. He immediately robbed another bank and recruited an unlikely partner in a Farmington, New Mexico, bar. Nova Guthrie was a short, average-looking 23-year-old mortuary science student and the youngest daughter in a large Fundamentalist Christian family. "It was the pull of a misunderstood love," explained Guthrie's minister to the *Denver Post*. "My observation is it was a love that put her into bondage, as opposed to a genuine love which brings freedom."

Soon, like Clyde Barrow before him, Pritchert had talked Guthrie into helping him launch a series of takeover-style bank robberies in the Pacific Northwest, Texas, Arizona, New Mexico, and Colorado. On August 13, 1997, they hit a Norwest Bank in Scottsdale, Arizona. On Halloween 1997, the Bank of the Southwest in Durango, Colorado. On February 19, 1999, it was the Klamath First Federal Bank in Bend, Oregon, where the robber-lovers peeled away with more than $100,000.

"A lot of bank robbers are opportunists, and Craig is more planned than that," FBI detective Steve Vogel told ABC News. "He doesn't just act on emotion and just jump off and rob a bank. It's a well-planned operation."

First, the lovers rent a motel room from which they can eyeball the target bank, sometimes for as long as two or three weeks. They take breaks only to stop by a Radio Shack to buy police scanners and two-way radios or to read local want ads to pick up cars, guns, and clothes. Then, on the day of the raid, either Pritchert or Guthrie will enter a bank with a semi-automatic weapon—the other will stay in the getaway car—and demand to be taken to the vault. (FBI agents say that asking for a tour of the vault is the duo's "signature" move.) "The robberies always occur either right after the branch opens, or just prior to closing," explained one FBI agent familiar with the case. If customers or employees get mouthy, the robber will use plastic handcuffs, duct tape, or a hard poke of his gun to quiet them.

The planning has paid off, since Pritchert has a knack for telling when the bases (the banks) are loaded. Where most modern-day bank robbers rarely net more than $2,000 per robbery, Pritchert and Guthrie averaged about $10,000 per heist. Afterward, the two burned everything—radios, cars, clothes, sacks, scanners—except for the money. Then they fly away, usually to swank ski resorts for a little snowboarding or tropical resorts for sunbathing and scuba diving. Pritchert is a big fan of day trading and uses his laptop from wherever he's hiding to invest in the stock market. The FBI has been able to track his trades, but not pinpoint his locations. By all accounts, Pritchert isn't exactly the world's luckiest trader; some believe he continues to rob banks, in part, to cover his trading losses. "Craig is not a very successful trader," said one FBI agent.

But it's also about the thrills, claims one psychologist. "They are 'Type T' personalities," said Frank Farley in an interview with ABC News. "The T stands for thrills. They're risk takers, thrill seekers, stimulation seekers, arousal seekers. These are people who live on the edge." And Farley believes the excitement runs through Pritchert and Guthrie's personal relationship as well. "There's probably a lot of sexuality going on there, too. I mean, I can imagine them hitting the sack after one of these robberies and just laughing their heads off and having fun."

Sometimes, planning and pleasure mix. Depending on the town, Pritchert and Guthrie would hit the area's hottest restaurants and chat up local notables. Once in 1999, the pair joined a Gold's Gym in Bend, Oregon, because it offered a nice view of the Klamath First Federal across the street. Pritchert and Guthrie would do butterfly presses and carefully note the comings and goings of bank employees. Willie Sutton would have probably admired the pair's ingenuity (and their abs).

Pritchert and Guthrie had a clean, two-year run, until April 1999, when Guthrie apparently felt a twinge of conscience and left her man. She returned home to her parents. Guthrie even allowed a Baptist minister to turn her in to the Denver FBI office, where she seemed ready to sing. "She seemed to have maybe internally come to terms with her involvement or participating in the robberies and was very, very cooperative," Denver FBI agent Janna Monroe told ABC News. Thinking that she would eventually help reel in Pritchert, the FBI let her go without an arrest.

Bad move. Guthrie quickly reteamed with her bank-robbing lover, and in August 2001, there were some reports that the fugitive lovers were hiding out in Canada—which makes sense, since that country provides plenty of skiing opportunities. "The climate in Canada could be ideal for them," FBI Agent Ed Hall told the *Toronto Sun*. "They could mingle with people at any resort."

As of press time, Pritchert and Guthrie were still on the run. The price on their heads: $50,000.

## Cool Fact from the Vault

Unlike Bonnie Parker, Guthrie has tattoos and a pierced belly button. Unlike Clyde Barrow, Pritchert owes $93,000 in back child support.

# 40 THE WORLD TRADE CENTER HEISTERS

**Number of bank vaults robbed:** None

**Estimated lifetime take:** $0

**Claim to fame:** Even in America's darkest hour, men were still trying to liberate large amounts of money from bank vaults

## "IT LOOKED LIKE THEY USED A BLOWTORCH, A CROWBAR."

Immediately after the devastating terrorist attacks on the World Trade Center and Pentagon on September 11, 2001, people couldn't help but think that life had suddenly turned into a Bruce Willis movie. But only after November 1 would people realize that life was imitating a particular Willis movie: *Die Hard: With a Vengeance.* In that movie, a criminal mastermind (Jeremy Irons) creates a series of explosions throughout New York City that culminate in a blast beneath a federal bank. Everyone assumes it's the work of terrorists, but it turns out to be an elaborate plot to steal billions of dollars worth of gold.

In real life, it was the international terrorists who took care of the explosions and devastation, but professional bank robbers appear to have tried to pull off the heist.

Beneath what used to be 4 World Trade Center, the Bank of Nova Scotia kept a giant vault containing $200 million worth of gold and silver. When a security team made a survey of the area beneath the rubble a month after the attacks, they were shocked to find scorch marks on a basement doorway leading to the vault. Apparently, someone had gotten there ahead of security and tried to cut their way to the $200 million. Not long after, the bank hired a New

York–based security firm, Knoll, Inc., to transport the precious metals to another, more secure location than a federal disaster area.

Of course, the bank denies that anyone tried to rob the gold and silver. "The contents remain safe and intact," said a Bank of Nova Scotia spokeswoman. "The contents are fully insured. It would be factually incorrect to say there had been any attempt to steal the contents of our vault." But on November 1, 2001, *The New York Times* quoted a "government official involved in the recovery efforts," who insisted there had definitely been an attempt to break into the vault. "It looked like they used a blowtorch, a crowbar," said the mysterious official. "The Port Authority police began periodic patrols, and then a closed-circuit television system was put in."

By November 2, the story of the attempted heist spread throughout the world. *The London Times* reported that the heisters were professional thieves who posed as rescuers. *The London Daily Telegraph* reported the attempt was "an inside job." The *Vancouver Sun* pointed out that there were other valuables stored in the basement, but the locations of those items "have been kept quiet for fear of encouraging burglars."

The identity of the heisters—if they even exist at all—remains a mystery.

## Cool Fact from the Vault

Would-be heisters would have succeeded had they tried to rob the vault beneath 5 World Trade Center. There, the Morgan Stanley Dean Witter safe was left open during the hurry to evacuate, and inside were billions in stocks and bond certificates. All the money was recovered more or less intact, save for a few scorch marks.

# PART 2

## A TREASURY OF BANK HEISTS

# 41 HOW TO ROB BANKS IN THREE EASY LESSONS

*Theoretically speaking, of course.*

Let's get this on the table right away: Don't rob a bank. "The bottom line is that bank robberies are a foolish crime," said one FBI agent to *The New York Times*. "There are easier ways to get more money." Truth is, you'll most likely get caught—the national conviction rate hovers between 60 and 70 percent. "The probability of success is very low," agrees one criminologist. Even if you don't get caught the first time, you'll most likely try to rob another bank, and another, and eventually you will get caught. Nobody beats the odds forever—just take a look at the list of the 40 most infamous bank robbers in history. (Notice anybody who robbed banks and went on to live a long carefree life in the Bahamas?) Get caught, and you're looking at a long stretch in prison—at least seven years, if your judge follows federal sentencing guidelines. Your family will be ashamed. Friends will laugh at you behind your back. And for what? A couple grand? Even minimum wage pays better than that. Not to put too fine a point on it: Don't rob a bank.

That said, here's how one *might* rob a bank.

## 1. BEFORE THE ROBBERY

First, you have to decide if you want to do a note job or a takeover. **Note jobs** account for the majority of all bank robberies (about 75 percent), according to FBI statistics. All you need is a pen, a piece of paper, a decent disguise, and a jigger of attitude. The drawback, of course, is that you're limited to the amount of money stored at one teller's station—never more than a few thousand dollars.

**Takeovers** involve you, a handful of willing accomplices, weapons, a getaway car, and a detailed plan. There's much greater risk of capture or things spiraling out of control, but the rewards can be worth it, especially if you are able to force employees to allow you access to the vault, and a fresh load of unmarked cash has recently been delivered. According to a short item in *The New York Times Magazine*, "How to Rob a Bank" by Shane Dubow, takeover heists earn criminals an average of $28,000 per job.

Either way, you'll want to **case your target bank.** If you don't, you might end up robbing a bank that doesn't deal with much cash or has a security measure you're not prepared to deal with. Successful bank robber Paddy Mitchell says he would case a bank day-in and day-out for as many as six months until he knew the bank's routine better than its own employees. This is also how he knew the hour and the day his target bank would receive a pile of virgin money—cash that hasn't had a chance to be loaded down with dye packs or electronic markers.

Study the bank for other details, too. Look for bulletproof bandit barriers (for more, see "Casing the Joint"); if you see one, don't bother; if you threaten to use a gun, the teller might just laugh at you. Try to pick a bank with as few windows as possible to avoid attracting attention from the outside. Dubow's *New York Times Magazine* article suggests picking a bank where your ethnicity will blend in. Some robbers today favor bank branches located in supermarkets, which usually lack bandit barriers and make casing easy: All you have to do is spend time food shopping every day. After all, everybody has to eat.

Some additional notes: It helps if you're **not a crackhead.** Some experts believe that 80 percent of modern bank robbers are strung-out junkies in need of quick cash for a fix, and are not what you'd call expert planners. Hence, they move fast, make stupid mistakes, and are captured rather quickly. Also, **don't forget the proper gear.**

According to depression-era robber Al Karpis, no professional bank robber went without a couple of army barracks bags to hold the stolen loot. (Though if you're pulling a note job, a simple backpack will do.) Krazy Glue is great for obscuring fingerprints, according to bank robber David Grandstaff, who pulled the second largest bank heist in U.S. history. A coating of glue allows you to break down weapons with dexterity, something that can be cumbersome wearing gloves.

There are two more options, by the way: **bank burglaries** and **electronic heists.** These kinds of robberies demand specialized training and tools—do you happen to have microflame torches, oxygen regulators, and a core drill handy?—but they also involve less risk than a daylight stick-up. Electronic heists are especially tempting for those who don't want to dirty their hands with a real-life bank robbery. "Banks are under the false impression that by eventually moving to electronics—e-commerce; ACH-Automated Clearing House; EDI-Electronic Data Input; wire transfers—they will do away with fraud," says Frank W. Abagnale, fraud expert and author of *Catch Me If You Can* and *The Art of the Steal.* "This couldn't be farther from the truth. The one thing about paper is that it leaves an audit trail. Electronic transactions do not. By moving to electronics, you create a faceless criminal, one who attacks you from thousands of miles away and with speed in a matter of seconds."

## 2.  DURING THE ROBBERY

*Note jobs:* You want to **appear as nondescript as possible.** Wear clothes with logos and labels that tellers and witness can remember, then remember to ditch them right after the robbery, so you'll look like a different person. Is it cold outside? Load up with hats and gloves and scarves, then ditch them afterward. A hat with a wide brim can sometimes obscure your face from surveillance cameras above you. Overall, the goal is to keep the robbery between two people: you and the teller. Speak quietly, if you speak at all. Don't make sudden, threatening movements. But make it clear that you mean business and intend to do harm if your demands are not met; bank tellers are trained to give money to anyone who threatens violence. Keep it under two minutes. If a silent alarm is pulled, the police will be on their way, but will most likely not arrive before 120 seconds have elapsed.

*Takeovers:* Here, the goal is to **make as much noise as possible,** shouting obscenities and frightening every person in that bank to the point that they'll hang on your every command. Paddy Mitchell was known as a gentleman robber, but not when he was on the job. "Nice bank robbers are not taken seriously," he writes. Keep your getaway car around the corner from the bank and have another getaway car stashed a few blocks away so you can make a quick change in the minutes after the robbery. If you're using a getaway driver, consider employing a woman, since she can sit in the driver's seat and fuss with makeup and not draw too much attention.

## 3.  AFTER THE ROBBERY

*Note jobs:* Pray you haven't picked up a dye pack. Some bandits keep a fish tank full of water in their getaway cars. The cash—along with any dye packs or electronic tags—go into the water; the security devices are (theoretically) disabled, and the cash can be dried out and used later. **Change out of your stick-up clothes** as quickly and discreetly as possible. If you can stop at just one bank job, do it. The FBI is actually counting on you to pull another. And another. And another, until you mess up.

*Takeovers:* **Change getaway cars** as quickly as possible. Paddy Mitchell used to hide in the trunk for as many as 24 hours until the heat died down. Sometimes, he would even leave everything—the money, the weapons, the disguises—in the trunk of the car for an extended period of time, then fly back later to collect. If all else fails and the heat is bearing down upon you, try fleeing to a country that doesn't extradite.

## *Notes from the Underworld*

Demand notes used in actual bank robberies across the country:

**Direct**

> "I have a gun."

> "All the large bills."

> "Give me all your money."

> "This is a robbery. Do as I say."

> "This is a stick-up; give me all the money."

**Threatening**

> "This is a hold-up. I have a gun."

> "I have a gun. Give me all your money—or else."

> "I have a gun. Don't do anything stupid. Give me all your money."

> "Put the money in the bag or I'll kill you."

> "Don't be fooled. I will shoot you."

> "Put all the money on the counter and you won't get shot."

> "Don't f... up. You have only two seconds to give me your money, three seconds, and I'll blow your head off."

**Specific**

> "This is a stick-up. Give me $3,000 and no ink."

> "I want your $20s and big bills, too. I have a gun and will shoot."

> "I have a gun, give me your $50s and $20s or you won't go home."

> "This is a stick-up. Fill the bags with $20s and $50s. No alarm. No police."

> "This is a stick-up. Give me your $20s, $10s and $50s now."

> "I have a gun. I want $20s, $50s and $100s."

> "I have a bomb. Put 20 dollar bills and 100 dollar bills in the bag."

> "Robbery with bomb, $100,000 demanded."

### Clever

"Put money in envelope, no dye packs, no alarms and no one gets hurt."

"Hello, this is a robbery, I am armed, keep smiling and don't push any alarm buttons."

"I have somebody watching you. Give me the money."

"Be calm. Don't turn this into a murder."

"This is a robbery. Don't make it a homicide. Put the money on top of the counter with no dye. Don't make me shoot."

### Eccentric

"This is not fun. I have a gun."

"I have a gun and a bomb. I have nothing to loose [*sic*]."

"Look at me! Any moves that looks [*sic*] like you're pushing any security buttons and I will blast you and anyone around me at random! Give me the loot and go to the bathroom and count to 1,000!"

"In the name of Allah, I have a bomb and I am willing to give my life for the cause of Islam. Put all the money in the bag, and don't be a hero."

"Voices in my head are telling me I need money. So give some or else. I'm robbing this bank. I need $2,500 now."

"No joke! This is a robbery. All I want is the money from the cash draws [*sic*] ... No one has to be hurt or shot at but me ... all will be over quickly you put money on the counter ... Hurry please!!! I must be on my way and that leaves you in the clear. I must go to a higher elevation ... your cooperation will be appreciated. My time is getting short. Sorry for your inconvenience."

### Just Plain Wrong

"Pook the money in the bag."

"Give me all of your brains or I'll blow your money out!"

"This is a robbery. Call the cops." [*Note: The author apparently forgot to include the word "Don't" at the beginning of the second sentence.*]

## 42 CASING THE JOINT

*A rundown of the ways banks have protected themselves against robbery since 1798.*

Now that you know the basics of bank robbing, let's detail the many methods banks use to make sure you never get away with it.

### VAULTS AND SAFES

This may seem obvious, but federal law requires every bank to have a vault or safe (sorry, but that cardboard box just *won't* do), with appropriate lighting and an alarm system. What kind of vault or safe is best? Manufacturers and bank robbers have been playing cat and mouse for over 200 years. When small safes were first used, robbers would simply rope 'em up and take 'em away. When they started to bolt safes to the floor, robbers simply cut away the bolts. When safes were made bigger and heavier, robbers like the Newton Boys began to use nitroglycerine (invented in 1867 by Alfred Nobel). When they started to manufacture safes and vaults with a layer of concrete between two layers of steel, robbers like Willie Sutton started using diamond-bit drills and chisels to bust though each layer. When safes and vaults were made thicker, robbers started using acetylene torches. Even thicker walls? Water-cooled core drills. Thicker still? A burning bar, which acts like several electric cutting torches at once.

Today, impossibly thick vaults are kept behind walls of steel-reinforced concrete, which is why there aren't as many bank burglaries as there used to be. Still, there is no such thing a robber-proof vault. "Anyone who believes they have a foolproof system has failed to take into consideration the creativity of fools," says fraud expert Frank W. Abagnale. "If a man or a woman creates something, there is a man or woman who will defeat it."

## ARMED GUARDS

You might think nothing says "Don't mess with this financial institution" more than a couple of hard-looking, thick-necked men with pistols strapped to their waists. But statistics show guards are the least effective security measure. All you need is an extra man on a heist team to cover him; robbers since the days of John Dillinger have been using guards as ready-made hostages. "Let's face it," said one police source to *The New York Daily News*. "Bank security guards are a thing of the past. Banks don't want confrontations. They don't want anyone to get hurt."

## ALARMS

The first bank alarms were cowbells attached to ropes, so that bank managers could warn the town to be on the lookout after bank robbers had fled the premises. Today silent alarms, triggered by employees in case of a robbery, flash a message instantly to local police departments or private security companies. Cutting the power to a bank before robbing it doesn't disable an alarm, since most have back-up battery systems. And since banks don't exactly make the location of their silent alarm triggers public information, a heister will have no idea whether one has been pressed. All a bank robber can do is keep the job under a predetermined amount of time—usually no more than two minutes—and hope that a squad car isn't in the immediate vicinity; or hire a professional who studies modern bank alarms and can disable the one in the target bank in exchange for a cut of the loot.

## SECURITY CAMERAS

In 1957, the St. Clair Savings and Loan Co. in Cleveland, Ohio, became the first bank to set up a surveillance camera—an ordinary 16mm movie camera. That same year, three unlucky robbers hit the St. Clair bank and, thanks to their debut on film, were caught the very next day. A banking trend was born, with cameras popping up like dandelions in banks all over the United States. In response, bank robbers started to carry cans of black spray paint to use during takeover heists. Sometimes, a heister would simply use a broom handle to tilt the camera out of position.

But sometimes, a robber doesn't have to do anything to disable a surveillance camera. Many banks today still use outdated, poorly maintained cameras that yield grainy, useless images in the event of a robbery. And sometimes, banks are just plain careless. After one heist in the Bay Area, the FBI retrieved the single photo taken by the surveillance camera. The image? A potted plant.

Modern law enforcement officials highly recommend digital cameras, because the images are extremely high quality and data can be stored on a single card rather than a stack of VHS tapes. "Very sophisticated security cameras with digital imaging and high-intensity zoom capabilities have helped identify robbers, even with masks," says fraud expert Frank W. Abagnale. Also, digital cameras can be tiny, making it difficult for a bank robber to use his trusty can of spray paint on it.

One enterprising cop, Sgt. Dean Zanone in Seal Beach, California, thought up a new way to discourage bank robbers: Install cameras that will broadcast an in-progress robbery to police departments over a secure Internet line. (If college kids can train webcams on their hungover roommates, why can't cops do the same with bank robbers?) Sgt. Zanone's department began testing it in 2000, and other departments across the country have since inquired about setting up a similar system.

# DYE PACKS

Bank robber passes a note to teller. Teller passes a pack of cash back to bank robber. Bank robber leaves bank, and ... SPLAT. Another victim of the infamous dye pack. Most banks use "SecurityPacs" from a company called ICI Security Systems; the device itself is made of thin, flexible plastic so it can be hidden in the middle of a stack of $10s and $20s without anyone being the wiser. Every teller in most banks has stacks of dye-packed-rigged money within reaching distance. In the event of a robbery, the teller makes every effort to discreetly sneak one of these packs into the robber's bundle.

While the robber is still inside the bank, the dye pack remains in "safe" mode. But once he passes through a doorway, a small transmitter activates it, and about 10 seconds later—depending on how much lead time the bank has set—the dye pack does its stuff. Not only is there a messy splattering of red dye (1-methylamino-anthraquinone, to be precise), but the device itself burns at 400° F, making the loot literally too hot to handle. So far, dye packs have helped police nab more than 2,500 robbers and return more than $20 million to bank vaults.

Once in a great while, however, dye packs can backfire. In the early 1990s, one young bank teller accidentally carried his cash drawer through a doorway with a transmitter in it. The dye pack exploded.

The teller panicked, then grabbed the dye pack from the drawer. "What should I do with this?"

"Outside!" his co-workers yelled.

The red-splattered teller ran outside with his burning, smoking dye pack, where a store owner saw him and called the fire department. After some careful explaining, the firefighters were nice enough to drop him off at a hospital to treat the burns on his hand.

But when a doctor asked him what happened, the teller replied: "Well, I had this pack of money and it blew up." Right away, the doctor called the police. After more careful explaining, the police were nice enough to let him go.

Another surprising downside of dye-packs: bank managers' reluctance to use them. One police source told *The New York Daily News* that fewer banks are permitting tellers to hand them out to robbers, for fear that the resulting explosion might injure someone and lead to a costly lawsuit—even from the bank robber himself.

## BAIT MONEY

Any bank that is federally insured is required to keep packs of bait money at every teller station. These packs of bills—say, a dozen $10 bills—have had their serial numbers and series year recorded by the bank. In the event of a robbery, police spread the numbers around to area merchants, hoping to catch someone trying to pass a stolen bill, or at least develop a paper trail that investigators can follow.

## ELECTRONIC TRACERS

The latest tracking device is Pro-Net, a thin piece of plastic that can be hidden in a stack of money. It works the same way as Lo-Jack systems on cars: A signal is emitted that lets cops zero in on the fleeing robbers. When bank robber Scott "Hollywood" Scurlock was hitting Seattle like mad in 1996, the FBI urged every bank to lace their money with electronic tracing devices. While these devices didn't directly lead to Scurlock's capture, they did rattle his gang enough during their last bank heist that they made crucial errors during the getaway.

## ENCLOSED BULLETPROOF TELLER AREAS

These so-called "bandit barriers" are clear, bullet-resistant partitions made of Plexiglas that completely surround the bank teller like a see-through vault, and they have been wildly successful. "Takeover robberies are virtually unheard of at banks with bandit-barriers," said one FBI agent. (In G-men lingo, installing these barriers is called "hardening a location.") The drawbacks: Barriers go for $1,000 a running foot, and some banks think they make customers feel like they're entering a fortress.

## ACCESS CONTROL UNITS (ACUS)

Some banks have two sets of doors—one when you first enter the building, and another set just a few feet later. But that's not so you have some place to stomp your wet shoes and unbutton your jacket. These banks may have installed devices—automatic magnetometers— in the vestibule that searches your body for weapons. If it detects one, the inner doors immediately lock. If you try to shoot your way into the bank anyway, good luck—that second set of doors is bulletproof. Some earlier models featured a "capture" mode, so that the unlucky criminal would be detained for arrest, but according to the FBI, many bank administrators strongly discourage this feature, fearing that a trapped heister will turn into a violent, shooting heister. (Instead, the criminal is allowed to escape back outside.) Like bandit barriers, ACUs have proven to be a very effective way of reducing the number of bank robberies.

## HASH-MARKED EXITS

Ever wonder how some bank employees are able to accurately gauge a man's height, especially when that man is sticking an Uzi in their faces? Some banks—and stores, for that matter—have installed discreet hash marks near the exits. (Look for them in your local branch.) Employees are trained to take a look at the fleeing robber, then match the top of his head to the closest corresponding hash mark: five and a half feet, six feet, six and a half feet, and so on.

## DRESS REHEARSALS

Some banks have local police departments or security firms take their employees through a simulated bank robbery. These mock bank heists can be as traumatic as the real thing. "These guys were intimidating," said one executive after a simulation at the North Island Federal Credit Union in San Diego, California, as reported by the *Credit Union Journal*. "I've done 13 of these and I was still teary-eyed during this because it is a very emotional experience. When you start hearing the guns shooting in the air around you and the screaming, you don't think *practice*." (The North Island FCU even provided trauma counselors on the scene.) The employees learned how to remember key details—height, clothes, identifying scars or tattoos—as well as how to protect evidence by placing red cups around spent bullet casings.

## WANTED POSTERS AND TV ADS

After a bank robber has made off with the loot, law enforcement's most effective tool is often a good old-fashioned wanted poster—especially one offering a cash reward for information leading to an arrest. That's how a majority of bank robberies are solved in major cities like Boston and Detroit. Since bank robbers tend to be average Joes—and not supercriminals protected by organized crime syndicates—there's a far greater chance someone they know will happen to see their mug on a post office wall somewhere. And that someone may be perfectly willing to trade in a buddy for $5,000 in reward money.

## THE INTERNET

Bank robber Leslie Rogge pulled off a bunch of heists, then holed up in Antigua, one of the oldest cities in Guatemala. It was a clever move: The feds—knowing that Rogge was a die-hard sailor—wouldn't think to look for him in a land-locked city like Antigua. During the six years Rogge was hiding out as "Bill Young," along with his wife "Anna," his story was featured repeatedly on *America's Most Wanted,* as well as placed on that show's website and the FBI's fledgling Top Ten website. Nothing.

Then Guatemala got access to the Internet in the mid-1990s, and Rogge made the mistake of helping a neighbor and his 14-year-old son make their first trip into cyberspace. Two weeks later, the teenager logged on to the FBI home page and was shocked to discover that "Bill Young"—a friendly handyman who never forgot to buy him a birthday present—was actually a wily thief who'd busted out of an Idaho prison and robbed banks all across the United States. "He just flipped out," said John Biskovich of his son's reaction. "But he insisted we turn him in." Rogge, knowing he was about to be thrown off-line for good, called his American lawyer and arranged for a surrender at the U.S. Embassy in Guatemala.

## INSURANCE

You might have seen the stickers on the windows at your own bank: Each depositor insured by the Federal Deposit Insurance Corporation (FDIC) up to $100,000. But that doesn't mean that the FDIC writes your bank a check if a bandit clears out the teller cages. That insurance is for *you* if your bank happens to fail. To protect themselves from the financial hit of robberies, banks are required by law to buy their own insurance, and most buy a type called "banker's blanket bond" (or "fidelity insurance"). Like life insurance, banker's bond insurance depends on all kinds of factors: risk, location, and size of the institution. In the event of a robbery, it's the bank shareholders who feel the pinch—not the U.S. government. Still, bond insurance is better than nothing at all. Before the insurance law was enacted, some banks were so desperate to hang on to their money that they equipped tellers with a cruder form of insurance: pistols.

## SECURITY GADGETS OF THE FUTURE

Think bank robbers have it tough now? Wait a few years, says Dick Soloway, CEO of NAPCO Security Systems, one of the top electronic security system manufacturers in the world. According to Soloway—who started his career in the 1960s designing amps, effects pedals, and psychedelic gear for Eric Clapton and Jimi Hendrix—an increasing number of banks will soon have access to units that use biometrics. The principle is simple: Unless you have the right fingerprint, handprint, or eyeball, you won't be allowed in the bank's front door. "I would say that the handprint is going to be the one that will predominate," says Soloway. "The hand is simply a larger target for the scanner to look at."

Even if a bank robber scams his way into a bank, he might not make it very far. Security companies are working on video recognition systems that will snap a photo of everyone entering a bank. That image would then be compared to thousands in law enforcement databases. If you're wanted by the law for anything—say, serial bank robbery—the proper agency will be notified.

If a robber somehow makes it past these security devices, he might find that the teller has a new trick up her sleeve. Or more precisely, around her neck. "Another trend is wireless silent call for help buttons," says Soloway. If a heister orders a teller to back away from her station, fearing that she'll press a silent alarm, the teller will be able to sound an alarm anyway by pushing a button that's near her watch or worn as a necklace.

## BEING NICE

One bank president in Thousand Oaks, California, has instructed all of his employees to say hello to as many entering customers as possible. "Nobody who's casing a joint wants a couple of people to come up to them and say hello," he explained to the *Los Angeles Times*.

### TIME IS MONEY

Before you start composing that perfect demand note, take a look at how much jail time you'll be facing.

A polite bank robber who never uses a gun and vows not to steal more than 10 grand may not be unambitious; he simply might be thinking ahead. Every component of a bank robbery—how much money is stolen, whether or not a gun is used—is factored into a convicted heister's sentence.

Here's how it breaks down, according to the 2001 Federal Sentencing Guidelines Manual. Keep in mind that these numbers are just that: merely guidelines. But you can guesstimate a sentence by using the following list and table, Chinese-menu style. Take the basic term (41 to 51 months) and add various offense levels—the unit of measure in sentencing—which translate into a suggested sentence*. For instance, if you rob a bank (offense level 22) while threatening to use a bomb (add 3 offense levels) and walk away with $1.5 million (add 5 offense levels), you end up with an offense level of 30. Consult the sentencing table, and you'll see that an offense level of 30 for a first-time offender can mean 97 to 121 months. That's more than eight years of hard time, hombre. And that's just if it's your first time.

Offense level for a first-time bank robber: **22**

Steal $10,000 or less? **Add 0 offense levels**

Steal $10,000 to $49,999? **Add 1 offense level**

Threaten to kill somebody? **Add 2 offense levels**

Steal $50,000 to $249,999? **Add 2**

Hurt somebody? **Add 2**

Threaten to use a weapon—be it knife, gun**, or bomb? **Add 3**

Steal $250,000 to $799,999? **Add 3**

Use a dangerous weapon, other than a gun? **Add 4**

Seriously injure somebody? **Add 4**

Steal $800,000 to $1,499,999? **Add 4**

Show a gun**, or have one on you? **Add 5**

Steal $1,500,000 to $2,499,999? **Add 5**

Use a gun** in a threatening manner? **Add 6**

Give someone a permanent or life-threatening injury? **Add 6**

Steal $2,500,000 to $4,999,999? **Add 6**

Fire a gun**? **Add 7**

Steal more than 5 million bucks? **Add 7** (and pat yourself on the back—you just broke the record)

* *End up in federal prison? Expect to serve at least 85 percent of your jail term. That's because there is no parole in the federal system any more; the best you can hope for is 54 days off every year for good behavior.*

** *Carry or use a gun? You'll be slapped with an additional five years on top of your bank-robbery sentence.*

## Sentencing Table

| Offense Level | Sentence (in Months) |
| --- | --- |
| 22 | 41–51 |
| 23 | 46–57 |
| 24 | 51–63 |
| 25 | 57–71 |
| 26 | 63–78 |
| 27 | 70–87 |
| 28 | 78–97 |
| 29 | 87–108 |
| 30 | 97–121 |
| 31 | 108–135 |
| 32 | 121–151 |
| 33 | 135–168 |
| 34 | 151–188 |
| 35 | 168–210 |
| 36 | 188–235 |
| And so on. | |

# 43 SHUT UP AND LIVE

## How to survive a bank heist.

One minute you're standing in a bank line, waiting to deposit that $35 check Aunt Carol sent for your birthday. The next, somebody's sticking a gun in your face, telling you to kiss the floor or else he'll blow your brains out. What should you do, aside from asking Aunt Carol to send you a gift certificate next year?

Listen to the advice of Richard J. Ottenstein, Ph.D., CEAP, CTS. He's the founder of the Workplace Trauma Center, an organization that specializes in helping people cope with nerve-rattling situations such as bank robberies. Ottenstein has counseled hundreds of bank-robbery trauma victims, but some of the stories he hears still surprise him. "Once, a perpetrator asked for an exact amount—say $500," says Ottenstein. "The teller handed him a stack of cash that exceeded that amount, and he returned the excess funds before leaving." Don't let bank robbers take you by surprise. Here are Ottenstein's strategies for anyone who walks into a bank in the morning and finds himself in the middle of Dog Day Afternoon.

1. **Don't make any false moves.** "The customer should stay calm, comply with the orders of the perpetrator, and avoid making any sudden moves," says Ottenstein. "In almost all instances, clear, calm compliance with the perpetrator's demands is the best way to keep the robbery from turning violent." Are the bandits telling you not to be a hero? Listen to them. According to Ottenstein, most bank injuries happen when someone tries to stop the robbery.

2. **Remember: It will all be over quickly.** "Unlike in the movies, most robberies are over within a few minutes—although it may seem like a lifetime to the victims," says Ottenstein. And try to relax; the odds that you'll be held up by a raving, kill-crazy maniac are fairly remote.

3. **If things get ugly, find a safe haven.** Okay, let's say you are faced with a raving, kill-crazy maniac. "If the perpetrators are assaulting or shooting victims," Ottenstein says, "try to escape or hide—barricade yourself in a room or hide in a closet." Is one of the thugs in your face, trying to make an example of you? Ottenstein recommends that you try not to react to it. "But if it becomes apparent that you are going to be killed—that is, others have already been killed," he says, then all bets are off. "Do anything you can to survive."

4. **Avoid becoming a souvenir.** Does one of the bad guys want to take you along with him? That's not good news—statistic show that your odds of being killed are greatly increased if you are taken hostage. "Faking a heart attack, or falling and then having trouble walking can discourage the potential hostage taker," says Ottenstein. "But this could also anger the perp, so the victim should use his best judgment."

5. **Take careful mental notes so you can help nail the bastards.** "As soon as it is safe, write down your description of the perpetrator before talking to anyone about what you saw," says Ottenstein. Things to look for during the robbery: the robber's clothing, tattoos, scars, mannerisms, unusual gait, or other distinctive physical characteristic. Things to listen for: accents or speech defects. If there's more than one perp, concentrate on the one nearest you. And of course, if you happen to see the getaway car, memorize the color, make, and license plate. But be careful not to stare directly at the robber—take quick, unobtrusive glances. If a bandit thinks you're trying to ID him, he might become more aggressive.

# 44  HURRY UP!
## IT'S THE LAW

*Two national agencies made it their business to catch bank-robbing bad guys: first the Pinkertons, and then J. Edgar Hoover's FBI. But who will be chasing them in the future?*

It's 1875. You own a large bank that's just been robbed by a band of good-for-nothing hooligans. Who do you call? Not the FBI—they don't exist yet. Local law enforcement? Please. They couldn't track a one-legged dung beetle in a snowstorm. And many cities didn't even have a dedicated police force. Nope, your best bet is to call in the Pinkertons.

For decades, the Pinkerton Detective Agency, founded in 1850, was America's *de facto* national police force. It was founded by Allan Pinkerton, a Scotland native who left his homeland after gaining a reputation as a labor agitator. He immigrated to a small town near Chicago, where he stumbled into a band of counterfeiters and helped capture them. This led to a job as the local sheriff, then a gig with the newly formed Chicago Police Department in 1850. Even though he was a public official, Pinkerton that same year created a new kind of police force for hire: a private detective agency. Pinkerton also had some amazingly innovative ideas to bring to the table. The Pinkertons were the first to collect books of criminal mugshots and trade information with foreign law officials, and the agency's organizational system would later serve as the inspiration for the FBI's own structure.

Within 10 years, Pinkerton's men and his symbol (an open eye with the motto, "We Never Sleep") became famous nationwide, especially after the agency helped foil a plot to assassinate Abraham Lincoln in 1861. By the 1870s, the Pinkertons had turned their attention to train and bank robbers, tangling with Jesse James (who swore to kill Allan

Pinkerton after some of his detectives accidentally killed James's half-brother), the Reno Gang, master thief Adam Worth, as well as Butch Cassidy and the Sundance Kid. "I couldn't do that," says Butch Cassidy (Paul Newman) in the 1969 film, surprised to learn that the Pinkertons were still hot on his trail after days of tracking. "Could you do that? Why can they do it? Who are those guys?"

Even the U.S. Justice Department, formed in 1870, hired Pinkerton men to conduct investigations. But by 1907, Congress was having conflict-of-interest doubts about hiring freelancers to do its detective work, and some within the Justice Department lobbied for the creation of their own small, investigative team. It was the birth of a small bureau that would eventually become the mighty FBI. Meanwhile, the hundreds of Pinkerton ops situated all over the country were concentrating on other assignments—labor troubles, especially. In 1915, Dashiell Hammett, the godfather of hardboiled detective fiction, became a Pinkerton operative and would later base his landmark novel, *Red Harvest,* on his strike-breaking days. Bank robberies increasingly became the bailiwick of local police departments, which were growing in strength and manpower all over the country. (Pinkertons never slept—and they never closed, either. In March 1999, the Pinkerton Agency merged with Securitas AB, the largest security company in the world, and now largely deals with Fortune 500 clients.) Prior to 1934, a bank robber's getaway strategy was simple: Pull a heist, then flee by horse or automobile across state lines. Local cops couldn't legally follow you, and interdepartmental cooperation was virtually nonexistent. The FBI (then still the "Division of Investigation") was on the hunt, but they couldn't touch you until you drove a stolen car across state lines. All that changed on May 19, 1934, when Congress officially made bank robberies a federal offense, giving the FBI the legal muscle to pursue bank robbers to the ends of the earth—or at least to the borders of the United States. Since then, the FBI has been a bank robber's worst nightmare, compounded in recent decades by newly formed joint task forces, where the FBI and local police departments team up to solve cases with maximum efficiency. Crooks everywhere knew that the moment they slid a demand note across the marble counter, they would have the dreaded G-men on their tails for a long, long time.

Then came September 11, 2001, and the FBI's manpower was suddenly refocused on the war on terrorism. Priorities shifted. And it's very likely that in 2002 the FBI—after nearly 70 years of hunting bank robbers—might ease up the chase. A December 2001 report in the *Washington Post* revealed that FBI Director Robert S. Mueller III was considering ceding certain investigations—bank robberies among them—to local authorities. As this book was going to press, no firm decision had been made, but there was no doubt that bank robbers quickly took a backseat to international terrorists. "Some divisions may not be responsive to each and every bank robbery due to other things going on, obviously such as terrorism," said John McEachern, an FBI special agent in the L.A. bank-robbery squad, in *American Banker*. But McEachern quickly adds that in L.A.—the bank-robbery capital of the world—the FBI will continue to dispatch agents to every single heist. Another FBI spokesman said that the agency will measure each crime against a bank and deliver the appropriate manpower. An elderly man pushing a demand note? Maybe not. A well-honed strike force of six armed robbers? Definitely.

Still, the policy shift worries many bankers. "Our biggest fear is that Congress redirects the FBI not to do any more bank robbery investigations," said Bill Wipprecht, director of security for Wells Fargo & Co., in an interview with *American Banker*. "We're seeing reports from all over the country of increased bank robberies in major metropolitan areas, and some people are attributing it to the fact that some law enforcement is distracted by a high-alert status related to the September 11 attacks," added Rob Drozdowski, a specialist with trade group America's Community Bankers.

The worry is that without the FBI, other agencies (local police, as well as bank security officers) will be left in a lurch without the FBI's coordinating skills and their centralized databases, which have helped nail countless serial robbers over the years, especially bandits who moved across various jurisdictions—the very reasons national agencies like the Pinkertons and the FBI went after bank robbers in the first place.

# 45 MEET THE GOLDILOCKS BANDIT

## Why do the FBI and local law enforcement officials give bank robbers goofy nicknames?

Are you a pro heister who desperately wants your 15 minutes of fame? You're in luck. If you rob enough banks, the FBI will slap you with a nickname to help you stick in the minds of the agents hunting you. Gangster nicknames are nothing new (take "Machine Gun" Kelly and "Pretty Boy" Floyd, for example), but depression-era handles usually originated in the underworld. Today's bank robber nicknames are specifically designed by the FBI to quickly identify you based on your most obvious trait—a quirky habit, a funny tattoo, a physical deformity, a resemblance to a celebrity—and help speed your capture.

Bandits started receiving special names in the early 1980s, largely thanks to a Los Angeles FBI agent named Bill Rehder, who during his 30-year career nicknamed hundreds of bank robbers. "We're working on maybe 35 or 40 cases at any one time," he explained to the *Los Angeles Times* in 1988. "And the average bandit will hit six or seven times before he's caught. So we need some kind of an easy reference point for agents." (Plus, a funny name couldn't hurt when hoping for a bit of press attention.) The old method was to name the bank robber after the agent assigned to the case; but it got confusing when half a dozen robbers were all referred to as "Bill Rehder's bandit."

Rehder would spend a small part of each day thinking up names for bank robbers. He would watch bank robbery flicks for inspiration, or sometimes hold up a photo of the suspect and ask co-workers, "What actors does this guy resemble?" But most often, the nickname would make itself obvious, based on interviews with bank tellers, repeated viewings of surveillance camera footage, or a plain old wicked sense of humor.

The result? A generation of criminals who sound like they've popped out of a Dick Tracy comic strip: the Bad Breath Bandit, the Fireplug Bandit, the Ugly Robber, the Clearasil Bandit, the Happy Face Bandits, the Nerd, the Mummy Bandit, the Shamu Bandit, the Shadow, the Dumb and Dumber Bandits, and yes, the Goldilocks Bandit, the poor bastard who wore blond wigs when knocking over banks in San Diego. Other memorable bandits from the last 15 years include the following:

- **Acne Bandit:** A San Diego bank robber with a complexion like a 13-year-old boy. Amazingly, this pizza-faced pro tried to sue the FBI for giving him an embarrassing nickname. (A judge later squeezed the case out of court.)

- **Bad Breath Bandit:** One bank teller couldn't wait to give this San Diego bank robber his money—just so he would make a quick getaway.

- **Beer-Bellied Bandit:** This 70-year-old bank robber was fond of his chrome-plated, 25-caliber revolver … and frosty pints of beer, from the looks of his belly. He hit several banks in the Chicago suburbs in the mid-1990s, but was caught when police trailed his car to a tavern a few blocks away from his house. "He stopped for a drink on the way home [from a hold-up]," explained one arresting officer. "Orange juice and vodka."

- **Both Hands Bandit:** A meticulous bank robber in Ventura County, California, who always gingerly handed his demand note to a teller with both paws, careful not to leave any fingerprints behind.

- **Bulbous Nose Bandit:** Not only did this robber of seven banks in Chicago have a pudgy proboscis, but he made the unfortunate mistake of wearing a pencil-thin moustache, as if to underline it.

- **Charlie's Angels Bandits:** Three young women—aged 18, 21, and 22—robbed 11 banks by convincing L.A. bank tellers that they all had pistols in their purses, just like the fictional *Charlie's Angels*. But the 1970s TV show didn't inspire the robbery spree. "They saw an article in [the paper] about a bank robber," explained one cop, "and they thought it would be easy to do."

- **Chevy Chase Bandit:** This L.A. bank robber once tripped and fell during a stick-up, and the FBI never let him forget it. Gerald Ford would probably sympathize.

- **Dr. Seuss Bandit:** During his 1997 robberies in the Chicago area, this heister wore a tall, brightly colored hat, which reminded people of the main character from Dr. Seuss's *Cat in the Hat*. He changed his disguise shortly after earning the nickname, but that didn't prevent Chicago's finest from bagging this cat on July 28, 1998, after a short car chase.

- **Grandpa Bandit:** This cranky, white-haired, 50-something heister hit at least seven banks in Chicago in the mid-1990s. (Then presumably went home to watch *Matlock*.)

- **Groundhog Bandit:** For over six years, the FBI saw his shadow: The Groundhog hit over 22 banks during that time, starting with a heist on Groundhog Day, 1995.

- **Guido Sarducci Bandit:** A bushy moustache? A dark felt hat? How could San Diego FBI agents resist naming this bank robber after Don Novello's popular *Saturday Night Live* character?

- **Happy Face Bandits:** This bank-robbing duo in L.A. were fond of inserting stupid little happy face symbols all over their little demand notes.

- **Hardboiled Bandit:** This Denver-area bank robber had a large boil on his left cheek. (If his life were a movie, Hardboiled would have been captured by a cop named "Lance.")

- **I Spy Bandits:** A pair of bank robbers—one white, one black, just like Robert Culp and Bill Cosby in the hit 1960s TV show.

- **Itty Bitty Bandit:** This bank robber was extremely short and wore glasses. (Which would explain the booster seat he installed in the getaway car.)

- **Kangaroo Bandit:** An extremely successful—24 banks in under two years—serial bank robber in L.A. who always wore a knapsack around his waist.

- **LAX Bandit:** A bank robber fond of banks near the Los Angeles International Airport. (Not to be confused with the Ex-LAX Bandit, who takes frequent breaks during a hold-up.)

- **Marx Brothers Bandits:** These mid-1980s heisters went out of their way to earn a cool nickname, wearing Harpo Marx–type wigs, vintage suits, and Groucho moustaches during their bank jobs. "It's kind of fun to watch them and try to figure out at what point they're going to make their first mistake," commented Rehder at the time.

- **Michael Jackson Bandit:** This smooth criminal was named for the single black glove he wore during his L.A. robberies.

- **Mild-Mannered Bandit:** No barked commands or blazing Uzis from this bank robber; instead, he was known around Minnesota for his "quiet and polite" demeanor.

- **Miss America Bandit:** The handle of a wig-wearing, bank-robbing cosmetologist who was actually attractive. "Most of the women robbers are quite a bit less than good-looking," said Rehder in the *Los Angeles Times*.

- **Miss Piggy Bandit:** She was 5 foot 4. She weighed over 300 pounds. She robbed banks, then stuffed herself and the loot into a tiny Volkswagen bug to make her getaway. Later, it turned out that Miss Piggy was not only the weight of two women: She *was* two women—sisters, who looked an awful lot alike.

- **Nightstalker Bandit:** In late fall 2001, this Chicago bandit robbed seven banks, all in the evening. The publicity caused Nightstalker to try a Saturday morning heist, but cops noticed a busted taillight on his 1987 Oldsmobile, and pulled him over. When they searched the car, police found $4,000 from the LaSalle Bank branch he'd just robbed.

- **The Pervert:** A scruffy, rumpled bank robber who one teller described as "looking like he just stepped out of an adult bookshop." (It didn't help matters that his demand note was written on the back cover of *Celebrity Hooters* magazine.)

- **Post-Graduate Bandit:** An L.A. lone wolf robber whose demand notes were always ridiculously misspelled. "This is a rabbry," read one note. "Don't pull anytrix."

- **Rainbow Coalition:** A bank-robbing trio consisting of a white, an African-American, and a Latino bandit.

- **Still Learning Bandit:** First, this L.A. bank robber tried using a demand note. The teller walked away. Next, he tried a tougher demand note, one that claimed he had a gun and wouldn't be shy about using it. The second teller didn't buy it, either, and the robber walked away with nothing. Finally, he tried using a real gun, and this time actually got his hands on some money, but a few seconds after exiting the bank, a dye pack exploded. According to Rehder, the Still Learning Bandit got frustrated and either retired or lammed out of L.A.

- **To-Go Bandit:** Some bank robbers think ahead and bring a knapsack to haul away their stolen loot. Not this L.A. heister. He always asked the teller for a doggie bag.

- **Typed Note Bandit:** Named for the typewritten demand notes he'd slide to bank tellers. Upon his arrest, Typed Note seemed upset. "He wanted to know why we named him that," explained one FBI agent. "He didn't think it was flashy enough."

# 46 RESERVOIR DORKS

### Bank jobs gone horribly, horribly wrong.

"They're not on the high end of the intellectual spectrum," said FBI spokesman Bob Long to the *Chicago Sun-Times*. "If we ever had bright bank robbers, we'd have real problems." Amateur heisters' most common goof: writing their demand note on the back of their own deposit slips—sometimes complete with name and address. Other, more original blunders include ...

◆ The heist at a Community Bank went off without a hitch. The robber ran to his getaway car, placed his gun and sack of money on the passenger seat, then reached for his car keys ... wait a second. **Where were his car keys?** They were sitting on the carpet inside the bank, right where he'd dropped them. "You don't pay attention to that kind of stuff when you are robbing a bank," noted Purcellville Police Chief David Simpson. The robber tried to hide in some bushes about 100 yards away from the bank, but a bloodhound sniffed him out. (Purcellville, Virginia, 2001)

◆ A bank robber walked into a bank and demanded money. **The weapon in his hand: a brick.** The bank guard did a double take, then walked over and slapped handcuffs on the would-be robber before he started building a wall or something. "It was just some screwball standing there with a brick in his hand," said FBI spokesman Bob Long to the *Chicago Sun-Times*. "Your classic bank robbery weapon." (Chicago, Illinois, late 1980s)

◆ A trio of ski-mask–clad bank robbers with silver handguns hid in a parking garage beneath a bank, then ambushed two workers, planning to force them to open the bank. **Too bad they**

**weren't bank employees.** And since the bank was not scheduled to open for at least an hour, the gunmen had no choice but to let their hostages go and flee the scene. (Garden City, New York, 2000)

- A 19-year-old robber walked into a bank on New Year's Eve and handed the teller a demand note. On one side: a threat of explosives if the bank didn't hand over money. **On the other side: the man's arrest sheet,** dated December 15, 1999, when he was charged with opposing an officer. The robber was caught two blocks away. (Jacksonville, Florida, 1999)

- A bank manager looked out of his front window and saw a guy wearing a false nose, scruffy blond wigs and gold-rimmed clown glasses pacing up and down the sidewalk. The clown would approach the bank, seem to change his mind, then head back to his car—which had its license plate covered with a rag. This happened several times. Something was obviously up, so the manager called the police, but a passing fire truck scared the clown before they could arrive. The manager gave them a description anyway, and the very next day, **the same clown showed up at a different bank.** Thanks to a police alert to area banks, the clown was nabbed before he could so much as make a balloon Tommy gun. (Cary, North Carolina, 2000)

- A 22-year-old man was unlucky enough to get splattered with fluorescent orange paint from a burst dye pack after he robbed a bank. He hid in an apartment building lobby and switched jackets. Then he saw a police car drive by and realized that he knew the officer. He ran outside and raised his arm—**still painted bright orange**—to wave at him. (Wilmington, Delaware, 1998)

- A bank robber carried a bag into the Hudson City Savings Bank and handed the teller a note claiming that he had a bomb. The bag, which he left behind after fleeing with some money, didn't have a bomb inside. **But it did contain a photograph of the robber.** And outside the bank, the robber dropped a deposit slip with a traceable alias written on it. (Newark, New Jersey, 1999)

- A heister plucked $1,400 from a ripe bank along the Chicago Loop. But on the way out, a dye pack burst, splattering the robber in red. That made him an easy target for the **dozens of police and Secret Service agents** who were providing security for then-President George Bush, who was speaking at the Board of Trade—right next door. (Chicago, Illinois, 1991)

- A 49-year-old man walked into the Independence Savings Bank in Bensonhurst and handed the teller a note: "Be fast. I have a gun. Give me all your money. Don't make me pull it." The teller gave him $2,100, which the robber stuffed in a brown paper bag. He had run a few blocks before somebody tripped him. The same person started kicking him in the face and chest, and then grabbed his paper bag. **It was a mugger,** who had seen the bank heist going down, and decided to hang around to take advantage of the situation.

  Once the mugger fled in a station wagon, the angry bank robber climbed to his feet, then immediately walked to the 62nd Precinct station house to report the incident. "He said that he had robbed a bank and that he himself had been robbed," said a police spokesman. "Only a psychiatrist would know why he did it." Despite a detailed description, the mystery mugger was never found. And the bank robber was charged with first-degree robbery, criminal possession of stolen property, and criminal possession of a weapon. (Brooklyn, New York, 1989)

- A 43-year-old comedian was deep into his routine at the Comedy Cafe in Macon when he tossed out this line: "I have something on my mind I want to share with you. **I'm the one who has been robbing all the banks** in middle Georgia." Thing is, he wasn't kidding. The club manager called the police. (Macon, Georgia, 2001)

- A man walked into a bank and threatened to detonate a pipe bomb unless he was given money. "Hold on a moment," a teller responded, and left the man **to wait for 20 minutes.** By the time the cash appeared, so did the police. (Fort Lauderdale, Florida, 1997)

◆ One 23-year-old bank robber was so pleased with his knockover at a People's Bank branch, he decided to spend the next day at the beach getting drunk. So drunk, in fact, that he started urinating in public. Police nabbed him, hauled him into the station, then started emptying his pockets. There, **they found the demand note** he had used the day before. "We're fortunate that some of these crooks aren't too intelligent," said one police captain. (Gulfport, Mississippi, 1999)

◆ A week before their wedding, an engaged couple found that they were desperately short on money to pay for the reception. **"They didn't want to disappoint family members,"** later explained one cop. So they decided to rob a Chase Manhattan Bank near Coney Island with a demand note and the threat of a bomb. "Our child is sick and we have nothing to lose in robbing this bank," the note read. But the teller stalled, and the couple had to flee without so much as a dime to go toward the champagne cocktails. They were arrested minutes later when the blushing bride-to-be stopped the getaway car to use the bathroom at a doughnut shop. (Brooklyn, New York, 2000)

◆ A call came into the Longview police station: The bank just down the street had been robbed. A description of the suspect was issued, and on a whim, Sgt. Ed Jones took a peek out of his window. There was the bank robber, **sitting on a bench, drinking a cold can of beer.** His brilliant getaway plan: Buy beer at a convenience store and try to fade into the background. Sgt. Jones simply walked across the street and slapped the cuffs on him. (Longview, Washington, 2001)

◆ A man used the old thumb-and-forefinger trick to simulate a gun with a teller at a Bank of America branch. Unfortunately, the teller could clearly see he was holding ... **well, just a thumb and forefinger.** The bank job, having quickly devolved into a hand job, ended in the man's arrest. (Merced, California, 1997)

◆ A 46-year-old man heard an interesting tip: **If you smear lemon juice on your face,** it will blur the image on any surveillance camera. So he robbed a bank with nothing but a spritz of lemon covering his mug, but shockingly, the cameras were still able to clearly record his face. The guy received 24 years in prison, which probably soured him on the whole bank robbery business. (Pittsburgh, Pennsylvania, 1995)

◆ A Queens bank robber left a very unusual accomplice in the get-away vehicle parked outside the bank: **his 86-year-old father, who suffered from Alzheimer's disease.** Then again, it was unlikely that Dad would—or could—squeal to the cops. The son was caught when he sped away and nearly clipped a police radio car. (Queens, New York, 2001)

◆ He looked like Alfred E. Neumann, he only wore black, and he was very good at knocking over banks—over 12 in one year. So what possessed the "Gap-Toothed Bandit" to **attend a Halloween party in the same costume** he used to stick up tellers? "I'm a bank robber," he said proudly, when someone asked what he was supposed to be. Someone else at the party remembered seeing a wanted poster for the "Gap-Toothed Bandit" that very morning. One phone call later, Gap-Toothed had a new costume: handcuffed prisoner. (San Diego, California, 1999)

◆ Normally, I would withhold the names of dumb robbers, but if Ronnie Bell didn't worry about it, why should I? Bell approached an armed bank guard and handed him a note: "This is a bank robbery of the Dallas Federal Reserve Bank of Dallas, Texas, give me all the money. **Thank you, Ronnie Darnell Bell.**" The guard immediately hit an alarm button, but Bell didn't seem to be in too much of a hurry, so he started chatting with him. "Well, I'm here to rob you," said Bell. "Is this where the money is? I tried to rob the post office, but they threw me out." (Dallas, Texas, 1998)

◆ A man walked into a bank and promptly handed a teller a note that was two pages long, full of bad handwriting and what appeared to be poetry. **It also demanded "19 trillion dollars."** After telling him that his demands were being considered, the teller summoned security, and the man was arrested without incident. He seemed genuinely surprised. "I guess they denied my robbery request," he said. "But I would have settled for $100 million!" (Des Moines, Iowa, 1995)

◆ The three bank robbers were well-prepared: ski masks on, rifles loaded, nerves steeled. They burst into the Sterling Bank & Trust, screamed, "Everyone hit the floor!" then immediately started looking for the cash. The only problem: **Sterling didn't have any cash.** It never does—the bank strictly deals in checks and electronic transfers. Frustrated, the robbers fled in their van and went off in search of a bank with real money in it. A bank executive told a reporter, "The police detective assures me that word's out on the street that we don't have cash on the premises." (San Francisco, California, 1997)

◆ A 69-year-old widower walked into a bank, prepared to rob it. Of course, "prepared" is a loose term. For starters, he chose to knock over his own branch of the GreenPoint bank, where **every employee knew him by name.** He didn't wear a mask. He slid the teller a note asking for $1,500 and claiming he had a gun. He received the money, but obviously didn't give much thought to a getaway; once outside, he started looking for a cab. In the meantime, the dye pack hidden in his loot exploded, splattering the old man with red paint. After much effort, a cab finally did stop, but by that time a police officer was already on the scene, and halted his escape. "I would have never expected him to do something like this," said one neighbor. "He looked like he could barely walk." (Queens, New York, 1999)

◆ A 25-year-old bank robber **didn't have a getaway car of his own,** so he called a cab to take him to his next job. The first bank he tried, however, was closed. So was the second. Finally, he asked the cabbie to drive him to a third bank, which was actually open and gave him $1,500 after he slid a teller a note that read, "I have a gun. Give up the money." The note, however, was written on Civic Center Days Inn stationery. Police tracked down the cabbie, who remembered the room number of his morning pick-up, which yielded the robber's name. "I can't believe he used his real name when he registered at the Days Inn," one cop remarked. Police finally found the robber at another motel, showered and ready to split town—presumably, via another cab. (St. Paul, Minnesota, 1993)

◆ One bank robber hit three banks in a lightning 25-minute spree, netting $10,300 from a Midlantic Bank, PNC Bank, and Meridian Bank. But he was captured just as quickly, when witnesses later spotted him wandering around a bus depot just around the corner from the Meridian, **his pockets bulging with cash.** (Philadelphia, Pennsylvania, 1995)

◆ One 51-year-old man seemed **hell-bent on spending the night in prison.** First, he smacked his pickup truck into a police car. After being charged and released, the man walked a few blocks away to the First Source Bank and told the teller to hand over "all of the large bills." Taking the money, the man walked back to the jail and told the cops what he did. Police escorted him back to the bank, confirmed that he had robbed it, and finally granted his wish. (South Bend, Indiana, 1998)

◆ Two bank robbers hit a downtown bank at high noon, then took off. It would have been a clean getaway, except for the fact that an FBI agent in a fast food joint saw them flee, as did a city cop who happened to be in the area. Both lawmen took off in hot pursuit. The G-man quickly nabbed one of the robbers, but the other managed to stay free long enough to reach the getaway car ... which had been parked illegally, and was being ticketed by **yet another city cop.** (Baltimore, Maryland, 2001)

◆ The robber walked up to a teller at 8:45 A.M. and said, "Give me money. I have a gun. Don't push the alarm." He also slid her a note that said pretty much the same thing. After the teller slid him some twenties and fives, the robber shook his head. "Give me more." The teller did—still more twenties and fives. "Give me more," he repeated. "I don't have more," the teller explained. **"I just opened."** The robber believed her, and fled with only $845. (New York City, 2002)

◆ Three men stormed into the lobby, looking to pull a bank robbery. They were forced to leave empty-handed, however, because they didn't realize that **Coldwell Banker wasn't actually a bank.** (Hacienda Heights, California, 2000)

◆ While cops searched a bank robbery suspect, they found a thick stack of $20 and $100 bills "rolled into a tight wad" and **hidden between the man's buttocks.** The robber had been the target of a 10-hour manhunt involving four trucks and a helicopter after robbing a First National Bank, and obviously took a moment from the chase to stash his loot in the safest place he could imagine. (Cleveland County, North Carolina, 2001)

# 47 ALL ABOUT THE BENJAMINS

### The 50 largest and lamest robbery paydays ever.

A bank robber these days can count on glomming at least a thousand dollars from the average bank teller. True, bank jobs are not as lucrative as jewel heists or bank fraud scams. But they're also not as risky as knocking over a neighborhood bodega, where the take might be $25 bucks—and the counterman might blast you with a sawed-off shotgun to get it back. Today's bankman plays the averages, rolls the dice, and hopes to walk away with a decent amount of change.

However, once in a while some bank robbers beat the odds, and end up stealing an astounding amount of cash. Still others beat the odds, but in the opposite direction. Here are the highs and lows of American heists—along with a handful of other big nonbank and worldwide heists, just for comparison's sake.

## $31,400,000

In the biggest bank robbery in world history, guerrillas blasted through the vaults of the British Bank of the Middle East in Beirut in 1976 and stole valuables worth this staggering amount.

## $11,500,000

The score from France's largest bank robbery in history, stolen from the Caisse d'Epargne in Paris in 1980. Another bank robbery, which took place on the Brittany coast of France in 1986, was almost as large.

**$11,000,000**

The largest U.S. cash robbery in history, lifted from a Sentry Armored Car Courier in New York on December 12, 1982.

**$10,200,000**

Stanley Rifkin's haul from the Security Pacific Bank computer robbery. (The bank recovered only $6.4 million.)

**$10,000,000**

The amount Russian computer hacker, Vladimir Levin, transferred from Citibank to bank accounts in the United States, Israel, Finland, Sweden, Germany, the Netherlands, and Switzerland in August 1994. More than $400,000 was cashed out before the transactions were frozen.

**$8,000,000**

The haul from the infamous Lufthansa Heist at Kennedy Airport on December 11, 1978. None of the money has ever been recovered.

**$8,000,000**

The score from a Hudson Armored Car job in Greenpoint, Brooklyn, in 1992. All but $250,000 was recovered.

**$7,000,000**

The amount of cash stolen by Victor Gerena, a Wells Fargo bank guard, and his accomplices on September 12, 1983. The money has never been recovered, and as of this printing, Gerena is still on the FBI's Ten Most Wanted list. At the time, this was the second largest cash heist in U.S. history, though not technically a bank robbery.

**$4,461,681**

The largest amount ever stolen in a single U.S. bank robbery. The bank: a Seafirst branch near Tacoma, Washington, which was flush with money from nearby banks, businesses, and a nearby casino. The perps: the infamous Trench Coat Robbers, a.k.a. William A. Kirkpatrick and Ray A. Bowman.

## $4,000,000

The estimated amount of cash stolen from the Societe Generale bank in Nice, France, in 1976. ($14 million more in valuables were also stolen from safe deposit boxes.) This bank burglary was inspired by Robert Pollack's novel, *Loophole,* which detailed a similar sewer tunnel break-in. (See "Let's Book 'Em.")

## $3,300,000

This much cash, when piled into a tower, is 4 feet tall, 3 feet wide, 5 feet long, and weights about 350 pounds. That's what David Grandstaff and his two partners stared at after they robbed the Valley National Bank in Tucson, Arizona, in 1981—at the time, the largest cash heist in history.

## $3,000,000

The estimated amount of cash, bonds, and diamonds stolen by the Newton Boys during a 1924 train robbery near Roundout, Illinois. (The brothers later traded most of it for decreased jail sentences.)

## $2,747,000

For three years, bank-robbing genius George Leonidas Leslie struggled to case the elusive Manhattan Savings Institution. Leonidas's hard work paid off when he and his gang busted into the bank's hidden vaults on October 27, 1878, and took this amount, which at the time was the largest theft in U.S. history.

## $2,700,000

The take from the infamous Brink's robbery in Boston in 1950.

### $2,678,700

The amount stolen from the Lincoln National Bank in Lincoln, Nebraska, on September 17, 1930. Heist king Harvey Bailey was thought to be behind it, but claimed he was nowhere near Nebraska on that day.

### $1,600,000

The proceeds of the "Big Dance" robbery of a Brink's truck, all in the name of funding the Black Liberation Army's revolutionary conquests.

### $1,500,000

Over Memorial Day Weekend 1980, a crew of cops and robbers worked together to steal this amount from the Depositors' Trust Bank in Medford, Massachusetts. And this was just the cash portion; the gang also stole an estimated $18 million in jewels.

### $1,492,000

The take from a robbery of a Chemical Bank Branch in New York City on December 21, 1993. In the confusion during the getaway, however, the gang responsible left behind a third of the money. At the time, it was the largest bank robbery in New York City.

### $1,380,000

The score from the largest bank robbery in Brazilian history, perpetrated by five men who had disguised themselves as bank auditors.

### $1,000,000

This is how much Seattle bank robber Scott "Hollywood" Scurlock stole from the Lake City Seafirst Branch the day before Thanksgiving 1996. It would be Scurlock's biggest—and last—heist.

## $1,000,000

The estimated amount—in cash securities—that master thief Adam Worth stole from the Boylston National Bank in Boston after an elaborate bank burglary.

## $786,879

The amount that George Leonidas Leslie stole from the Ocean National Bank on June 27, 1869—at the time one of the biggest takes in U.S. history.

## $750,000

The loot from one of the largest bank robberies in southern California history, which took place at a Bank of America branch in Santa Clarita in July 1995.

## $414,000

The score stolen in a College Park, Maryland, heist, thanks to the inside help from a bank teller. At the time, it was the most lucrative bank robbery in the state's history.

## $224,000

The haul from a still-unsolved heist at a Chase Manhattan Bank on Northern Boulevard in Little Neck, Queens, in the summer of 2001.

## $200,000

The score from the Denver Mint Robbery of 1922, all the money in fresh, unmarked $5 bills.

## $162,821

The take from the first recorded bank robbery in U.S. history.

**$160,000**

The amount stolen by Paddy Mitchell before his last American heist on February 22, 1994.

**$160,000**

Willie Sutton's biggest score, taken from the Corn Exchange Bank in Philadelphia.

**$74,782**

The Dillinger Gang's largest haul, stolen from the Central National Bank in Greencastle, Indiana.

**$35,000**

The amount taken in Pampa, Texas, in 1927 when Matt and George Kimes, along with Ray Terrill, plowed their truck through the front windows of a bank, attached a cable to the safe, and simply drove away with it.

**$22,000**

The largest bank haul of the infamous Reno Brothers Gang.

**$15,567**

The take from Herman "the Baron" Lamm's last heist, at the Citizens' State Bank in Clinton, Indiana, on December 16, 1930.

**$10,900**

That's how much Patty Hearst and Symbionese Liberation Army stole in their infamous Hibernia Bank heist in San Francisco.

## $6,024

The amount Harvey Bailey—who had been accused of at least two multimillion-dollar heists—stole when he teamed up with the sloppy, violent robber Wilbur Underhill.

## $5,000

The take from the first daylight bank stick-up in American history, perpetrated by drunkard Edward W. Green on December 15, 1863.

## $5,000

The largest amount of money the Average Joe Bandit ever requested in a stick-up. (The smallest amount was $3,000.)

## $3,500

The Dillinger Gang's smallest haul, stolen from the Commercial Bank in Daleville, Indiana.

## $2,500

The largest amount of money Clyde Barrow and his gang ever stole; most of his small-town robberies resulted in tiny paydays.

## $700

That's how much Henry Starr stole from the Byards State Bank in Oklahoma in 1914. Starr would earn nearly 20 times that amount in 1919, when he produced and starred in a movie about his own life.

## $400

The take from Wilbur Underhill's robbery of the International State Bank in Haskell, Oklahoma, on October 11, 1933.

## $160

The amount Bobby Wilcoxson and Al Nussbaum were stuck with after a bank teller in Philadelphia locked herself—and the big bills—in the vault.

## $140

This was all that Butch Cassidy, along with Matt Warner and the McCarty brothers, stole during his first train robbery. (Don't feel too bad for them; a year and a half later, they hit a train for $20,000.)

## $115

The take from Clyde Barrow's first bank robbery in Orango, Missouri, on November 9, 1932.

## $51

The amount Machine Gun Kelly once filched from the wallet of a kidnapping victim.

## $10

On September 18, 1991, a bank robber in Philadelphia handed the teller a note that read: "I want $10." The teller handed over the bill. Thinking this was easy, he asked for more money, but the teller said no. The robber then tried another teller, who also refused. Finally, the robber decided to quit while he was ahead, and left the bank.

## $3.50

The score from Pretty Boy Floyd's first heist at a post office in Akins, Oklahoma, on May 16, 1922. The haul was in pennies, dimes, and nickels. (Today, that haul wouldn't even buy a "Pretty Boy" wanted poster on eBay.)

**$0**

The amount the James Gang took from the First National Bank in Northfield, Minnesota, after residents fought back. (Jesse James thought he might be helping himself to at least $200,000 in the bank's vault.)

**$0**

The amount the Dalton Gang stole from Coffeyville, Kansas, after trying to hit two banks at once; they ended up in a bloody ambush.

**$0**

The amount one group of mystery bandits carried away after trying to torch their way into a bank vault beneath the rubble of the World Trade Center in October 2001.

# 48 THE NAKED CITIES

*The lowdown on America's bank heist boom towns.*

Bank robberies tend to fluctuate year to year. The last peak year was 1996, with about 9,500 heists nationwide. By the turn of the millennium, it was back down to about 6,500 per year. But that downward trend suddenly reversed in 2001, with a number of cities and states reporting an upkick in robberies. Was it the new recession? Aftershocks of the September 11 terrorist attacks? Increased drug use? Or just a statistical quirk, with no rhyme or reason? Recently, every bank robbery "boom town" has had its own set of statistics—and explanations.

## LOS ANGELES, CALIFORNIA

L.A. is the bank robbery capital of the world, and has been since 1978. Back in the 1960s, L.A. saw an average of only 400 bank heists a year. That number doubled in the 1970s, then nearly doubled again during the 1980s, with an average of 1,400 per year. (During this time, L.A. bank robberies accounted for 20 to 30 percent of the total bank jobs in the United States.) The peak year was 1992, when there was an astounding 2,641 bank heists in the Los Angeles region, which basically meant that FBI agents scrambled to a robbery scene every 42 minutes of each business day.

Why the astronomical number of Hollywood-area heists? Surely, Winona Ryder can't be blamed for all of them. According to a 2000 report in the *FBI Law Enforcement Bulletin,* two factors are to blame: a booming population and California laws that permit unlimited bank branches. (More branches equal more opportunities for stick-ups.) Also, drug addicts in need for cash for their next heroin fix, and L.A. street gangs, who see bank heists as fund-raising opportunities, only add to the problem. For instance, in September 1991, a gang called the West Hills Bandits robbed a bank of $436,000, one of the largest takeover heists at the time. Suddenly, every gang wanted to muscle in on the bank-robbing business.

The good news: The number of bank robberies has plummeted since the early 1990s, falling in 1998 to only 656, the lowest number in three decades. There was a **slight upkick in the year 2000, with 694 bank robberies,** but the FBI attributes the increase to gang activity and the work of serial robbers. "If you get the right 10 bank robbers off the street," assistant FBI director James DeSarno told the *Los Angeles Times*, "you're going to have an incredible effect on the numbers."

## DETROIT, MICHIGAN

In 2000, Motor City placed **second (to L.A.) in highest number of bank robberies, with 326.** There's an average of one heist every two days in Detroit and the surrounding Wayne County suburbs; FBI and local police blame a surplus of serial robbers on the prowl. To make matters worse, only 131 of the robberies committed in 2001 have been solved, leaving many drugged-out bank robbers free to strike and strike again. "They do it until they get caught," said Detroit FBI agent Terry Booth in an interview with the *Detroit News*.

## SEATTLE, WASHINGTON

The city that was once full of grunge bands now seems full of robber gangs. Seattle had **311 bank robberies in the year 2000,** placing it third on the list of most bank heists in the country (after L.A. and Detroit). Blame the 1990s boom of millionaire tech barons and the dozens of new bank branches opening up to accommodate them. And even though dot.com mania has fizzled since March 2000, bank robberies haven't.

## NEW YORK, NEW YORK

There were **224 bank heists in the Big Apple** during the year 2001—the highest number since 1997. By year's end, there were 55 armed robberies in the 5 boroughs, up from 31 the year before. Some speculated that the increase was due to the redeployment of FBI agents—now too busy looking for terrorist cells to worry about old-fashioned bank robbers. But the FBI disagrees and blames the recession. "This is actually pretty predictable," FBI spokesman James Margolin told the *New York Daily News*. "Whenever there is an economic downturn there is an increase in bank robberies."

## CHARLOTTE, NORTH CAROLINA

Bank robberies were also on the rise in the Tar Heel state, with 350 throughout the state (up from 339), and **over 100 in the Charlotte region** (up from 91). City officials were at a loss for an explanation, but told the *Charlotte Observer* that they hoped a new publicity campaign promoting a reward program and stiffer jail terms would help deter would-be robbers.

## BOSTON, MASSACHUSETTS

Between September 11 and November 30, 2001, there were **an amazing 81 bank robberies in southern New England.** (During the same time the year before, there were only 33.) "We have to say there is a connection to 9-11," said FBI special agent Charles Prouty in an interview with the *Boston Herald*. Most robbers here tend to be drug addicts who pick banks without armed guards and use demand notes, and it is speculated that they believe the FBI to be too busy combating domestic terrorism to bother with bank robbers any more.

## SAN FRANCISCO, CALIFORNIA

Halfway through 2001, Bay Area counties were reporting an increase of bank robberies. Santa Clara County, for instance, had **70 robberies by August, 2001,** as compared to only 55 in all of 2000. Local experts blame a number of high-profile bandits—such as "the Bag Lady," a bank robber who lived in her car, and the "Robust Robber," a former air traffic controller turned heister—for the boost. "Certainly these latest cases are more colorful," said San Francisco State University criminalist Mike Rustigan in an interview with the *San Jose Mercury News*. "They are getting a lot of publicity and that may give people the impression that bank robbery is on the rise. I don't believe it is."

## NEW ORLEANS, LOUISIANA

By early November 2001, in the Eastern District of Louisiana there were **over 64 bank robberies,** up from 58 the previous year. "This year is the highest in recent memory," said FBI special agent Bob Tucker in the *Times-Picayune*. "I expect it will level off and go back down in the years ahead." As for cause, local criminologists point to economic troubles, rather than the assumption that FBI agents are too busy to go after terrorists. "I don't think your garden-variety armed robber operating in this area has put the world of terrorism down to the perspective of the bank he'll rob," said William Thornton, professor of criminology at Loyola University.

*Other major cities reporting a rise in bank robberies:* **Dallas,** with 88 in 2001, nearly double the previous year; **Indianapolis** with 54 in 2001, also double the previous year; Twin Cities **St. Paul** and **Minneapolis** reported 85 bank robberies in 2001, up from 70 the year before; **Kansas City** had more bank robberies in 2000 than the four previous years combined; and **Pittsburgh,** between April 2000 and April 2001, reported 98 bank robberies—double the yearly average.

# 49  LET'S BOOK 'EM

Consult this survey of sure-fire bank robbery novels and curl up with a good 211.

"Parker is very popular in prison," wrote 1960s bank robber Al Nussbaum. "Despite the fact that almost everyone can find some nit to pick with the criminal methods he describes, the strength of the Parker character overshadows any small flaws." Nussbaum was referring to the hardboiled crime series by Richard Stark (a pseudonym of mystery writer Donald Westlake) featuring a professional heister named Parker—no first name, thankyouverymuch. The Parker novels are crisp, cold, suspenseful ... and apparently, inspirational. "I've not only read them," wrote Nussbaum, "I've even tried to live a couple of them."

Of course, Nussbaum wasn't your average crime buff—he had a vested interest in the topic. But what might modern-day Nussbaums be reading in the slammer these days?

*Blood Money* (1927) by Dashiell Hammett. The hero of this short novel—and many other short stories, first published in *Black Mask* magazine during the 1920s—is a balding, middle-aged operative who works for the Continental Detective Agency (think: Pinkerton Agency). In *Blood Money*—which is actually two related novellas, *Big Knockover* and *$106,000 Blood Money*—the Continental Op tangles with a criminal mastermind named Popadopalous who organizes an audacious double-bank heist perpetrated by no less than 150 (!) criminals. The $106,000 refers not to the take from the robbery, but rather the bounty on Popadopalous's head. Hammett's seminal hardboiled novel **Red Harvest** also features a bank robbery as a subplot.

*Thieves Like Us* (1937) by Edward Anderson. Three escaped convicts resume their careers as bank robbers in Oklahoma, but things become complicated when the youngest bandit, Bowie A. Bowers, falls in love with a cousin of one of the older robbers and decides to make a run at the straight life. Anderson got the idea for the novel after interviewing his cousin Roy Johnson, who was in the Huntsville State Penitentiary for armed robbery; the original title was *They're Thieves Like Us*. The novel was later filmed as Nicholas Ray's *They Live by Night* (1949) and Robert Altman's *Thieves Like Us* (1974), starring Keith Carradine and Shelley Duvall.

*Hell Hath No Fury* (1953) by Charles Williams. A drifter named Madox wanders into a small town and finds work at a used car lot, but is just biding his time until he can devise the perfect bank robbery by setting diversion fires all over town. But someone's already set a fire for Madox: the used car lot owner's wife. In 1990, *Hell* was turned into a Dennis Hopper–directed movie called *The Hot Spot* starring Don Johnson (as Madox), and Virginia Madsen (as the boss's wife, Dolly Harshaw).

*The Big Caper* (1955) and *Steal Big* (1960) by Lionel White. White was the king of pulp caper novels—his racetrack robbery thriller, *Clean Break,* was the basis for Stanley Kubrick's early film noir *The Killing*. In *The Big Caper,* White details a complex bank heist, complete with a safecracker, an arsonist, a pair of tough guys, and a phony husband and wife whose job it is to case the bank. But what happens when that couple decides they'd rather live as man and wife for real than pull the bank job? White described another bank heist gone south five years later in *Steal Big*, where a hardened con named Donovan puts together what he considers the ultimate bank robbing gang—but all of them turn out to be the ultimate collection of sociopathic losers. White has some fun with in-jokes; one Manhattan black market gun dealer operates under the front, "Kubric Novelty Company."

*The Getaway* (1958) by Jim Thompson. A bank heist perpetrated by a pair of married ex-cons—Doc and Carol McCoy—goes sour, and suddenly a clean getaway is the only thing that matters. Of course, this is a Jim Thompson novel, and in Thompson's sordid little corner of the universe, nothing is clean or easy. Still, Doc McCoy has a few clever heist techniques up his sleeve. As one thug named Rudy explains early in the novel: "First, [Doc] looks for a bank that ain't a member of the Federal Reserve System."

"Oh. Oh, I see," says another criminal. "The Feds don't come in on the case, right, Rudy?"

"Right," says Rudy. "So anyway, he checks that angle, and then he checks on interest rates. If a bank's paying little or nothing on savings, y'see, it means they got a lot more dough than they can loan out. So that tips Doc off on the most likely prospects, and all he has to do then is check their statements of condition—you've seen them printed in the newspapers, haven't you?"

*The Devil Wears Wings* (1960) by Harry Whittington. It's a shame that Whittington is largely forgotten among today's mystery readers. Only he could have come up with a bank heist like the one in this book, where an alcoholic World War II vet named Buz Johnson is recruited by a bank robber to serve not as the getaway driver, but the getaway *pilot*. That's right: These heisters plan to abscond with the money via Cessna plane. Then again, Whittington insisted that this novel was based on a true story. "This botched, bourbon-laced crime was one I wrote for editor Joe Corona at *True Detective*," wrote Whittington. "But I could not get this tragic-comedy out of my mind, so I structured the true events enough to give them form, a beginning, middle, end and desired emotional effect."

*The Name of the Game Is Death* (1962) and *One Endless Hour* (1969) by Dan J. Marlowe. These two books are the *Godfather* and *Godfather II* of bank robber novels. Earl Drake successfully knocks over a jug in Phoenix, but catches a bullet in his upper-left arm during the getaway. While he recovers, Drake entrusts the loot to his partner, who lams out for Florida and promises to send Drake some money every week. For a while, the money arrives right on schedule. Then one day it stops, and Drake sets out for Florida to find out why. It's impossible to say more without ruining the plot; needless to say, Drake has a hell of time trying to recover his loot. And just when you think the ending leaves Drake no possible escape, along comes *One Endless Hour,* which picks up exactly where *Death* leaves off and manages to equal—if not surpass, in some scenes—the original.

Marlowe later turned Drake into a series character ("The Man with Nobody's Face"), but in novels like *Operation: Flashpoint* and *Operation: Drumfire* he stopped acting like a ruthless bank robber and became more of a Bondian secret agent. Still, Marlowe's later missteps take nothing away from the brutal one-two punch of the originals.

***The Sour Lemon Score*** (1969) by Richard Stark. Even though *Sour Lemon* is professional thief Parker's twelfth novel appearance, this is the first time we actually see him robbing a bank. (The previous 11 novels focused on payroll, jewels, and other assorted heists.) Everything goes smoothly enough when Parker and three others hit the Laurel Avenue Branch of the Merchants' and Farmers' Trust Bank. But the take is not quite what the group expected—a measly $33,000—and suddenly, one gang member gets greedy and pulls a double-cross. In many ways, this novel is a flashback to the very first Parker novel, *The Hunter,* in which our anti-hero is screwed out of his share of a payroll heist and left for dead, then goes after the syndicate to get it back. (You may remember the film versions of this novel—*Point Blank* with Lee Marvin and *Payback* with Mel Gibson.) A bank robbery also kicks off Stark's ***Flashfire*** (2000), in which Parker firebombs a convenience store in order to distract cops while his accomplices pull a bank heist. Another double-cross is pulled this time, too, but not in the way you might think.

***Bank Shot*** (1972) by Donald Westlake. One reviewer called this book "*The Thomas Crown Affair* meets the *Three Stooges.*" It's the second in Westlake's series about John Dortmunder, a serious-minded yet bumbling thief who decides to gather his crew to steal a bank. That's right—not the money in the bank, but the bank itself. "I was commuting weekly between New Jersey and New York," recalled Westlake to an interviewer. "There was a bank on Route 23, they were tearing down the old bank and putting up a new bank. It took about a year, and they were operating the bank out of a mobile home next door. And after several months of watching this twice a week driving back and forth, I said, 'Wait a minute. An enterprising guy could back a truck up to that thing and drive the bank away.'"

*The Friends of Eddie Coyle* (1972) by George V. Higgins. Eddie Coyle is a small-time crook supplying pistols to a bank robber named Jimmy Scalisi. But Eddie's also being squeezed by cops to offer up some underworld dirt, and Coyle, with a wife and three kids to support, has some tough decisions to make. Higgins's first (and arguably best) novel is a masterwork of gutter-tough dialogue, at its best when two characters are simply sitting around a table, talking business—or, for that matter, being held up. "It's not all unusual," says a bank manager who's fallen victim to a Scalisi heist. "I've been in this business for thirty-six years. I've been held up, this is the fourth time. It's been my experience that people like this're generally telling the truth. They want the money. They don't want to hurt us. If we can keep calm, we'll be all right."

*Bank Job* (1974) by Robert L. Pike. Lieutenant Jim Reardon is called in to solve a grisly bank heist in which a San Francisco cop was gunned down. The bandits steal away with a quarter of a million bucks in small, unmarked bills—but they also leave behind some interesting videotaped evidence, which starts Reardon on a dizzying manhunt. Pike, a joking pseudonym of writer Robert Fish, also wrote *Mute Witness,* which was the basis of the Steven McQueen cop thriller *Bullitt.*

*Let's Hear It for the Deaf Man* (1973) by Ed McBain. McBain's popular 87th Precinct series, set in the fiction city of Isola (read: Manhattan), occasionally features a Moriarity-like villain dubbed "the Deaf Man" who loves sparring with the detectives. In this installment, the Deaf Man tells Detective Steve Carella that he's going to steal $500,000 on the last day of April—with Carella's help. Then, the Deaf Man starts mailing clues: a portrait of George Washington. A photo of J. Edgar Hoover. Another photo of an obscure actress. What does it all mean? And can the boys of the 87th figure it out before one bank loses half a million bucks?

*Loophole, or How to Rob a Bank* (1973) by Robert Pollock. While the other novels on this list may have served as inspiration for real-life bank robbers, Pollock's *Loophole* definitely did—just ask the French police. "Some French political criminals read the book and used the plan to pull two of the largest bank vault robberies in history, in Nice and Paris," says Pollock. "The Chief of Police in Nice, Albert Moure, confirmed in a press interview the gang got their idea from the book." Which is not surprising, considering that Pollock based *Loophole* on an actual heist plan cooked up by England's foremost bank robber. "We did a deal where I paid him a percentage of my possible income from a novel based on the plan," says Pollock, who met the crook while reporting for the *Sunday Times*. "Then I did extensive research which included going down the London sewer and obtaining photographs of the bank vault locking systems." Meanwhile, his robber friend checked the technical details.

The result was a knockout novel that achieved worldwide acclaim and was later made into a movie starring Albert Finney and Martin Sheen. "My informant took me to the London premiere in his Jaguar," adds Pollock.

*Roses Are Red* (2000) by James Patterson. Series detective Alex Cross (who has been portrayed by Morgan Freeman in the movies *Kiss the Girls* and *Along Came a Spider*) squares off against the Mastermind, a psychotic jugmarker who seems to be getting his jollies from killing bank employees and their families. Patterson is the king of the ultra-short chapter, making for ultra-readable thrillers. It doesn't hurt that Patterson seems to have done his bank robbery homework, dropping references to real-life heisters like Joseph Dougherty, Terry Lee Conner, and David Grandstaff.

**"The Death of Jack Hamilton"** (2001) by Stephen King. Yeah, this list promised novels, but one short story for the road can't hurt. This humdinger, which appeared in the December 24–31, 2001, issue of *The New Yorker*, details the aftermath of a John Dillinger heist, and King manages to weave a yarn that's riveting, gory, suspenseful, and touching—not to mention true to history. A must-read for Dillinger junkies.

# 50 REPEAT OFFENDERS

### The weird, wild world of bank robbery reenactment.

A bank robbery can be a traumatic event for employees and innocent bystanders alike. The memory of a flashed gun, a harshly barked command, maybe even physical violence can haunt a robbery victim for years. So why is it that so many Americans enjoy recreating bank robberies in a series of annual festivals? For your next vacation, you might break off a chunk of your stashed loot and check out ...

## DEFEAT OF JESSE JAMES DAYS

Every September since 1948, Northfield, Minnesota, has been throwing a four-day bash in honor of the day that their ancestors got the drop on Jesse James and his gang. The 2001 festival, the 125th anniversary of the actual raid on Northfield, included such decidedly noncriminal events as a horseshoe hunt, tractor pull, car show, Western Style Steak Fry, bingo, a noncompetitive "Fun Walk," and most importantly, the beer tent. ("Always the star of the show as I far as I was concerned," reported one attendee.) But gunslinging fans needn't worry: There is also a reenactment of the raid by actors, with real horses and guns and everything. A $3 button gets you a front-row seat in the bleachers, but you can also stand elsewhere for free.

For information, visit www.defeatofjessejamesdays.org. You can contact the organizing committee at djjdinfo@djjd.org, or by writing to Defeat of Jesse James Days, PO Box 23, Northfield, MN 55057.

## DALTON DAYS

After nearly all his brothers were wiped out in that ill-fated Coffeyville, Kansas, raid in 1892, Bill Dalton—with no previous bank robbery experience—joined up with Bill Doolin and his gang. Later still, Dalton split from Doolin and formed his own gang to rob the First National

Bank in Longview, Texas, on May 23, 1894. But Bill Dalton was no more successful than his brothers: Soon after, lawmen trailed Dalton to his hideout and shot him to death.

Exactly 100 years later, citizens of Longview started celebrating the raid and Dalton's demise with Dalton Days, a festival full of cowboy storytelling, chuck wagon demonstrations, trick roping, horseshoe pitching, and of course, a reenactment of Dalton's assault on the First National Bank. Some historians argue that Bill Dalton may not have even been involved in the First National robbery, but that's no reason not to kick back and have a little trick roping fun with the kids, is it?

The sixth annual Dalton Days celebration (the 2001 festival was cancelled due to the September 11 attacks) is scheduled to take place on September 28, 2002. For more information, contact the Gregg County Historical Museum at 903-753-5840 or visit the Longview, Texas, tourism website at www.longviewtx.com.

## AUTHENTIC BONNIE AND CLYDE FESTIVAL

Every year, the town of Gibsland, Louisiana, picks the weekend closest to May 23 and stages this two-day celebration, starting with a lively gumbo dinner and ending with the bloody end of Bonnie and Clyde in a forest a few miles outside of town. Usually, the event draws 300 people, and, shotgun deaths aside, is meant to be fun for the whole family. Writer Ron Geraci traveled to the festival in 2000 and met a group of Bonnie and Clyde fans who were serious—"*Trekkie* serious," Geraci wrote—about every last detail of the lives of Bonnie and Clyde, as well as the ambush. "It sounded just like dee-namyte," recalled Olan Jackson, the 89-year-old street commissioner of Gibsland, who was working in a nearby field at the time of the ambush. "It was loud and lasted maybe ten seconds. It wasn't until they pulled the bodies through town in the car to show the school kids that I realized what I'd really heard." The car used in the reenactment isn't the real Bonnie and Clyde deathmobile—that's on display at Whiskey Pete's Casino in Las Vegas—but rather the replica used in the 1967 Arthur Penn movie, which is now owned by Dallas historian Ken Holmes Jr.

If you'd like to attend the next festival, call Gibsland City Hall at 318-843-6141 or Ken Holmes Jr. at 214-741-5241.

# THE STICK-TIONARY

Don't break the box in the jug unless you've talked to a peterman and have a mace ready to run the cat roads, lest you end up in the big sneezer. In other words, here's a glossary:

**211**   police code for armed robbery

**access control units (ACUs)**   entry doors often used by banks that automatically lock shut when they detect someone with a weapon

**bandit barrier**   a bulletproof partition that separates the teller and the money from the bank robber and a gun

**barking irons**   pistols

**the big sneezer**   prison

**boodle**   a quantity of money

**breadsville**   a bank

**breaking the box**   cracking into a bank safe

**caravan**   a lot of money

**casing the joint**   watching a bank in preparation for a robbery

**chopper**   a submachine gun

**dime**   a 10-year jail sentence

**G-men**   FBI agents; this term was supposedly coined by Machine Gun Kelly during his arrest, as in "Don't shoot, G-men, don't shoot!"

**getaway sticks**   legs

**glom**   to steal

**gonif**   thief

**hardening a location**   installing a "bandit barrier" in a bank

**heat**   the law

**heist**   to steal; most likely a bastardization of the word "hoist"

**jug** a bank

**jugmarker (also jugger)** a professional thief who will plan a bank robbery for a gang in exchange for an up-front fee or a piece of the action

**knockover** a heist or robbery

**mace** a car with phony license plate and registration that will pass a quick once-over by the law

**nicked** stole

**note heist** robbing a bank with a demand note

**on the nut** broke

**peterman** a safecracker

**playing center field** in a daylight stick-up, working the floor of the bank

**playing the tiger** daylight stick-up, acting as the gunman at the bank doorway during a daylight stick-up

**running the cat roads** making a getaway along dark, small country roads. Harvey Bailey called them "cat roads" because cats were the only ones who could use them after dark

**screwsman** a burglar who works with keys

**soup job** cracking open a safe with nitroglycerine

**stick-up** an armed robbery

**takeover heist** seizing control of a bank and its employees with guns and/or threats of violence

**tapping a jug** robbing a bank

**wholesale banking business** robbing a bank

**yegg** a safe-cracker, bank robber, or another assorted criminal ("You know, the aristocracy of the criminal profession," said master jugger Eddie Bentz. Writer Raymond Chandler, however, had a more specific definition in mind: "A yegg is a safe-cracker, a box man," he wrote in a letter to friend Hamish Hamilton. "He wouldn't go near a bank, because he couldn't open a bank safe, even if it didn't have a time lock. He could only open a rather cheap and vulnerable safe.")

## Hand Over the Balsam, Jack

**synonyms for money**  balsam, berries, blunt, boodle, brads, brass, bread, cabbage, chips, clams, cush, dead presidents, dinero, dough, ducats, friends in the bank, geets, geetus, gravy, greenbacks, heap of jack, heavy sugar, iron men, long green, mazuma, rhino, scratch, sheckles, spinach, spondulix, stuff with the dead ones' pictures, sugar, wearing the green

**two bits**  25 cents

**a half**  50 cents

**ace, can, fish, push note**  $1

**deuce**  $2

**fin**  $5

**sawbuck**  $10

**double sawbuck**  $20

**half a yard**  $50

**century note, yard**  $100

**a pair of Cs**  $200

**G**  $1,000

**large**  $1,000

**twenty large (etc.)**  $20,000

*Sources: William Denton's excellent* Twists, Slugs and Roscoes: A Glossary of Hardboiled Slang *(www.mistaktonic.org/slang.html), Max Décharné's* Straight from the Fridge, Dad: A Dictionary of Hipster Slang, *as well as innumerable crime novels and true-crime books.*

# THE HARD NUMBERS

## The FBI's bank robbery breakdown and other fun stats.

According to most law enforcement officials, bank robbery statistics defy any kind of logic. "You'll see that there is no real rhyme or reason to bank robbery stats," explains Special Agent Linda Vizi, spokesperson for the Philadelphia FBI office. "They could be up in burbs and down in the city one year and the next year, just the opposite. You can have one serial bank robber that really throws the numbers off for a particular area and when he is caught, the numbers take a big drop."

## TOTAL NUMBER OF BANK ROBBERIES

This includes those of commercial banks, mutual savings banks, savings and loan associations, credit unions, and armored-car companies. "Bank robberies peaked in 1991 and have dropped every year since 1996," says Erma Rabusa, spokesperson for the American Bankers' Association.

| | |
|---|---|
| 1984 | 6,067 |
| 1985 | 5,427 |
| 1986 | 5,672 |
| 1987 | 6,078 |
| 1988 | 6,549 |
| 1989 | 6,691 |
| 1990 | 7,837 |

| 1991 | 9,388 |
|------|-------|
| 1992 | 9,063 |
| 1993 | 8,647 |
| 1994 | 7,029 |
| 1995 | 6,758 |
| 1996 | 8,046 |
| 1997 | 7,876 |
| 1998 | 7,584 |
| 1999 | 6,599 |
| 2000 | 7,546 |

## THE HAUL

In 2000, the average amount of money stolen by a bank robber was **$4,437. That same year, bank robbers walked away with a total of $78,011,622,** not quite as much as in 1997, when **$103,072,136** was stolen.

## MISSED OPPORTUNITIES

In 2000, about **642** bank robberies ended up with the heister getting doodly squat, which was better than 1998, when **659** robberies were duds, and 1996, when **679** robberies were duds.

## THE METHODS

Demand notes are usually in popular ... er, demand.

|                   | 1998  | 1997  | 1996  |
|-------------------|-------|-------|-------|
| Demand note used  | 3,999 | 3,989 | 4,127 |
| Gun used          | 2,482 | 2,671 | 2,602 |
| Other weapon used | 37    | 87    | 108   |

|                          | 1998  | 1997  | 1996  |
|--------------------------|-------|-------|-------|
| Weapon threatened        | 3,693 | 3,645 | 3,774 |
| Bomb used or threatened  | 292   | 322   | 328   |
| Oral demand              | 4,189 | 2,791 | 1,102 |
| Vault or safe theft      | 79    | 93    | 52    |
| Inside job (till theft)  | 122   | 128   | 100   |

## A BANK ROBBER'S DAY MINDER

"Can I squeeze in that FirstAmerica heist between my Friday morning ballet lessons and my weekly church group lunch?" Bank robbers seem to like Mondays and Fridays the most.

| Day of the Week | 1998  | 1997  | 1996  |
|-----------------|-------|-------|-------|
| Monday          | 1,487 | 1,544 | 1,542 |
| Tuesday         | 1,441 | 1,482 | 1,522 |
| Wednesday       | 1,329 | 1,369 | 1,410 |
| Thursday        | 1,376 | 1,506 | 1,414 |
| Friday          | 1,751 | 1,804 | 1,901 |
| Saturday        | 469   | 519   | 481   |
| Sunday          | 84    | 85    | 60    |
| Unknown         | 54    | 63    | 53    |

## STUFF THAT DIDN'T FIT ANYWHERE ELSE

◆ The most popular time and day to hit a bank? Between 9 A.M. and 11 A.M. on Friday.

◆ The number-one reason people rob banks? To buy drugs.

◆ The overwhelming majority of bank robbers hit branch offices, as opposed to a main office or a remote facility. Most robbed banks are in a commercial district, not shopping centers or residential burbs.

- Few attempt the late-night back-door method anymore—only 10 percent of total bank robberies every year take place when the bank is closed. And only about 1 in 20 try to crack a safe.

- In 1999, bank robbers took 100 hostages. In 2000, 108 hostages were taken.

- In 2000, there were 62 armored car jobs. Forty-eight of them were successful, the loot totaling $9,255,922.

- Guns or other weapons were used in 72 percent of reported bank robberies in 2000. Heisters got violent in 412 of those cases, resulting in 166 injuries and 23 deaths.

- In 2000, 68 percent of the solved bank robberies were committed by people who were responsible for multiple bank robberies.

- In 2000, Western states accounted for 33 percent of reported bank heists; Southern states 32 percent; North Central states 21 percent; and Northeastern states 14 percent.

- When caught, bank robbers almost always have less loot than the amount stolen—even if it's only a day since the heist. (Maybe it was the White Sale at Macy's?) Of the $78,011,622 that was stolen in 2000, only $13,208,476 (about 17 percent) was recovered.

- Also in 1999, 22 bank robbers were gunned down.

- Four of five people informally polled agree that *Point Break* was a very stupid movie.

# THIS HERE'S A BIBLIOGRAPHY

Still hungry for more bank-robbing action? Check out these related titles:

Abagnale, Frank W. *The Art of the Steal*. New York: Broadway Books, 2001.

Asbury, Herbert. *The Gangs of New York*. New York: Alfred A. Knopf, 1927.

Caren, Eric C. *Crime Extra: 300 Years of Crime in North America*. New Jersey: Castle Books, 2001.

Clemente, Gerald W. *The Cops Are Robbers*. Boston: Quinlan Press, 1987.

Cooper, Courtney Ryley. *Ten Thousand Public Enemies*. Boston: Little, Brown and Company, 1935.

Cromie, Robert, and Joseph Pinkston. *Dillinger: A Short and Violent Life*. New York: McGraw-Hill, 1962.

Décharné, Max. *Straight from the Fridge, Dad: A Dictionary of Hipster Slang*. New York: Broadway Books, 2000.

Deloach, Cartha D. *Hoover's FBI: The Inside Story by Hoover's Trusted Lieutenant*. Washington, D.C.: Regnery Publishing, Inc., 1997.

Drago, Henry Sinclair. *Outlaws on Horseback*. New York: Dodd, Mead, 1964.

Edge, L. L. *Run the Cat Roads*. New York: Dembner Books, 1981.

Hearst, Patricia Campbell. *Every Secret Thing*. New York: Avon, 1982.

Helmer, William, with Rick Mattix. *Public Enemies*. New York: Facts On File, 1998.

Hynd, Alan. *We Are the Public Enemies*. New York: Fawcett Publications, 1949.

Karpis, Alvin. *On the Rock: Twenty-Five Years in Alcatraz*. New York: Beaufort Books, 1980.

Karpis, Alvin, with Bill Trent. *The Alvin Karpis Story.* New York: Coward, McCann & Geoghegan, 1971.

King, Jeffrey S. *The Life and Death of Pretty Boy Floyd.* Ohio: Kent State University Press, 1998.

Kirchner, L. R. *Robbing Banks: An American History 1831–1999.* New York: Sarpedon, 2000.

Louderback, Lew. *The Bad Ones: Gangsters of the '30s and Their Molls.* Greenwich, Connecticut: Fawcett Publications, 1968.

Macintyre, Ben. *The Napoleon of Crime: The Life and Times of Adam Worth, Master Thief.* New York: Dell Publishing, 1997.

MacNee, Marie J. *Outlaws, Mobsters and Crooks: From the Old West to the Internet.* Detroit: UXL, 1998.

Meadows, Anne. *Digging Up Butch and Sundance.* New York: St. Martin's Press, 1994.

Metz, Leon Claire. *The Shooters.* New York: Berkley Books, 1976.

Muller, Eddie. *Dark City: The Lost World of Film Noir.* New York: St. Martin's Griffin, 1998.

Nash, Jay Robert. *Almanac of World Crime.* Garden City, NY: Anchor Press/Doubleday, 1981.

———. *Bloodletters and Badmen: A Narrative Encyclopedia of American Criminals from the Pilgrims to the Present.* New York: M. Evans and Company, Inc., 1995.

Newton, Joe, and Willis Newton, as told to Claude Stanush and David Middleton. *The Newton Boys: Portrait of an Outlaw Gang.* Texas: State House Press, 1994.

Newton, Michael, and Judy Ann Newton. *The FBI Most Wanted: An Encyclopedia.* New York: Dell Publishing, 1989.

Patterson, Richard. *Butch Cassidy: A Biography.* Lincoln, Nebraska: University of Nebraska Press, 1998.

Phillips, Charles, and Alan Axelrod. *Cops, Crooks and Criminologists: An International Biographical Dictionary of Law Enforcement.* New York: Facts On File, 1996.

Phillips, John Neal. *Running with Bonnie and Clyde: The Ten Fast Years of Ralph Fults.* Oklahoma: University of Oklahoma Press, 1996.

Reynolds, Quentin. *I, Willie Sutton*. New York: Farrar, Straus and Giroux, 1953.

Roth, Andrew. *Infamous Manhattan: A Colorful Walking History of New York's Most Notorious Crime Scenes*. New York: Citadel Press, 1996.

Sabljak, Mark, and Martin H. Greenberg. *Most Wanted: A History of the FBI's Ten Most Wanted List*. New York: Bonanza Books, 1990.

Sante, Luc. *Low Life*. New York: Random House, 1992.

Sifakis, Carl. *Encyclopedia of American Crime*. New York: Smithmark, 1982.

Smith, Robert Barr. *Daltons! The Raid on Coffeyville, Kansas*. Norman: University of Oklahoma Press, 1996.

Sutton, Willie, with Edward Linn. *Where the Money Was*. New York: Viking, 1976.

Theoharis, Athan G., with Tony G. Poveda, Susan Rosenfeld, and Richard Gid Powers. *The FBI: A Comprehensive Reference Guide*. New York: Checkmark Books, 2000.

Time-Life Books, editors. *The Wild West*. Alexandria, Virginia: Time Warner, 1993.

Toland, John. *The Dillinger Days*. New York: Random House, 1963.

Treherne, John. *The Strange History of Bonnie and Clyde*. New York: Cooper Square Press, 2000.

Under, Robert. *The Union Station Massacre: The Original Sin of J. Edgar Hoover's FBI*. Kansas City: Andrews McNeel Publishing, 1997.

Volkman, Ernest, and John Cummings. *The Heist*. New York: Franklin Watts, 1986.

Wallis, Michael. *Pretty Boy: The Life and Times of Charles Arthur Floyd*. New York: St. Martin's Press, 1992.

Weyermann, Debra. *The Gang They Couldn't Catch*. New York: Simon & Schuster, 1993.

Wolf, Marvin J., and Katherine Mader. *Fallen Angels: Chronicles of L.A. Crime and Mystery*. New York: Facts On File, 1986.

# INDEX

## A

access control units. *See* ACUs
Acne Bandit, 237
"Actor, the." *See* Sutton, Willie
ACUs (access control units), 225
Adams Express robbery, Reno
   Gang, 20
alarms, security, 221
Alexander Mitchell and Company
   raid, James Gang, 12
amateur heists (blunders), 241-247
   69-year-old widower, 246
   Bell, Ronnie, 245
   Coldwell Banker, 248
   Gap-Toothed Bandit, 245
   mystery mugger robbery, 243
   Sterling Bank and Trust, 246
armed guards, 221
Ashley, John, 57-59
Average Joe Bandit. *See*
   Schwarberg, Daniel

## B

Bad Breath Bandit, 237
Bailey, Harvey, 70, 255
   accomplices
      Barker, Freddie, 73
      Holden, Tommy, 72
      Karpis, Alvin, 73
      Kelly, George "Machine
         Gun," 72
      Stein, "Jew Sammy," 72
   arrest of, 73-74
   gas station business, 72
   prison escape, 74-75
   robberies
      Fort Scott (Nebraska), 73
      Great Denver Mint, 71-72
      Hamilton County Bank
         of Ohio, 71

Lincoln National Bank
   (Lincoln, Nebraska), 73, 252
People's National Bank of
   Kingfisher, 75
"running the cat roads" getaway
   method, 70-71
Urschel kidnapping, 76
bait money, 224
Baker, George, 57-59
Bank of America robbery (Santa
   Clarita), North Hollywood
   Gunmen, 193-194, 253
Bank of Commerce robbery,
   Wilcoxson and Nussbaum, Inc.,
   156
Barker, "Arthur Dock," 136
Barker, Fred, 135-136
   association with Harvey Bailey,
      73
Barker, Herman, 136
Barker, Lloyd, 136
Barker, "Ma," 135-136
Barker-Karpis Gang, 135, 140
   FBI ambush, 141
   gang members, 135-139
   kidnappings, 140
   robberies
      Cloud County Bank
         (Concordia, Kansas), 139
      Fairbury Bank (Nebraska),
         139-140
      Mountain View Bank, 137-138
      Northwestern National Bank
         (Minneapolis), 138
      Wahpeton bank (North
         Dakota), 139
Barkerm, Arthur "Dock," 135
Barrett, Arthur "Bucky," 170-173
Barrow, Clyde (Bonnie and Clyde),
   83-92, 255-256, 269
Bassett, Jack, association with Willie
   Sutton, 143

Holden, Tommy, 138
  association with Harvey Bailey,
    72
"Hollywood" Scurlock. *See*
  Scurlock, William Scott
Hoover, J. Edgar, 106
Hope, Jimmy, association with
  George Leonidas Leslie, 23
Hudson Armored Car robbery
  (Greenpoint, Brooklyn), 250
Hughes and Madison Bank rob-
  bery, James Gang, 13
Hunter, Freddie, 62, 135

# I

I Spy Bandits, 239
insurance coverages (banks), 227
  Federal Deposit Insurance
    Corporation, 227
  fidelity insurance, 227
International State Bank robbery
  (Haskell, Oklahoma), Wilbur
  Underhill, 255
Internet, resource for capturing
  criminals, 226-227
Itty Bitty Bandit, 239

# J

Jackson County Vigilante
  Committee, 22
James, Alexander Franklin
  Civil War guerrilla raids, 9-10
  death of, 17
  James Gang. *See* James Gang
James, Jesse Woodson
  Civil War guerrilla raids, 9-10
  conspiracy theory, 17-18
  death of, 16
  James Gang, 9
  repeat offender, 268
James Gang, 9-10, 13-17
  raids
    Alexander Mitchell and
      Company, 12
    Northfield, 15-16, 257

robberies
  Daviess County Savings Bank,
    13-14
  Hughes and Madison Bank,
    13
  Liberty, 10, 12
  Sexton Bank, 16
  St. Genevieve Bank, 14
Jones, Payne, James Gang, 9

# K

Kangaroo Bandit, 239
Kansas City Massacre, Charles
  "Pretty Boy" Floyd, 119-121
Karpis, Alvin, 135, 137
  association with Harvey Bailey,
    73
Kelly, Bill, association with George
  Leonidas Leslie, 23
Kelly, George "Machine Gun," 83,
  127-130, 256
  association with Harvey Bailey,
    72
  college education, 132
  First Trust and Savings Bank
    robbery (Colfax, Washington),
    129
  relationship with Kathryn Kelly,
    127-128
  Urschel kidnapping, 76, 130-131
  Woolverton kidnapping attempt,
    129
Kelly, Kathryn, 127-128
Kerrigan, Michael. *See* Dobbs,
  Johnny
Ketchum, Jack, association with
  Butch Cassidy, 39
kidnappings, Barker-Karpis Gang,
  140
Kimes, George, 254
Kimes, Matt, 254
King, Nathan, association with
  "Pretty Boy" Floyd, 114
Kinkaid, Cecil, association with
  Patrick "Paddy" Mitchell, 181

# T

# DUANE SWIERCZYNSKI

**Number of banks robbed:** 1 (piggy)

**Estimated lifetime take:** $13.75

**Former occupations:** Piano player in a wedding band, maintenance worker, model interviewer, newspaper bundler, and fact-checker

**Claim to fame:** Duane and his brother Gregg were named after the Allman Brothers

## "READ THIS BOOK AND NOBODY WILL GET HURT."

Swierczynski is a senior editor at *Philadelphia Magazine* and has worked as an editor at *Men's Health* and *Details*. He is believed to be holed up with his lifelong accomplice, Meredith Swierczynski, not far from Philadelphia's former Eastern State Penitentiary, from which bank robber Willie Sutton escaped in 1947. You can reach the author at duane.swier@verizon.net or at www.bankrobbers.org.

### Cool Fact from the Vault

Swierczynski's grandfather, Louis Wojciechowski, grew up in South Philly with Frederick Tenuto—the slab of mob muscle who most likely murdered the man who snitched on Sutton. "Know him?" Wojciechowski asks. "Guy still owes me five bucks."